The Image Factory

New Technologies/New Cultures Series

General Editor: Don Slater, London School of Economics

New Technologies/New Cultures will draw together the best scholarship, across the social science disciplines, that addresses emergent technologies in relation to cultural transformation. While much contemporary literature is caught up in wild utopian or dystopian pronouncements about the scale and implications of change, this series invites more grounded and modulated work with a clear conceptual and empirical focus. The series draws on a wealth of dynamic research agendas, from Internet and new media scholarship to research into bio-sciences, environmentalism and the sociology of consumption.

Series ISSN: 1472-2895

Previous titles published in this series:

Brenda Danet, Cyberpl@y: Communicating Online
Elizabeth Shove, Comfort, Cleanliness and Convenience: The Social Organization of Normality

The Image Factory

Consumer Culture, Photography and the Visual Content Industry

Paul Frosh

Oxford • New York

First published in 2003 by
Berg
Editorial offices:
1st Floor, Angel Court, 81 St Clements Street, Oxford, OX4 1AW, UK
838 Broadway, Third Floor, New York, NY 10003-4812, USA

Berg is an imprint of Oxford International Publishers Ltd.

Library of Congress Cataloging-in-Publication Data
A catalogue record for this book is available from the Library of Congress.

British Library Cataloguing-in-Publication Data
A catalogue record for this book is available from the British Library.

ISBN   1 85973 637 8 (Cloth)
       1 85973 642 4 (Paper)

Typeset by JS Typesetting Ltd, Wellingborough, Northants.
Printed in the United Kingdom by Biddles Ltd, Guildford and King's Lynn.

www.bergpublishers.com

For Caroline

Contents

Acknowledgements

This book would not have been possible without the support and interest of colleagues, students and mentors at the Department of Communication and Journalism at The Hebrew University of Jerusalem, especially Yosefa Loshitzky, Brenda Danet and Yeshayahu Nir who provided wise counsel and consistent encouragement throughout my original research on stock photography. Various branches of The Hebrew University of Jerusalem provided essential help at crucial moments: the Authority for Research and Development generously contributed to the purchase of images for this book, the Smart Family Communications Foundation funded much of the fieldwork, and the Fellowship Committee generously supported a very productive and pleasant stay at the Centre for Cultural Studies at Goldsmiths College, London, during which I extended and refined some of my original ideas. I was also helped greatly by the stimulating and constructively critical comments of participants in the various gatherings at which I have presented aspects of my work: in Israel at the Hebrew University of Jerusalem, Haifa University and Tel Aviv University; in the UK at the University of Westminster, at Goldsmiths College, and the University of Edinburgh's Institute for the Advanced Studies in the Humanities; and in the USA at the University of Pennsylvania and the University of Indiana. More recently, Don Slater's astuteness and enthusiasm have been invaluable, as have the professionalism, amicability and patience of Kathryn Earle and the staff at Berg.

I am also extremely grateful to the many professionals – too numerous to name – who acted as sources and guides to the world of stock photography, and who generously gave time and consideration to my unusual requests and often naive questions. Here I owe a special debt for my initial exposure to the stock business (first as a client and only later as a researcher) to Marcus Sheff, Cheral Druck, Ilan Peeri and Andrea Stern.

Finally, I would like to thank my family for their understanding, tolerance and (very) occasional excitement while I have been working on this book. Caroline, to whom the book is dedicated, for love, good sense and even better humour. Gefen and Tomer for the happiest of distractions, however cross I might occasionally have seemed, and baby Nitzan for the alternating exhaustion and excitement that accompanied revisions to the final draft. My father for his periodic but effective *nudging* about the book's progress and for a lifetime of moral support. And my mother, who would have been made so happy by this book's publication and who is so sorely missed by us all.

This book has been written as a cohesive, and I hope coherent, work. Nevertheless, some parts of it have been published elsewhere as shorter articles. Sections of Chapters 2 and 3 draw on material that was first published as 'Inside the Image Factory: Stock Photography and Cultural Production', *Media, Culture & Society*, 23(5), 2001: 625–46 and 'To Thine Own Self Be True: The Discourse of Authenticity in Mass Cultural Production', *Communication Review* 4(4), 2001: 529–45. Parts of Chapter 6 refine arguments first aired in 'Rhetorics of the Overlooked: On the Communicative Modes of Advertising Images', *Journal of Consumer Culture* 2(2), 2002: 171–96, while Chapters 7 and 8 use some of the material that appears in 'And God Created Photoshop: Digital Technologies and the Stock Photography Industry' in Larry Gross, John Stuart Katz and Jay Ruby (eds), *Image Ethics in the Digital Age*, University of Minnesota Press, 2003.

1

Introduction: The Making of Ordinary Images

This book is about the making of ordinary, mass-produced, photographic images. The kinds of image that we encounter many times each day as we pass by advertising billboards, turn the pages of newspapers, flick through magazines, glance at publicity brochures, and – increasingly for many of us – traverse windows and websites on our computer screens. Yet although these images are ubiquitous, they are also so unexceptional that our encounters with them seem to have no duration, and are not marked off as noteworthy events or experiences. They are, in fact, the sort of everyday images that we hardly give a thought to, that escape our attention, that we barely recall and that we struggle to place. Neither compelling nor arresting nor intriguing in any way, they can seem almost deliberately inconspicuous, as though designed *not* to attract attention or detain the eye. Part of the background, unremarkable and effectively 'invisible', they are routinely *overlooked* by most of their viewers, most of the time. They are the wallpaper of consumer culture.

Of course, calling such images 'ordinary' begs quite a few questions. What does being ordinary entail? What distinguishes ordinary, overlooked images from those which stand out, catch our eye, grab our attention, and become the focus not only of our personal interest but even of public discussion? Is 'ordinariness' a quality of the content of certain photographs, of their placement within particular media contexts and viewing situations (making them potentially extraordinary in other circumstances), of our viewing habits and attitudes toward them, or of all these things together? And since, by our own admission, these images *are* ordinary, why bother writing a book about them? Surely the fact that they escape our notice indicates their insignificance within the greater scheme of things: pictures so banal and uninteresting that they have no value for us in the present, let alone any lasting importance for our culture and society.

A chief theme of this book is that the ordinariness of these images is neither naturally given nor easily achieved. Rather, it is a result of an elaborate system of manufacture, distribution and consumption that is itself largely concealed from view. Just as these images are so unremarkable as to seem invisible, so the system that creates them is for the most part unknown outside a relatively small coterie of 'image specialists' in advertising, marketing, design and a number of other media professions. And this despite the fact that this system is actually quite big business: a billion-dollar industry, known variously as 'stock photography' and 'the visual content industry', which is not only responsible for an estimated 70 per cent of the images used in advertising, marketing and design, but which owns some of the most important historical photographic archives and the digital reproduction rights to much of the world's fine art.[1] So our ordinary, everyday visual environment is the product of hidden forces.

It is tempting to conclude from this that we are the victims of some horrific conspiracy. Obscure powers systematically producing the images that constitute the visual background to our lives while escaping our conscious attention: it almost sounds like the plot of a paranoid sci-fi thriller. This book does not entirely endorse such a view. The creation of visual ordinariness is not a streamlined and predictable affair, and while there are certainly crucial political dimensions involved – who creates our visual environment, for what purpose and with what effects – there are plenty of muddles and messes generated by the conflicts, misunderstandings and indifference that exist between various parties, not to mention the internal contradictions inherent within the production system itself. But it does endorse the idea that we need to know something of how our everyday visual environment is manufactured in order to understand just how it comes to seem everyday, and what its significance might be for us.

The form that this endorsement takes can be traced through the three elements that make up the book's sub-title: consumer culture, photography and the visual content industry. 'Consumer culture' is an important term here because it suggests that the industrially manufactured visual environment of complex media societies is dominated by the treatment of viewers as consumers of commodities, and by the sense that their social identities and roles are shaped substantially in relation to consumption (rather than, say, in relation to work or political power). Equally, this environment is dominated by the production of visual images both as commodities in their own right and as promotional vehicles for other commodities: objects whose primary value is realized in their purchase and whose goal – much of the time – is to persuade viewers to buy products with which they have been associated.[2] The relevance of photography is more immediately obvious. It is one of the chief media by which ordinary images are produced (television is another), although – as we shall see at various junctures in this book – defining what precisely constitutes photography can be a matter of some dispute. And the least familiar term, 'the visual content industry', emphasizes the centrality of an industrialized system of image-production to our everyday visual world, and the way it conceives of images as 'content'. In fact, the visual content industry (and its precursor, the stock photography business) is really the main subject of this book: for it contains within itself both an orientation toward consumer culture and the routine employment of photography as a cultural practice.[3]

These three elements also serve to situate the book within previous research and thinking. Much of the stimulus for my interpretation of the visual content industry was the surprising absence of research on commercial and advertising photography, whether within historical studies on the medium or among theoretical accounts of its status and impact. Related to this was my dissatisfaction with most of those investigations of advertising and commercial photography which *had* been undertaken. These were almost exclusively restricted to textual (usually semiotic) analyses of advertisements or other cultural 'texts', with little or no reference to the ways in which advertising images were manufactured. (This is generally true of 'critical' research on advertising: studies of the institutional and practical contexts in which advertisements are made are seriously outnumbered by formalistic and semiotic analyses (Soar 2000).) Both of these concerns, however, were symptomatic of a broader worry, which served as my starting point in approaching the visual content industry: the feeling that the empirical investigation of cultural industries and production processes *in general* had been seriously neglected within cultural studies, certainly when compared to textual analyses and reception studies.

I will expand on these frustrations in due course. It would be counter-productive, however, to do so in a vacuum. Since very little is known of stock photography outside the professional worlds of advertising, marketing, design and publishing, I will begin with a brief preliminary description that – while it can only allude to issues that are explored in detail in subsequent chapters – I hope will prevent confusion later on.

What is Stock Photography?

Stock photography is a global industry which manufactures, promotes and distributes photographic images for use in marketing, advertising, sundry editorial purposes, and increasingly for multimedia products and website design. The industry is dominated by a small number of multinational 'super-agencies' based in the United States and Europe: The Image Bank and Tony

Stone Images, both owned by Getty Images PLC (The Image Bank and its associated businesses were acquired in September 1999 from Eastman Kodak), Visual Communications Group (owner of FPG International, Telegraph Colour Library and others) which was owned by United News and Media PLC until February 2000, when it too was bought by Getty, and Corbis, privately financed by Microsoft President Bill Gates. These compete alongside a much larger number of smaller and medium-sized agencies, around 2,500 altogether (www.imagebank.com, March 1999).

Traditionally, stock-photography agencies acquire licences to sell the reproduction rights of photographic images in return for giving photographers a share of the revenue generated from these sales:[4] the percentage for non-digital domestic sales is customarily 50 per cent, although after deductions made by the agencies to cover marketing and administrative costs, it can reach as little as 36 per cent ('ASMP's Stock Survey Results – May 1999', The American Society of Media Photographers (ASMP) Press Release, www.asmp.org).[5] These images are kept in 'stock' by the agency, duplicated, filed and cross-referenced according to general categories such as 'The Family', 'People', 'Lifestyle', 'Business', Nature', 'Sports', 'Scenics' and 'Abstract'. A selection of them are marketed – through printed catalogues, CD-ROMs, and increasingly the agency website – to prospective clients (usually advertising agencies, marketing divisions and graphic designers) who can purchase the reproduction rights relatively inexpensively and quickly for negotiable periods and areas of exclusivity.[6] Until recently, purchased photographs were supplied to clients as prints or slides, although this has changed as a result of digital technologies.

This production and distribution system is called 'rights-protected', 'managed rights' or even 'traditional licensing' stock photography, and it has proved mutually beneficial to photographers, stock agencies and clients: the photographer bears the production costs of the image but does not incur significant marketing and distribution costs, and can expect a steady income from repeated sales of the same image without relinquishing copyright. The agency, on the other hand, can draw on a large pool of virtually free 'content' which it can sell worldwide over a long period, without having to worry about production expenses. The client benefits by being able to acquire, extremely quickly and relatively cheaply, the image of his or her choice, evading the organizational and financial quagmire of the assignment photo shoot and the danger of disappointing results. (Commissioning photographers for specific assignments is the traditional method of creating advertising photographs, and is still essential for product shots.) As Diane Fannon, then Vice President and Managing Director of The Image Bank's Still Image Division, noted: 'the only difference now between stock and assignment photography is that, with stock, the photographer has already gotten lucky! I've been on enough bad-weather shoots to know that's a hell of a guarantee to give a client' (Zoom 1994: 13). In terms of image-content and style, the system has traditionally encouraged conservatism and the constant reproduction of formulaic and stereotypical 'generic' images (smiling, white middle-class families at the beach, well-groomed businessmen shaking hands) which both reflect and construct cultural stereotypes.[7]

In the last decade, however, stock photography has entered a period of rapid and radical change. This change is connected to three overlapping types of transformation: cultural, technological and structural-financial. Briefly (again, each of these will be dealt with in much greater detail later on), shifts in advertising and marketing practices have led, in the last decade, to the appearance of less obviously stereotyped and more diverse image styles and content, including 'artistic' images, more 'realistic' (i.e. grainy and black and white) images and images of 'ethnic' and minority (e.g. gay and lesbian) subjects. It is tempting to connect such changes to broad historical claims of a 'post-Fordist' transformation in production and in commercial culture as a whole: the rise of consumption-driven, flexible, 'small-batch' production (Harvey 1989: 141–72), 'hyperrealist' and 'hypersignificant' advertising (Goldman and Papson 1994), and lifestyle research and niche marketing – all conceivably elements of what Baudrillard contends is an epochal shift in the relationship between the economy and culture, the collapse of the economic into the symbolic (1981: 143–63; 1988: 29–56). Whether or not we accept such grand claims – and it will be my inclination throughout this book not to stray too far from the specific material and representational practices of the visual content industry – these changes in stock images nevertheless occurred within a hegemonic framework, largely dictated by the cultural backgrounds of photographers and the 'cultural intermediaries' (advertising-art directors and picture editors) who are their primary clients, by advertising's continued promulgation of images of well-being, and by the orientation of many advertisements toward audiences with significant disposable income.[8]

Technologically, the advent of digital imaging technologies has augmented the power of image-producers to manipulate and 'enhance' their photographs. At the same time it threatens the 'artistic integrity' of photographs by giving users the ability to dismantle them and recombine their fragments with other images and media in unanticipated ways. Digital storage, search and retrieval technologies have allowed the phenomenal growth and integration of greatly differing categories of images, thus serving processes of cultural dedifferentiation and redifferentiation required by niche-marketing. Digital distribution via CD-ROM and websites promises to reduce duplication and distribution costs and at the same time has created a number of perceived threats: extensive violation of copyright in a global environment where both legislation and enforcement are failing to match the pace of technological change; the need to redistribute the burden and the profits of marketing through both conventional and digital channels which is endangering the delicate balance of power between photographers and agency management; the threat that global access to websites poses to the relationship of mutual dependency between large US and European agencies and their local suppliers and representatives on other continents; and the rise of an entirely new sector of 'royalty free' (RF) photography, initially on CD-ROM but increasingly via websites as well, which directly sells low-cost images to a broad consumer market as well as to professional cultural mediators, radically challenging the traditional operational structures, practices and assumptions of rights-protected stock photography.[9]

The initial capital costs of the new technologies, plus the potential rewards of 'synergy' between producers of technologies and producers of content, have led to a spate of mergers and acquisitions (culminating in Getty's $183 million acquisition of The Image Bank in late 1999 and $220 million acquisition of VCG in early 2000), resulting in the dominance of the multinational super-agencies mentioned above. These usually own, in addition to stock photography agencies, 'stock footage' companies (based upon the same principle as stock photography, only with generic video or film clips), historical and photojournalistic still and film footage archives, celebrity-image archives, fine-art archives, illustration archives, royalty-free companies, and in some cases developers of digital imaging, security and delivery technologies. Thus stock photography is being subsumed within a globalized and digitized 'visual content industry' (Getty Images, Company Overview, www.gettyimages.com, 1998), whose ramifications include, among many other things, the accelerated blurring of boundaries between previously distinct institutional and discursive contexts of production and distribution: in particular, between fine art, news and advertising images, and in a culture glutted with authentic and fabricated 'vintage' images, between historical and contemporary photographs.

The visual content/stock-photography business is currently estimated to have an annual sales turnover of between one and two billion dollars worldwide: the largest super-agency alone, Getty Images PLC, earned $484.8 million in 2000 and $451 million in 2001 (Annual Report, Getty Images PLC, 2000; 'Getty Images Reports Financial Results for the Fourth Quarter and 2001', Press Release 6/2/2002. Both at www.gettyimages.com), although this includes revenues from operations not always considered part of the stock photography business (such as the sale of royalty-free images).[10] This caveat indicates only one of the problems with the $1–2 billion figure, which has to do with the very definition and identity of the industry, an issue that will be dealt with in later chapters; the other major misgiving about the figure is caused by the almost paranoid reticence of agencies to provide reliable corporate figures (Getty, the only publicly quoted major company, is alone in publishing quarterly and annual accounts).

The figure's approximate nature should not, however, disguise its utility as an indicator of stock photography's significance. Rather – and despite its almost laughable modesty when compared with the $38.2 billion worth of sales done *alone* in 2001 by AOL-Time Warner (the world's largest media conglomerate) – the figure marks out the business as a principal 'site' for the production and distribution of photographic images in the culture as a whole. Once considered a poor, and cheap, alternative to commissioned assignment work, largely because of its reputation for producing visual clichés, stock photography has become more integrated and reputable as a source of images, for a variety of commercial, aesthetic and cultural reasons. Today, as the visual content industry, it creates a substantial proportion of the photographs encountered in commercial and consumer culture, supplying a majority of the images used in US advertising, marketing and graphic design and acting as a key provider of images for multi-media products and professional website design. For this reason it is continually and extensively discussed in the professional photographic, advertising and design trade journals, and is widely perceived in the marketing and design communities as an increasingly potent force in contemporary visual culture.

Finally, stock photography enjoys what appears to be a powerful ideological advantage over other sectors producing contemporary visual culture: *invisibility*. As I suggested earlier, most viewers have never heard of stock photography, and are blissfully unaware of the provenance of the pictures that surround them. The industry's system of production and distribution effectively shields it from the ultimate consumers of its images, veiling the beliefs, interests and power-relations that help shape their manufacture.

Photography as Product and Representation

This book seeks to integrate theories of cultural production and theories of visual representation through their application in a specific case: stock photography and the visual content industry. The choice of 'case study' is not, however, merely incidental to the theories employed, not simply a convenient empirical peg upon which to hang somewhat gaudy theoretical apparel. For stock photography represents an exemplary standardization and systematization of photographic practices on quasi-industrial lines, and a consequent abstraction of photographic images as exchangeable signs and cultural commodities. In fact, the very word 'stock' refers us to the systemic nature of cultural production *and* to semiotic questions of appearance and meaning. A stock image is literally kept 'in stock' in real agency archives, stored – ready for distribution – like a manufactured product in a warehouse; the word 'stock' also connotes, however, the predominant appearance of these images: instantly recognizable iconographic combinations which rely upon, and reinforce, 'clichéd' visual motifs and stereotypes that are drawn from a far broader cultural archive or image-repertoire. Hence the 'specific case' of stock photography is actually a privileged case. It provides the ideal conditions in which to comprehend the enmeshing of photographic practices and images within contemporary consumer societies.

This integration of approaches will involve bridging the gaps between semiotic accounts concerned with elucidating the creation of photographic meaning, and analyses in the tradition of the 'sociology of culture' and (very broadly) the 'political economy of communication' (Garnham 1986; Ryan 1992) which focus on the material processes and practices of cultural production: on the one hand, approaches that define photographic images as specific types of sign or text, as forms of representation and signification, and on the other models of cultural production that emphasize their nature as products and commodities, as the material of labour, and as tokens of exchange-value.[11] I attempt to situate stock photography within what Scott Lash calls a 'regime of signification', moving between its 'cultural economy' (relations of production, conditions of reception, mediating institutional framework and means of circulation) and its 'mode of signification' (characteristic relations between signifier, signified and referent) (1990: 4–5). In other words, my task is simultaneously to illuminate the production of photographic meaning and the meaning of photographic production.

Discourse, according to Paul Ricoeur, is 'realised as event and understood as meaning' (1981: 22). The integration and mutual transformation of sociological and semiotic accounts that I hope to perform in the pages that follow – the exploration of production practices interacting with the analysis of complex representational forms – expresses this inescapable duality, or dialectic, of discourse. The task of making such an integration and mutual transformation happen begins properly in Chapter 3. However, to give a sense of its implications, I want to make my position clearer by briefly staking it out in relation to (a) developments in photography history and theory, and (b) the (in)famous opposition between cultural studies and the political economy of communication.

Photography History and Theory

It is difficult, perhaps impossible, to make an absolute distinction between theories of photographic representation and the historical study of photography. To begin with, theories of photography frequently make use of historical evidence about photographic technologies and practices, while histories of photography necessarily make assumptions about the nature of the medium and technologies whose history they are describing. More profoundly, however, the recurring themes of photography theory and history display an underlying affinity that anchors their identities as intellectual endeavours. They are both fascinated by an elusive object: the *essence* of photography, the very thing that makes photography what it is and distinguishes it from other technologies and cultural practices (painting, writing, lithography, illustration, print, etc).[12] This fascination has enjoyed multiple incarnations: historically it is manifested as the quest for the true origin, originator and destiny of photography;[13] philosophically it is theorized as a new and unique relationship between reality and representation, referent and sign; and culturally and politically it is proposed as photography's instrumental roles within modern Western societies: to survey, copy, order and master the multifarious objects (and peoples) of the world. The public declarations of Daguerre and his supporter Arago, as well as of their English competitor Fox Talbot, testify to the unity behind this trinity of concerns, as their texts fuse partisan technical histories of the invention, claims regarding photography's status as a mode of representation, and predictions about its social and scientific uses.[14]

The orbital journey of photography history and theory around this core of 'ontological desire' (Barthes 1984: 3) has led in directions aesthetic and art historical (the writing of monographs, the codification of artistic criteria, the establishment of oeuvres and genres, the canonization of works and practitioners), and technical and technological. In recent years it has also been influenced – perhaps predictably – by literary analysis, semiotics, psychoanalysis, and the convergence of post-structuralist, deconstructive and Marxist approaches which can be conveniently labelled 'cultural theory'. These influences have proved especially fruitful, enriching the variety of ways in which photography is understood and discussed, and even allowing us to question the notion of 'photography' as historically and technologically self-evident and internally coherent.

Moreover, they have led to increasingly sophisticated analyses of the institutional and cultural contexts of photographic production and consumption, and their relationship to the formal and thematic conventions of images. Outstanding among these are investigations of domestic photography (for example Spence 1986; many of the essays collected in Spence and Holland 1991; Slater

1983; Slater 1995a, Kenyon 1992), the connection of photography to social status (Bourdieu 1990), the institutional contexts and cultural meanings of news and documentary images (Hall 1972; Sekula 1982; Tagg 1988; Lutz and Collins 1993; Kozol 1994) and art photography (Krauss 1982, 1984; Bolton 1989), the relationship of photography to positivist science and romantic aesthetics (Sekula 1981) and the use of photographs in police, medical and anthropological archives and projects (Sekula 1989).[15]

Despite this expansion in the concerns of photography theory and history, at least one significant gap remains in the recounting of photography's impact upon social experience. This, as I have more than hinted, is the systematic industrialization of photography as a ubiquitous part of contemporary Western commercial and consumer culture. As Rosetta Brookes notes, writing specifically but not exclusively of fashion photography, 'For historians and critics concerned with isolating "great" photographic images and according them enduring significance, the commercial sphere of photography – the domain of the everyday image – represents the debasement of a conventional history of photography' (1992: 17).[16] Even those scholars who reject the 'art historical' emphasis on the medium's aesthetic development have revealed an astonishing capacity for neglect. To take a canonical example, Gisèle Freund's pioneering work, *Photography and Society* (1980), published in France in 1974, includes chapters on 'Press Photography', 'Photography and the Law', 'American Mass Media Magazines', 'Photography as a Political Tool' and 'Amateur Photography' – among others. Despite its historical and social breadth, however, it barely mentions advertising or commercial photography.

More surprising, perhaps, is the fact that while virtually every semiotic or textual analysis of advertising has had, at least implicitly, to interpret photographs as part of whole advertisements, and even to engage with photographic conventions and the (controversial) notion of a specifically photographic form of signification, very little of substance has been written on the organized mass production of photographic images as part of advertising, marketing and commercial culture as a whole (Ramamurthy, 1997: 155). Commercial photography as an institutionalized section of 'the culture industry' (Adorno and Horkheimer 1979) has been largely ignored, with only a few exceptions.

Such alarming scholarly and critical neglect of what would seem an obvious subject accords, however, with the impression that both traditional photography history and theory, and many (though by no means all) of the more critical 'post-structuralist' approaches, ultimately circle about the contested but familiar terrain of photography's essential identity (including when they persistently claim that photography has no such identity), venturing beyond it mainly in gestural and programmatic ways in order to secure better positions on the old battleground of ontological debate.[17] In particular, there is a dearth of systematic analyses of contemporary commercial photographic production that can discern the complex connections and discontinuities between photography as a mode of representation and as an industry (some of the few that do exist are discussed in Chapter 3).[18] Needless to say, this scholarly inactivity has been paralleled, in the world of commercial practice, by the consolidation, growth and globalization of stock photography as an increasingly integrated photographic business and an increasingly important source of the images which surround us.

Cultural Studies and/versus Political Economy

The dearth of analyses of commercial (and other) photographic production practices, as well as advertising practices can be understood to be symptomatic of a double-headed malaise afflicting cultural studies in general since the 1980s: first, its preference for the formalistic analysis of 'texts' informed, with whatever caveats, by the legacy of structuralism (see Billig 1997); and second, its tendency toward abstract philosophizing based on a heady (and sometimes ill-starred) fusion of post-structuralist and postmodernist writings, rendered in an arcane style whose playful self-consciousness is severely obfuscatory. The accuracy or otherwise of this description – much attributed to writers in the 'political economy' tradition (notably Garnham) though also reproduced by some of the foremost figures in cultural studies itself (Hall 1992) – is not at issue here.[19] What is much less in doubt is that, compared with 'theory', textual analyses and more recently reception studies, empirical investigations of cultural *production* have been relatively marginal to the practice of cultural studies – if the topics of the central journals and anthologies are any indication. This is notwithstanding its seeming importance to some of the work of 'foundational' thinkers: Williams's writing on television springs to mind here, as does Hall's work in the 1970s on television programming and news photography, and – very obviously – Adorno and Horkheimer's critique of 'the culture industry'. And this is also despite the ongoing concern with the organization of cultural production in the sociology of culture and media sociology.

Studies of 'industrial' cultural production have, however, begun to make a comeback in recent publications (for instance, Du Gay 1997, Hesmondhalgh 2002, Negus 1997). In their diverse ways, and despite their different emphases and areas of interest, these works share cultural studies' concern with the multiple and dialectical relations between social power, cultural identity, material practice and symbolic representation as well as a distrust of attempts – stereotypically attributed to political economy – to reduce culture to 'underlying', usually economic, forces. Yet they also share a detailed engagement with production procedures (including financial imperatives) and a commitment to empirical research that appears closer to the political-economy tradition (and definitely to the sociology of culture) than to much of what currently passes for cultural studies (which just goes to show how simplistic the cultural studies/ political economy opposition is: see Hesmondhalgh 2002). What is most interesting, however, is the way they seem to conceive of production as a *privileged* yet *complex* 'moment' in the circulation of cultural goods and practices. Production is 'privileged' because, however much it may be subject to forces and influences at work more generally in a given society, it marks that point at which cultural forms acquire their ostensive fixity with respect to their ultimate audience, at which they achieve a 'closure' that is produced systematically, at which they are *sealed* much as an envelope is sealed or an object granted a seal of approval. An authorized version is created, a final mix, a master copy, a definitive cut. And however much consumers may be free to interpret, 'resist' or even alter these sealed forms, *it is these forms that they must receive and act upon.*

Now, such fixity is not the natural or inevitable outcome of production procedures. Rather, it is the result of culturally, socially, economically and legally sanctioned practices that grant key players (individuals, occupational groups and organizations), at particular sites, the authority and power to seal cultural products. The discourses that sanction this power also naturalize it, rendering it an invisible 'given' for consumers and – when it does appear (as, for instance, the privileges accruing to artistic talent, professional expertise and intellectual property) – making it seem instinctively 'right'.

If, then, production is privileged, why is it 'complex'? First, because production is itself analysable (i.e. can be broken down) into organizationally distinct processes and practices involving diverse and often *competing* agencies (individuals, occupational groups, companies). These fashion potential cultural products in *competition* with other potential cultural products embarked upon the same risky path to fixity and circulation. Second, because commercial cultural production, as a rationalizable system involving the calculation of risk and success (of this or that photograph/film/record/book in a competitive market) and the maximization of profitability and utility (through formatting and multiple reuse of component parts), requires the malleability, the openness, the *instability* of products as they progress – or fail to progress – from the moment of primary conception to their final appearance in approved manufactured form.

This systemic instability, and its relation to fixity and closure across the key boundary between cultural industries and mass audiences, will be described in later chapters under the rubric of 'materialization' and 'dematerialization'. What I want to stress here by these terms is the mutual transformation of semiotic and political economic approaches. How are these 'mutually transformed'? By overcoming the implicit opposition between 'matter' (the physical constitution of an object) and 'meaning', as well as between product and process. In the case of semiotics, this requires a rejection of so-called textual autonomy and a movement – to reverse Barthes's famous phrase – *from text to work*. For the treatment of representational and symbolic forms is thoroughly imbricated within material practices and non-symbolic dynamics and constraints: the meaning of a cultural product is neither inherent 'in' the product nor endlessly polysemic in some ideal abstract way. It is always meaning *for* someone within a specified interpretative and practical context. Moreover, meaning is not something that is put *into* the product as one fills a vessel with liquid, or that 'occurs' *after* the product has been produced: meaning is what *makes* the product. Cultural production is an intentional affair, and the multiple constructions of a potential product's meaning (by different people at different stages), and the anticipation of its diverse interpretation by others (both professional and non-professional), is integral to the design and manufacture process: meaning is not what is produced – meaning is always *in production* as part and parcel of a material-representational practice. Hence the 'semiotic' analysis of a product should also account for the ways in which meaning is contingent upon and generative of the product's material constitution in a particular context of production and in relation to other contexts.

At the same time, and in a reciprocal move, political economy becomes 'semioticized'. Administrative routines; professional norms; financial imperatives and constraints; personal and occupational identities and values; the power-relations between cultural managers, financial managers, technicians, primary creators, owners and shareholders; the overall structure of the market and the distribution of resources: these factors certainly bear upon the organization of production and upon product form. But to privilege them as constituting an 'underlying' process of material organization and manufacture, to which meaning and meaning-making are somehow supplementary, is to fail to comprehend cultural production as a dynamic process at once material *and* semiotic.

Let me spell this out. Cultural products are designed, produced and distributed in complex manufacturing environments which are increasingly composed of organizationally distinct yet interlinked sites, from the development systems and marketing departments of transnational corporations to the more fluid settings of freelance artists and independent specialists. A potential product – an advertising image, a pop song, a film script, a news format, a commercial photograph – must prove itself against alternative potential products as it develops and moves across these sites. This means that the product's path toward the consumer is fraught with uncertainty not just at the end stage

– its appearance before its ultimate audience – but at key junctures in its production.

Hence cultural products, as a result of their precarious existence, need to deploy and conspicuously display their *potential meaningfulness* to a range of different addressees well before they reach a mass audience. Such persistent and systematic display is an existential imperative, constituting a self-promotional rhetoric designed to propel products across the cultural and economic borders between manufacturing and distribution sites within the production system. This 'system rhetoric' is geared primarily toward meeting the economic considerations and cultural assumptions of diverse cultural managers, rather than toward the product's ultimate audience. The latter is addressed by a parallel 'mission rhetoric', the product's self-justification before consumers (its claim to their attention), which the system rhetoric structures, utilizes and subsumes within its own self-promotional strategy. (Thus a key meaning of an image to a cultural manager is its potential meaningfulness to consumers.) Something as 'intangible' as promotion, therefore, is no less important to the dynamism of the production process than, say, calculations of financial cost and return: indeed – both monetary and 'interpretative' calculations are intimately entwined.[20]

This brief outline marks my approach as broadly sympathetic to recent work in 'cultural economy' which 'challenge[s] us to think about the reciprocal interrelationship of what are often thought of as discrete "cultural" and "economic" practices' (Negus 2002: 504).[21] Much of it informed by 'actor-network theory', this work tends to endorse a view of reality as flux – and an ontology of *becoming* rather than of being (Chia 1996) – that privileges relationships, movement and processes over discrete and self-sufficient entities (objects, facts), events and effects. Things are not self-evidently and statically what they are: they have *become* (are always becoming) what they are, are subject to (momentary) stabilization and materialization, through incessant practices and performances of organization and ordering, codifying and classification. It is the notion of self-evidence that is chiefly under suspicion here, a suspicion which in the chapters to follow will lead me to stress the instability, malleability and contingency of cultural objects ('images', 'content', 'information'), values ('success', 'creativity') and activities ('photography') by treating them as 'black boxes' (Latour 1987) – entities whose complexity has been closed off to enable further operations – that need to be opened up to view. Indeed, I will argue that this very instability is what makes objects and activities *productive*. By opening up these black boxes in their particular contexts, we not only restore their dynamism but we also move away from the inertia of 'the production *of* culture' to an understanding of culture *as* production.

Such an understanding can be formulated in a number of key assumptions about stock photography:

1. Stock photographs are the product of certain kinds of professional practice. Those practices are systematized and institutionalized, both formally in legal and contractual relations between individuals and different kinds of organization, but also informally in the web of conventions, technological imperatives, financial and administrative routines, organizational norms, procedures and expectations, accepted professional wisdom, technical know-how and aesthetic intuitions that shape the course of production. This point expresses the essentially industrial approach to the production of culture. Its legacy can most obviously be traced back to Adorno and Horkheimer's (1979) critique of 'the culture industry', which suggests that the content and form of mass-produced cultural goods are substantially determined by the structures, goals and limitations of the corporations that produce them within the overall framework of capitalist commodity production. We can summarize this argument through the first part of Keith Negus' (1998: 359) useful axiom: 'an industry produces culture'.

2. However, this corporate or industrial systematization of professional practice is not isolated from broader cultural and social trends. 'Production does not take place simply 'within' a corporate environment created according to the requirements of capitalist production but in relation to broader cultural formations and practices that may not be directly within the control or understanding of the company' (Negus 1998: 360). This axiom is in opposition to 'filter-flow' (Hirsch 1972), 'organisational' (DiMaggio and Hirsch 1976), 'transmission' and other models of industrial cultural production – such as that developed by Rosenblum (1978: see my Chapter 3) – that treat cultural texts as solely or primarily determined by organizational factors. Cultural material is not merely, and somewhat tautologically, that which is made by the production process, but a participant in a dynamic network of symbolic forms that construct and express social experience (Jensen 1984). Specific cultural products, however original they are claimed to be, are therefore always in a sense pre-produced and pre-understood 'elsewhere' in the weave of symbolic forms, before and beyond the moment of specific production. Similarly, the very practices of material production (including, for example, technical preferences, economic calculations, contractual producer–client relationships, and preferred distribution channels) are themselves conditioned and limited by their wider socio-economic and cultural contexts. The overall idea expressed here can best be summarized through the second phrase of the axiom mentioned at the end of point 1: while 'an industry produces culture', it is also true that 'culture produces an industry' (Negus 1998: 359).

3. Production, like distribution and circulation, can be specified as a distinct 'moment' in 'the circuit of culture' (du Gay, Hall et al. 1997). These connected but separate moments are part of an analytic model that attempts to show how a continuous and circular cultural process 'can be sustained through a "passage of forms" (Hall 1980: 128). The expression of the cultural process through these distinct moments allows us to specify the form that the product – in this case, the commercial photographic image – takes as it moves through each stage, and also to emphasize the product's necessary *openness, instability and mutability* within the overall production process. Moreover, it should not be assumed that this model is a mere abstraction. In the case of stock photography, the separation between moments is manifested concretely in the discrete technical administration and distinctive milieu of each (see Chapter 3). And passage through and across these moments is crucial for the life of the cultural product, such that the individual image is shaped not only by its 'mission' – the necessity to communicate with an end user – but also by the anticipated interpretative frameworks and practical demands of agents within the 'system' of production-distribution-circulation itself.[22]

4. It must be noted, however, that as integral phases of a circuit, each moment carries traces of the others in varying ways: production is influenced by distribution and reception, which in turn are affected by the possibilities, conventions and limitations of production as well as by the form of the product. It is assumed, therefore, that these moments are not simple and self-contained, and that diversely complex processes of cultural mediation occur in each (hence my reservations regarding Lutz and Collins (1993)'s implicit emphasis on sequential linear process: see Chapter 3 below). Indeed, the precise terms used show how difficult the task of designating these moments can be. The trinity of 'production', 'distribution' and 'reception' actually presents a simplistic model of the circuit of the stock image, as I hope to show later on.

5. The creation of stock images is influenced by conceptions, often formulated as key terms, through which the connections across different moments are expressed and the cultural process is held in uneasy cohesion. Notions such as 'creativity' and 'originality', for example, may not only be relevant during the initial production stage (or 'success' during distribution or reception); rather, they articulate the continuity between moments by conferring cultural and professional legitimacy and by providing producers, cultural intermediaries and end-users with an authorized vocabulary for the aesthetic and commercial evaluation of images. Hence these terms are discursive in Foucault's sense (1972), providing a way of speaking about photography that also governs its practice. Apart from anything else, these terms place stock photographic practices and discourses within a more broadly cultural discursive

formation, connecting the production of stock images to the creation of other distinctively cultural and symbolic forms.

6. Production processes create multiple potentialities for image use and interpretation rather than determining a single meaning inherent to the image. Saying this does not, however, imply an unlimited diversity of potential readings but rather a limited plurality that can, to a certain degree, be planned by those producing the images through the use of pre-existing motifs and formulae. This tension between singularity and plurality, the attempted predetermination of meaning in production and its confirmation or transformation in distribution and reception, formulaic predictability as against profitable polysemy, appears to be at the heart of the visual content industry in general and stock images in particular. It is made particularly apparent by the fact that the process of cultural production manifested in stock photography seems to incarnate the (unrealizable) ideal of the decontextualized image, the image as artefact and sign 'in its own right', by presenting and promoting photographs as objects of contemplation in printed catalogues, on CD-ROMs and in selections of slides. These decontextualized images – replete with diverse signifying possibilities – are, however, made to be viewed instrumentally by cultural intermediaries, as potential vehicles for purposive meanings anchored in the final advertising or marketing text.

7. Stock images are products of photographic practices. They are subject to contextual influences, constraints and pressures that impact upon their production, distribution and reception, but they are also shaped by the specific historical conventions and technological capacities of photography.

A Brief Word About Research Methods

The ways in which I have researched the visual content industry reflect my dual concern with cultural production practices and representational forms, focusing on two separate but related objects of analysis: stock-photographic production procedures and categories of stock-photography images.

Data on *photographic practices* were gleaned from three sources: (1) Interviews with professionals connected to the stock photography industry, in Israel, the UK and the USA. The interviewees included photographers, agency management, activists in professional trade associations, industry 'observers', graphic designers and advertising 'creatives'. (2) Attendance at the Photo Expo East '98 conference in New York in November 1998, the East Coast version of the stock and commercial photography industry's most important professional gathering in the United States. Attending this conference meant that I could participate in seminars with some of the leading figures in the stock photography industry. In particular I was able to observe the (increasingly troubled) interaction between photographers and stock-agency management over creative, technological and financial issues. This proved an essential supplement to the information provided in the interviews. (3) Industry Publications: I have made extensive use of articles on stock photography published in trade journals such as *Photo District News*, *Stock Photo Report*, *PhotoStockNOTES*, *Communication Arts*, *Graphic Design USA* and *Creative Review*, among others. The websites of these magazines, and of the stock-photography companies themselves (in particular Getty Images and Corbis), have also been extremely important sources of information.

My analysis of *stock photographs* is organized around the catalogues of images that are used by agencies as their main marketing tool. Twenty such catalogues have been acquired, from a variety of US and European companies, spanning the last decade. These provide the basic material for the analysis of the images.

The rationale for using these catalogues as data sources is fourfold. First, the notion of the 'catalogue' is especially compelling in photography theory, for the medium is often accused of transforming the whole world into a spectacular catalogue of interchangeable signs (Sontag 1977), while its actual use as a format points to the way in which photography decontextualizes unique material objects and presents them as equivalent and exchangeable 'sights'. This kinship of critical cultural analysis and commercial photographic production – 'archive' in particular is deployed as a key term in both – will be explored more fully later on.

Second, the catalogues represent a pre-selected sample of the vastly greater number of images held in stock by the companies concerned. As such, they have been arranged according to subject-classifications chosen for their utility to the catalogue user and/or their cultural resonance, rather than for their fidelity to the structure of the agency archive as a whole: hence not only the content, format and style of these pre-selected images, but the differences in classification labels for particular content (such as, for pictures of people, 'Lifestyle' as opposed to 'People'), can serve as cultural indicators.

The third reason for relying on the catalogues as data sources is that this is chiefly how the immediate clients of stock agencies have traditionally encountered most of the images, including the few that they may ultimately purchase, although in recent years the printed catalogue has been augmented – and in some cases replaced – by CD-ROMs and websites. Ultimately, the images that are chosen and promoted in catalogues are those perceived by the agency as having the greatest sales potential and, moreover, they are also those that are most frequently sold in practice. Thus the catalogue, rather than the agency archive, most consistently articulates the connection between moments of image-production, distribution and circulation.

The final reason for relying on stock catalogues as a pre-selected sample is largely logistical. It is far easier to gain access to stock catalogues than it is to agency archives: they are distributed free of charge to potential clients, whereas the archive itself is normally amenable only to agency staff. Moreover, the archive is subject to constant, complex change, both incremental and momentous, much of which is unrecorded. The catalogues, on the other hand, provide a permanent record from different periods. They allow for effective comparison historically between diverse periods and synchronically between different companies during the same period, something that would be almost impossible to achieve were the research to be carried out directly on the larger archives.

Despite the fact that the catalogues offer a more manageable sample of images, their size still presents difficulties for qualitative cultural analysis. The average catalogue is around two hundred pages in length, each page containing from five to ten images: thus a conservative estimate puts the number of images per catalogue at around one thousand. Multiply that by twenty catalogues, and the sample has become too unwieldy for in-depth critical interpretation. A possible solution would be to focus on 'natural' classifications of images, by which I mean those named and used in the catalogues themselves, such as 'People'.[23]

The problem with this is that classification names come and go from catalogue to catalogue, with – to continue with our example – 'People' either not appearing at all or apparently taking over entire catalogues (and being subdivided accordingly). In order to create a manageable corpus of stock images while accounting for the impact of such shifts in classification I have further narrowed the sample, selecting a priori a key category of images promoted in stock-photography catalogues: 'romantic couples'. The rationale for this choice is discussed in Chapter 6.

Images and Words about Images

This dual approach to stock photography involves moving between – and comparing – two different types of 'data': the 'texts' of industry practitioners, including interviews, comments made at professional conferences and articles printed in trade journals; and the images that are the products of that industry. Hence an obvious but important difference between these data is their 'medium': one is verbal, the other pictorial. This distinction has important implications not only for the operations of the visual content industry, as I hope to show. It also means that the research itself will need to be sensitive to the complex and difficult history of encounters between images and words.

Such concern with the often fraught intersection of pictures and verbal texts is clearly nothing new. Their areas of reciprocity and friction, co-presence and intractability, equivalence and difference, are among the most vexed issues in the study of cultural artefacts and artistic works. These are weighty, time-honoured matters, subjects of extensive discussion across cultures and epochs, and they necessarily enliven (and plague) many critical encounters with visual, pictorial and 'multi-medial' symbolic forms.

Notwithstanding this venerable history, the advent of electronic and now digital communication technologies has made the image–word relationship, and its manifestation in contemporary cultural products – advertisements, newspapers and magazines, films, television programmes – a matter of increasing urgency to media analysts,[24] as well as a defining problematic of the new field of 'visual culture studies' (Mitchell 2002). Furthermore, these products have become grist to the mill of a semiotically informed cultural studies, both in their problematic appearance as 'texts' and through the apparently neutral notion of 'multimodality'. Yet a key problem besetting media and cultural analysts is that there is no obviously external 'vantage point' from which to observe the image–text relationship. For it is not simply a question of investigating the interactions between images and words. It also a question of how do this adequately *in words*. The study of images *on their own* is itself embroiled in the image–text problematic. Even if we set aside claims that verbal language informs almost all areas of subjective and inter-subjective experience, including visual perception and interpretation, the simple fact that academic scholarship is mainly rendered as written discourse means that the analysis of visual culture takes the form of words. We appraise pictures from *within* writing. We engage, ineluctably, in 'ekphrasis', broadly defined as the verbal representation of visual representation, the use of texts to describe images.[25]

At the most naive level this can involve an operational assumption of adequate code-equivalence between visual images and the discourse that interrogates them: the supposition that the analyst's verbal text can, at least approximately, 'grasp' the visual object and re-present it before a reader. Such an assumption, both necessary and largely inconspicuous, is open to serious challenge on theoretical and methodological grounds, although such challenges run the obvious risk of disabling critical investigation of non-verbal phenomena altogether. Upon these uncertain foundations, however, the edifice itself is unsteady, in particular with regard to that branch of semiotics or semiology in the Saussurean tradition that, for all the efforts of Peirceans, has been most influential in fields of inquiry which take 'visual' or multimodal media as primary objects of study: cultural studies, media studies, film history and theory, non-traditional forms of art and architecture criticism.[26] For the semiotic analysis of visual images bears within it a central crux – the claim that semiotics possesses 'supradisciplinary status' (Bal and Bryson, 1991: 176) and has freed itself from its (partial) origins in linguistics, making it suitable for application to non-linguistic 'texts', including pictures and photographs.[27] Such a claim clearly raises questions concerning the putative status of semiology as a 'science' (see Lefebvre's (1991: 130–47) trenchant critique), as well as about the relationship between disciplinary boundaries, representational forms and epistemological categories (such as modes of perception and cognition).

When the dust has cleared in these debates, it is still worth asking whether it is appropriate to analyse visual images using a theory that implicitly takes language as paradigmatic for meaning (for example, Barthes 1977a, b, c; Burgin 1982, a, b). Does not such a linguistic 'bias' threaten to reduce non-linguistic signs to linguistic categories, eliding the more fundamental question of the similarity – or otherwise – of images and words? And doesn't it tend to create a mystified and obscure 'remainder' of all that is irreducible to those linguistic categories, of everything that is left unexplained in the image after the various connotations and cultural codes have been peeled off and the semiotic analysis has run its course? (Thus Barthes describes the 'literal' meaning of an image as 'a message by eviction' (1977b: 42).) Examples of such a remainder might include Bryson's (1981: 6) figural 'being-as-image', or Barthes' 'obtuse meaning': 'what, in the image, is purely image' (1977c: 61). The key assumption behind this 'purely image' is that there is (or should be) a realm of pristine visuality unadulterated by language and signification, a *'this-side of language'* (Barthes 1977a: 30, original emphasis).

So a good reason for hesitating before accepting the claim that semiotics is a 'transdisciplinary theory' is that the relationship between images and language is very much unsettled: 'The visual has served, over and again, as the figure within textual analysis for the nontextual, within discourse for the nondiscursive . . . The image, in essence, becomes the figure in such analysis for the rupturing of linguistic totality' (Herbert 1995: 538). This linguistic intractability of the image underpins what W.J.T. Mitchell has called the 'pictorial turn' (following Rorty's 'linguistic turn') in philosophy and in the production and understanding of culture, in which ' pictures form a point of peculiar friction and discomfort across a broad range of intellectual inquiry' (Mitchell 1992: 90; see also Mitchell 1994).

The methodological implications of such friction and discomfort are as follows. To begin with, while linguistic-semiotic approaches are not only so ubiquitous as to be unavoidable, but are also genuinely compelling analytical tools, it is important to recognize the ways in which they are resisted by visual images, and to understand visual experience and the interpretation of images as not wholly explicable in terms of textual decipherment.[28] Equally, however, it is essential to resist the contrary temptation: the reification of 'the image' and its abstraction from material, social and linguistic contexts, which some have argued mirrors on the level of theory the decontextualization and commodification of images on a global scale that is so prominent a feature of current cultural practice (Foster 1996: 106–7).[29] Images may be very different to linguistic texts, but they are almost always contextually juxtaposed with words – whether captions, titles, advertising or editorial 'copy' – and it is reasonable to assume that their interpretation is in important ways inflected by language (see Barthes 1977a, b; Burgin 1986: 51–69).

In other words, word and image are not identical, but they are both mutually engaged and jointly embedded in broader discourses, making it rash to claim that the production and interpretation of images can be wholly detached from 'non-visual' sensory and signifying practices, especially language. The complexity of this relationship necessitates the sensitive application of a number of analytical approaches, recognizing the advantages, biases and limitations of each. That is why the analysis of the images undertaken in this research deploys a somewhat eclectic conceptual armoury, moving between modes of inquiry borrowed from cultural studies, film studies, history of art and photography theory, and well as from literary studies, textual hermeneutics, and linguistic-semiotic accounts of cultural signification.

Yet I will also make a further claim: that the friction between images and words is not really a 'problem'. Rather, it is actually *productive* in practice. It contributes to the ceaseless performance, intelligibility and utility of symbolic forms both as 'technical' media and as 'cultural' activity, and to the (precarious) coherence of cultural production processes. For intellectual uncertainty as to the equivalence or difference of words and images is paralleled by a similar – indeed, often far more intense – concern among particular groups of professional 'imageers' in contemporary popular culture. These occupational groups include image-makers who manufacture pictures, as well as – for want of a better term – professional 'image-exploiters' who buy and utilize them in further text-image ensembles (adverts, brochures, newspaper and magazine articles, product packaging, etc.). All of these groups use words systematically and deliberately in order to create, organize, understand, evaluate, promote and deploy that apparently most 'visual' of media – *photographs* – while occasionally placing a tactical distance between themselves and the verbal realm.

Stock photography provides a good example of this productivity. Not only is the evaluation of images heavily dependent on verbal language, but the professional literature is replete with advice to photographers to produce their images as visual counterparts to common verbal idiomatic expressions. More-over, the images are subject to (and *created* through) institutionalized forms of verbal classification and description in stock agency archives and catalogues (see Chapter 3) – forms which are being reconfigured as a result of the deploy-ment of 'keyword' searches to find images in digital archives, including web-sites (see Chapter 7). So in effect I will use the case of stock photography to explore a hypothesis: that among the engines driving the production of visual culture, especially in its 'mass' or 'industrialized' forms, is the systematic and dynamic intersection of images and words in a dialectic of symbolic generation. And this dialectic is both creative and propulsive: it helps to bring images into being as material objects and it drives their movement across institutionally distinct sites of production, promotion, circulation and reception.

Admitting Limitations

Any research on 'the real world' is bound to be incomplete. In addition to the extreme unlikelihood that an intellectual enterprise can fully convey the rich complexity of empirical phenomena, there are always organizational and logistical problems which can be as influential for the research as they are annoyingly mundane. It's best to be up-front about these before discussing any 'findings': my work on the visual content industry was beset by a number of logistical difficulties. The first was the secrecy, verging on paranoia, of many in the industry itself. This may have intensified recently as a result of the transformations sweeping the business which have heightened competition and increased both short-term and long-term uncertainty. As I mentioned earlier, only Getty Images PLC publishes audited accounts, and that is because it is legally obligated to do so as a publicly quoted company. The other large agencies are unwilling to provide detailed sales information, except where they can see a definite marketing advantage, a benefit that proved unlikely to arise in connection with this research. Thus, acquiring information as basic as sales turnover becomes a major obstacle. Regarding details of organizational pract-ices, such as relationships between agencies and photographers, criteria for image production and selection, the connection between the archives and the catalogues, and the impact of new technologies, the informants from smaller agencies proved extremely friendly and helpful, while (with the exception of Getty, who were initially very helpful) for the larger agencies I have had to rely mainly on articles in the trade press, the agencies' own press releases, and statements that slipped out during the sessions at Photo Expo East '98.[30] Some representatives of large agencies (mainly in Israel) were so suspicious that they either refused to meet me point-blank or turned down my requests to tape the interviews.[31] Overall, this has the effect of making my information on photographic practices less definitive and representative than I would have liked.

With regard to the analysis of photographic images, the biggest problem is the lack of chronological regularity and continuity in catalogue production, as well as the instability of the format. Overall I was aiming at a sample of images that would provide both diachronic continuity and synchronic range, so that I could compare changes over time within corporations and differences between diverse corporations at the same points in time. This proved to be impossible for a number of reasons. First was the unwillingness of many agencies to send me catalogues on the commercially sound grounds that catalogues cost money and I was not a potential customer, which meant that catalogues had to be begged and borrowed from contacts in the advertising and design world who no longer needed them. This led to a rather random selection, especially as it meant that I was unable to acquire or gain access to any except a handful of catalogues from the 1980s.

A more significant problem is that catalogues are not necessarily issued on a regular basis, nor do they possess the kind of uniform format that allows for easy comparison. Not only have catalogues been released with increasing frequency, but whereas in the past it was possible to point to a standardized 'general catalogue' format that included all the major image-classifications (people, landscapes, industry, business, sports, abstract), in recent years the larger agencies have taken to issuing specialist catalogues. For example, The Image Bank's Catalogue 16 (1995) was devoted solely to 'People', while Catalogue 17 (1995) focused on 'Ideas'. Likewise, Tony Stone Images released the *Wild* catalogue – their second catalogue to be devoted solely to wildlife and nature images (the first was called *Visions of Nature*) – in October 1998 (TSI Press Release 12.10.98, www.tonystone.com). Similarly, actual classification names and applications are in accelerated flux: 'People' is fairly self-explanatory, but the content and its meanings are subtly altered when similar images are classified under 'Lifestyle' in a later catalogue, and especially when they are dispersed throughout the sections of something like The Image Bank's *Perceptions* (Catalogue 24, 1998), whose headings are 'emotions', 'relationships', 'choices + changes', 'communication' and 'imagination'. Hence one advantage of the methodological decision to concentrate on a particular predefined category of images – romantic couples – is that it allowed me to stabilize the object of analysis despite this fluctuation in format and classification, and to account for the ways in which these fluctuations might impact on the images' meanings.

Finally, the principal limitation of the research is that it does not include an analysis of the reception of the images by actual 'end-users'. Indeed, it may strike readers as odd that I focus on the production of images and the mediation of their meaning by 'cultural intermediaries' but do not attempt to ascertain whether their projections of consumer interpretations are at all accurate or determining.

There are many reasons for this. Logistically it is very hard to track most of the images through to their final appearance in advertisements and marketing material, and in many cases the images have been hugely altered by the time they reach the final viewer. (This is actually a central concern in stock photography, one that will be explored in subsequent chapters.) At which point the research would be less concerned with questions of cultural production and the mediation of photographic meaning than with the formation of advertising audiences and modes of reading in the broader context of cultural consumption, questions which are extremely complex in their own right and – while clearly connected – legitimately beyond the scope of this project. I am not arguing for the absolute and eternal separation of production and consumption (as I think is clear from the theoretical assumptions outlined above), or for the primacy of production with regard to the determination of meaning, but for the *privileged complexity of cultural production*. Therefore I would stress the *methodological* value of making the production/consumption distinction when analysing specific cultural industries. In fact, I would argue that this is one of the strengths of this book. By refusing at the outset to join the zero-sum argument over the power of producers versus the power of consumers, it is able to take cultural production seriously without dogmatically insisting on its ability to impose meanings.

Nevertheless, although I shall not directly investigate the processes of consumption, perception and meaning-creation among empirical viewers, this book would be seriously incomplete if it did not address the possible implications of production processes for consumption, since production has consumption as its goal and both producers and intermediaries work with either an implicit or an explicit 'profile' of an 'ideal' (that is, imagined or projected) viewer. As Don Slater argues in his discussion of the production and marketing of 'mass' (amateur) photography: 'production might not create the consumer concretely, without overwhelming mediation, but there is definitely an abstract specific consumer at which it is aimed, and it is this abstract relationship – of the 'manner' of production to the 'manner' of consumption – whose mechanisms must be explored' (1983: 247). This abstract or ideal consumer is potentially structured into the final product itself, although I will argue that in the case of stock photography, if not in other sectors, the complexity of mediation in the production process creates a diverse range of amorphous and sometimes conflicting ideal viewers, including, for the stock photographer, the ideal cultural intermediary. Moreover, these projections are not simply about *who* the viewer is imagined to be, but about the optimum conditions for viewing and the preferred viewing mode for generating a particular meaning (the 'manner' of consumption). In other words, producers project discursively sanctioned contextual ideals: ideal *modes of viewing*. As I argue in several of the chapters (most explicitly in Chapter 6) these conflicting projections and ideals are created around 'system' and 'mission' rhetorics – the former addressing professionals in the production system and the latter addressing 'consumers' at the end of it – and which can be traced in the images themselves. It is in these chapters that I come closest to speculating about the reception of stock images in consumer cultures and their connection to visual ordinariness.

Whether or not ideal modes of viewing are actually adopted by empirical viewers will, of course, remain beyond the scope of this book, although I do *not* assume that the responses of empirical viewers are necessarily limited by the range of viewing modes offered by a particular image: consumption is not a simple mirror-image of production, nor is reception totally deducible from the structure of the image or text. (See Bal and Bryson 1991 for an analysis of the distinction between ideal and empirical viewers and its problems.) Indeed, one of the claims of recent studies of consumer culture is that in many ways cultural production aims to reflect consumption, and not the other way around. The increasing use of focus groups, psychographic profiles, lifestyle research and audience-targeting techniques mean that 'ideal' viewing modes, at least as far as the cultural intermediaries in advertising agencies and marketing departments are concerned, are understood as a distillation of characteristics gleaned from empirical viewers.

How This Book Works

In addition to this introduction, the book is divided into seven inter-linked chapters (Chapters 2–8) followed by a very brief conclusion. The chapters are as follows:

Chapter 2. From the Library to the Bank: The Emergence of Stock Photography

Analysing the social and historical context of stock photography, this chapter offers an account of the industry's historical emergence and the crystallization of its core values and discourses. Historically the stock industry emerges in the United States and Europe in the early 1970s with the establishment of stock agencies The Image Bank and Comstock. Despite elements of continuity with previous formations – editorial picture agencies, photo libraries and private collections of artistic images – the new stock industry transformed previous practices by organizing them around the central discourse of marketing and advertising. This discourse was articulated through four interrelated core values: the institutional priority of marketing and advertising clients and images; the emphasis on 'quality' production values, technical excellence and 'talent'; the adoption of professional marketing and branding techniques; and a global orientation. Despite the dominance of these values, expressed in particular through the rise of the 'super-agencies', the industry accommodated diverse approaches informed by alternative practices and discourses, especially those connected to art and documentary photography.

Chapter 3. Shooting for Success: Stock Photography and the Production of Culture

This chapter explores the intersection between the 'cultural economy' of stock photography and its 'mode of representation' (Lash 1990). Beginning with a review of studies of photographic production, it then explores the 'biography' (Appadurai 1986, Kopytoff 1986) of the stock image by tracing its path through configurations of production and distribution, and by analysing key terms (success, creativity, meaning, genre, the concept, the catalogue) in the discourses of different industry professionals (photographers, agency management). These are interpreted in the context of semiotic and post-structuralist approaches to photography and cultural studies.

Chapter 4. The Archive, the Stereotype and The Image Repertoire: Classification and Stock Photography

Beginning with a theoretical discussion of the broader connection between photography and forms of social categorization, this chapter explores stock photography as an archival system, its connection to classification and social hierarchies in modern societies, the targeting of audiences and lifestyles within advertising and marketing discourse, and the relationship between stock images, stereotypes, perceptual modes, and the organizational and cultural milieu of cultural intermediaries. In the course of this discussion I introduce a different term – the 'image-repertoire' – to emphasize that, unlike some other photographic practices, stock photography is a dynamic archival system informed by a rhetorical and theatrical tradition rather than by positivist or empiricist emphases on the 'truth-value' of the image.

Chapter 5. The Image of Romance: Stock Images as Cultural Performances

This chapter draws upon semiotic and post-structuralist approaches to interpret a selected category of 'romantic' stock images and its relationship, broadly speaking, to cultural stereotypes. The analysis employs three interconnected dimensions – content, style and textual placement – and interprets the images' cultural significance using the central concepts of performativity (of social categories), materialization (of normative and culturally intelligible bodies) and abjection (of excluded others), particularly with regard to representations of sex, sexuality, class and ethnicity.

Chapter 6. Rhetorics of the Overlooked: The Communicative Modes of Stock Images

Developing the conception of the image-repertoire as a performative process, this chapter focuses on the complex communicative properties of stock photographs, including the ways in which they conspicuously perform their potential as promotional tools before cultural intermediaries while at the same time intersecting with the creation of 'ordinariness' and 'the everyday' among consumers. These communicative properties include the images' temporality, their narrative potentiality and their stillness, the conspicuousness of their performance or staging, and their incessant repetition. Interpreting the communicative mode of stock images as fundamentally enmeshed within the temporality of contemporary consumption itself, the chapter reassesses the potentiality of notions such as 'myth' and 'pseudo-cyclical time' in accounting for the visual dimensions of consumer cultures.

Chapter 7. And God Created Photoshop: Digital Technologies, Creative Mastery and Aesthetic Angst

This chapter explores the impact of new digital technologies on the practices and discourses of industry professionals and on stock images themselves. It looks at the ways in which digital technologies have both transformed and been incorporated into pre-existing industrial systems and cultural practices, tracing elements of continuity and discontinuity through moments of 'production', 'storage' and 'distribution'. It also examines the ways in which the technologies impart a sense of creative mastery to professionals while reviving anxiety over the 'integrity' of their images.

Chapter 8. The Realm of the Info-Pixel: From Stock Photography to the Visual Content Industry

In this chapter I ask how we might understand the systematic digitization of cultural forms, and how the environmental dynamics of industrialized visual culture can be grasped in relation to cultural experience and the organization of power. What, in short, might the advent of a digitized, global 'visual content industry' *mean* for us and our culture? To answer this question I address the relationship between new technologies and organizational, structural-financial and cultural factors in the creation of the visual content industry, exploring the industry as an organizational mode for exploiting and containing the destabilizing effects of digital technologies on previously distinct media such as photography, illustration, fine art, film and video. Describing the dynamics of the visual content industry, and their impact on the economic relations between diverse types of professionals and organizations, the chapter raises questions about their social and cultural ramifications for image-diversity, cultural domination and creativity. Finally, it considers the ideological and ethical implications of these developments.

Most of these chapters are characterized by the presentation and close analysis of empirical material, whether historical accounts of industrial developments (Chapter 2), explorations of professional practices and discourses in pre-digital stock and the visual content industry (Chapters 3 and 7), readings of stock images (Chapter 5) and the 'political-economic' analysis of organizational trends and power relations within the visual content industry (Chapter 8). These 'empirical' sections, while they certainly engage with cultural and photography theory, are punctuated by two chapters that are more purely 'theoretical' (or possibly speculative) in character: Chapter 4 on the archival dynamics of stock photography and Chapter 6 on the communicative modes or 'rhetorics' of stock images and consumer culture. I say this because although the book is written to be read as a whole, readers whose principal aim is to glean some useful information about stock photography might wish to postpone reading the 'theoretical' chapters. I hope that other readers who – like me – want to look at stock photography and the visual content industry in order to understand more about contemporary consumer cultures will find these 'speculative' sections particularly interesting, if not necessarily convincing.

Notes

1. This very rough figure of 70 per cent is based on data for 1997 (*Communication Arts*, August 1998: 209).
2. I use the term 'consumer culture' rather than 'consumer society' because it specifically applies to my main subject: the industrial production of visual cultural products for consumers. I should add that the 'treatment' of viewers as consumers by cultural industries does not, of itself, necessarily dictate that viewers do indeed shape their identities primarily through consumption.
3. For the sake of brevity, I will use the terms 'stock photography' and 'visual content industry' almost interchangeably in this chapter, although they

are not identical. As later chapters will make plain, the latter term both includes the former and succeeds it chronologically.

4. This is the general practice, although some agencies employ salaried staff photographers and produce in-house images which the agency owns. Other agencies operate a mixed system, creating in-house photographs and buying the licensing rights (not the copyright) to other images from freelance photographers. Very recently a number of 'high-end' agencies, most notably Tony Stone, have instituted a type of assignment or 'work-for-hire' relationship with photographers: the agency develops a particular theme or idea for a catalogue, selects and approaches suitable photographers, and actively directs the shoots. This new (and, for stock photography, minority) practice will be discussed in Chapter 8.

5. As a rule, photographers' share of international sales are lower than for domestic sales, largely because foreign representatives or franchisees need to be taken into account. The allocation of revenue from digital sales will also be dealt with in Chapter 8.

6. Prices can range from a few hundred US dollars for a small brochure to several thousand for national advertising campaigns (Demystifying 'Rights Protected' Stock Photo Pricing, Comstock, www.comstock.com, 1999). According to the ASMP Press Release 'ASMP's Stock Survey Results – May 1999', the value of the average sale made by stock agencies in 1999 was $352.

7. The term 'generic image' is widely used in the stock industry.

8. The term 'cultural intermediaries' originates with Bourdieu (1986) – who actually wrote of '*new* cultural intermediaries', a new (petit-bourgeois) class fraction of 'knowledge workers' specializing in representation and the provision of symbolic goods and services in such areas as broadcasting, public relations, advertising, etc. The term has been adopted, refined and critiqued in subsequent explorations of cultural production and advertising (for cogent recent accounts see Nixon and Du Gay 2002 and Negus 2002), with writers such as Hesmondhalgh (2002) preferring the term 'cultural managers'. The debate around these terms, which is in danger of becoming arcane, has nevertheless focused scholarly attention on the collaborative and complexly structured nature of contemporary cultural production and its relation to commercial practices and new occupational groupings. I use the term to refer to those workers in stock agencies, and their clients in advertising, marketing and design, who are responsible for the distribution and circulation of stock images but not for their initial production (stock photographers are not therefore cultural intermediaries – they are primary-symbol creators), although the distinction is not always easy to make. As intermediaries these workers 'come *in-between* creative

artists and consumers (or, more generally, production and consumption)', and are continually engaged in articulating the connections between them (Negus 2002).

9. 'Royalty-free' images are sold on a single-fee, multiple-use, mass-distribution principle, which means that, in contrast to rights-protected stock photography, purchase of the image includes purchase of a broad, non-exclusive licence to use the image as, when and however often the purchaser sees fit (although there are more restrictions than immediately meet the eye). Royalty-free images are generally sold on CD-ROM for between $100 and $500 for several hundred and even several thousand images, and are also available individually via the internet. The relationship between conventional stock agencies and royalty-free companies – which has moved from animosity to incorporation – will be dealt with in Chapter 7.

10. Broadly endorsed within the industry in the late 1990s, the figure of $1 billion for total global sales was frequently mentioned during the trade conference Photo Expo East '98, although no one could point to a definitive source. (The Image Bank estimated the figure for 1998 at $650 million, reaching $1 billion by the year 2000, while Index Stock put the value of the 'visual content industry' at $2.5 billion in 2000, without spelling out how it calculated that figure: Index Stock, 'Corporate History', 19 November 1999, www.indexstock.com/press/history.htm.) It was confirmed as an acceptable though 'very rough, repeat very rough' estimate by Brian Seed, Publisher of Stock Photo Report (probably the most thorough, though not necessarily the most popular, industry monitor) in private correspondence with the author (30.1.99). In his keynote address at Photo Expo East '98, Jonathan Klein, CEO of Getty Images PLC, bemoaned the secrecy of his competitors with regard to publishing accurate financial figures (31.10.98).

11. 'Representation' is a troubling term but especially useful for figurative pictorial and photographic images, since it can mean simultaneously 'depiction' and 'standing in place of' (as in representative government). This is complicated by the basic semiotic proposition that an image, as a type of sign, frequently 'stands in place of' something other than what it 'depicts': advertising images, for example, often depict scenes and persons which not only signify undepicted concepts, but stand in place of the viewer.

12. Barthes's declared aim in *Camera Lucida*, probably the most influential contemporary meditation on photography, is 'to learn at all costs what Photography was "in itself", by what essential feature it was to be distinguished from the community of images' (Barthes 1984: 3).

13. The choice is usually between Nièpce, Daguerre and Fox Talbot.
14. Some of these central texts are usefully collected in Trachtenberg (1980).
15. To name only some of the most prominent books and articles.
16. Andrew Tolson (1996; 112–13) makes a similar point.
17. Geoffrey Batchen (1997) examines the 'binary logic' that manifests an underlying connection – an obsession with ontology – between two ostensibly opposed approaches to photography: a traditional 'formalist' insistence on the inherent, fundamental and determining characteristics of photography as a unique medium, irrespective of cultural context, versus a 'postmodernist' account that elevates the historical and cultural context as against the self-sufficiency of the image, arguing that photography has no essential identity. The obsession with the ontological foundation of the medium is not of course unique to photograph theory: precedents come to mind in painting and sculpture (see Foster 1996), not to mention literary writing. Similarly, the ontologically-obsessed opposition of 'formalist' medium-specificity and 'postmodernist' contextualization has arisen elsewhere: 'Where we once ontologized mediums to death, we now historicize them out of existence' (Foster 1996: 100).
18. This is in contrast, for instance, to the theory and history of film. Although frequently in conflict, especially over questions of reception, these projects embrace a range of both theoretical and historical investigations, including detailed analyses of film as both text and as industry, that far outstrips the range of photography theory and history. Balio's (1985) anthology on the US film industry provides some good examples, while Bordwell, Thompson and Staiger's (1985) analysis of classical Hollywood cinema remains probably the best-known integration of industrial and textual analysis. For a lucid discussion of these issues see Hansen (1991: 1–8).
19. The crucial debate – between Garnham (political economy of communication) and Grossberg (cultural studies), with various stabs at mediation by other writers – can be found in a special issue of *Critical Studies in Mass Communication* 12(1) (1995), as well as in Ferguson and Golding (1997). Hesmondhalgh (2002) gives a brief but sane overview and suggests an eminently sensible resolution, while Jones (1999) gives an interesting account of the complex relevance of Raymond Williams's writings on 'cultural materialism' to this debate.
20. This sense that production is in great part a rhetorical affair is a development of Wernick's (1991) insight concerning the (self-)promotional logic of contemporary consumer culture, one which, however, extends his notion of promotional logic back into the production environment itself.

21. The key publication here is the anthology edited by Paul du Gay and Michael Pryke (2002).

22. The distinction between notions of 'mission' and 'system' is elaborated in Chapter 6.

23. As a general rule in the discussion of stock photography catalogues, the term 'classification' describes the subject-headings used by stock agencies themselves. 'Category' refers to the a priori division and ordering of images according to the needs of the research.

24. See McLuhan (1994 [1964]), Postman (1985), Meyrovitz (1985), Bolter (1996), among many others.

25. The literature on the image-text relationship and on ekphrasis is extensive. My broad use of 'ekphrasis' follows Mitchell's superb account in 'Ekphrasis and the Other' (Miller 1994). For a discussion of ekphrasis as a literary device, and in relation to the yearning for 'the natural sign', see Krieger (1992).

26. It is sometimes claimed that Peircean semiotic theory offers a more appropriate framework for the analysis of images (and other non-linguistic signs) than the Saussurean tradition. Nevertheless, Peirce's distinction between the sign-types index, symbol and icon has left a problematic legacy, with 'icon' probably causing the most confusion and concern. See, among others, Eco (1975), Rodowik (1990), and Elkins (1995) for brief discussions.

27. This assertion by Bal and Bryson is unfortunate, since it appears to locate their essay on semiotics and art history in a direct line of descent from more 'scientistic' approaches. Equally unfortunate is their contention that the development of semiotics in conjunction with literary texts is 'perhaps largely a historical accident, whose consequences, while not unimportant, can be bracketed' (1991: 176). Notwithstanding the deployment of conditionals and negatives here – 'perhaps largely' and 'not unimportant' used to strengthen a weak argument through contrite candor – this claim remains unsupported, and is rightly criticized by Mitchell (1994: 14, note 10). Most unfortunate, however, is that the claim of 'transdisciplinarity' is actually unfaithful to the substance of their essay, which is acutely sensitive to the limitations and lacunae of semiotic theory, while arguing cogently for the utility and relevance of 'post-strucuralist' perspectives, critiques of Saussurean semiotics among them.

28. This renewed emphasis on the opposition between image and text both echoes Lessing's eighteenth-century antinomy of painting and poetry in *Laocoon*, and perhaps achieves its apogee in Lyotard's distinction between 'discourse' and 'figure' (for a discussion see Lash 1988). According

to Rodowick, the privileging of the verbal over the pictorial has been a central strategy of Western philosophy for at least two hundred years (1990: 10); Derrida (1976), of course, has argued that the graphic (which, crucially, includes writing) has been systematically excluded by a phono-centric Western philosophical tradition that can be traced back to Plato, although some dispute whether Derridean 'writing' itself includes or excludes the pictorial (for example, Elkins 1995).

29. The threat of 'reification' and 'abstraction' is at the heart of the controversy around the institutionalization of 'Visual Culture' as a separate field of inquiry. See the 'Visual Culture Questionnaire', *October* 77 (1996: 26–69). For a critique of the assumptions behind this questionnaire, see Irit Rogoff's article in Mirzoeff 1998: 14–26. Mitchell (2002) provides a characteristically lucid discussion of the issues.

30. Despite the cooperation of most of my informants, some asked not to be named or quoted. Since their views were almost always echoed either in the trade press, at Photo Expo East '98 or elsewhere in the public domain, I have preferred to use these 'on the record' statements wherever possible, including for informants who made no request for anonymity. The interviews, therefore, largely occupy the background in the chapters that follow (with a couple of exceptions): they were, however, crucial in directing me – as an outsider – toward an understanding of the industry's core values and dynamics.

31. 'Suspicion' is my interpretation of the following: I was required to bring convincing proof of my status as a researcher, and when I promised to do so, my potential informant suddenly became 'too busy' on a permanent basis.

2

From the Library to the Bank: The Emergence of Stock Photography

In 'Pictures for Rent: From Stereoscope to Stereotype' (1999), the only published scholarly critique of the contemporary stock-photography business, J. Abbott Miller outlines the extreme difficulty of tracing the industry's history.

> Stock photography is both a border activity – a stepchild of more respected forms – and a transient, commercially driven undertaking. Nor is stock photography a stable, continuous or discrete entity . . . There is no single point of origin for stock photography, which has grown out of the diverse areas of photographic production and consumption. (Miller 1999: 121)

This is an acute observation. The issue of stock photography's stability and identity, its coherence as a discrete phenomenon (whether defined as an industry, a marketing method, an archival procedure, a photographic style, etc.) anchored in identifiable historical origins, is still of some concern among professionals today. Nevertheless, however fragile the foundations, an ordered chronological account of stock photography – shot through with critical reflection – demands to be constructed. For the industry and its products cannot be materially and discursively grasped without a sense of their historical emergence.

It is worth the risk of either dignifying or deriding that emergence through the conjuring trick of periodization. Three stages stand out from the wealth of detail: (1) a 'primitive' age before the 1970s in which stock photography barely exists, or exists only in potential (a potential to be recovered retrospectively in the subsequent quest for legitimacy), consisting as it does of an inchoate mass of small agencies serving a diverse range of sectors and purposes (editorial, historical, scientific, geographical, educational, journalistic, commercial) with little consciousness of belonging to a greater whole and sharing a common project or a distinguished future; (2) 1974–1990, a 'classical' period in which, following the lead of agencies such as The Image Bank and Comstock, stock photography is consolidated as a unified industry and as an object of discourse, establishing its paradigmatic identity and mission as the image-producing arm of the advertising industry, and formulating a recognisable, consensual visual aesthetic manifested in the 'generic stock image'; (3) 1990 to the present, a 'modern' (or perhaps postmodern) period characterized by rapid and radical fiscal, organizational and technological change, corporate and cultural disorientation, fragmentation, restructuring and consolidation coupled with massive growth and global wealth-generation, partial dislocation from the immediate imperatives of the advertising industry and the construction of alternative (including consumer) markets, and an experimentation with the style, and to a lesser degree the content, of images.

The necessarily brief chronicle that follows focuses on the first two of these periods, although it will also touch upon the third (which has already been outlined to some extent in the Introduction) where relevant.[1] A more in-depth analysis of this 'modern/postmodern' period will be provided in later sections and chapters, concentrating on the continuities and changes in image-content and style, and on the impact of technological, commercial and organizational changes. Hence I have attempted to keep repetition to a minimum, while trying to provide some sense of historical order and breadth.

According to most accounts, stock photography assumes its definitive contemporary identity and structure in the 1970s, shifting from a largely 'editorial' orientation based on the supply of images for magazine and newspaper articles to one that served the needs of consumer advertising and corporate marketing.[2]

In the process it broke decisively with ancestors who, judging by the tone of some current commentators, were variously distinguished and vulgar. From the wrong side of the cultural tracks, if we accept the implied disdain of the description in *How to Shoot Stock Photos that Sell*, were the 'photo libraries' established 'early in the 20th Century . . . "selling" rights to stock images of such predictable subjects as babies, animals and staged photographs of people' (Heron 1996: 13). Similar libraries are described by Naomi Rosenblum as 'companies that during the 1890s had stocked large selections of photographs, including stereographs, to meet the demands of middle-class viewers and burgeoning magazines' (1997: 467), apparently catering to a bourgeois taste for the sentimental, the exotic and the mildly shocking.

More venerable progenitors can be found among the news archives established by newspapers and wire services and in the documentary and art photography collections assembled by individual collectors. Probably the most famous private collection is that created by Otto Bettman, which began its life as two trunks containing 25,000 photographs, prints and negatives spirited (along with Bettman himself) out of Nazi Germany in 1935, and is today, with nearly 17 million images, the flagship historical archive of Bill Gates's Corbis Corp: the contemporary archive also includes material from United Press International and Reuters. Another esteemed forebear of stock photography, related to newspaper archives and private collections, is the 'picture agency' of the type established in Europe and the United States between the two world wars. Frequently founded by photographers themselves, these agencies were designed 'to serve the thriving market for news picture magazines such as Life, Paris Match and Picture Post' (Visual Communications Group Web Page 1997, no longer available). They focused primarily on the editorial market and worked broadly within the framework of photojournalism. Significantly, they were more than mere archives of 'out-takes' (unused images) from commissioned assignments. Rather, picture agencies were proactive with regard to their clients, and 'concerned themselves with generating story ideas, making assignments and collecting fees in addition to maintaining files of pictures from which editors might choose suitable illustrations' (Rosenblum 1997: 467). Significantly – from the point of view of the subsequent development of stock photography – many of their images were shot with multiple sales in mind. This had an effect on visual content and style: in the case of news photo agencies in Weimar Germany, for example, overt political imagery was discouraged 'since a neutral picture had more potential to be sold to both liberal and conservative publications' (Miller 1999: 125).

A good example of such a picture agency, and its destiny, is provided by the Freelance Photographers Guild, founded in the United States in 1936 in response to demand for photo-essay material for picture journals. Today, operating under its abbreviated title FPG International, it has evolved into one of America's largest stock-photography companies, its images and ethos now geared primarily to the needs of the advertising industry. Its ownership has also changed. No longer an independent stock agency, let alone a photographer's collective, FPG was bought in 1997 by Visual Communications Group (VCG), at that time one of the multinational super-agencies, which also owned stock agencies, fine art collections and historical archives in Europe, as well as a 'royalty-free' image division. VCG was itself owned by United News and Media PLC, owner of the UK's Express Newspapers and an international media and information conglomerate comprising consumer publishing, broadcasting, financial and business services.[3] Then, in 2000, FPG – along with the rest of its parent company – was acquired from United News and Media by Getty Images.

These historical antecedents – popular photo libraries, news archives and private collections, and picture agencies – are important for three reasons. First, each has contributed in identifiable ways to the contemporary stock industry:

the photo libraries have imparted their profitable sensitivity to popular taste, including for the conventional and the sentimental; the news archives and private collections have imparted a rhetoric of quality which refers both to seriousness of content and to technical proficiency; and the picture agencies have bequeathed creative and commercial energy in generating images based around saleable marketing concepts and specified target audiences. Second, they have 'returned', in a transformed constellation, as integral components of the advertising-oriented 'visual content industry' into which stock photography, as their independent offspring, is itself being subsumed: this is especially apparent from the affiliations and ownership structures of the multinational 'super-agencies', where stock photography, royalty-free image producers and historical and fine-art archives are being combined synergistically to serve corporate sales. Finally, this reconfiguration within the visual content industry represents an ironic historical reversal of stock photography's 'decisive break' with its forebears in the 1970s, emphasizing areas of continuity and mutual transformation rather than those of absolute rupture and difference.

The pioneer of that 'decisive break' is generally thought to be The Image Bank, established in New York in October 1974 by businessman Stanley Kanney and photographer Lawrence Fried, although Abbott Miller reports that the founders of Comstock – Tom Grill and Henry Scanlon, another photographer–businessman coupling – also claim credit (1999: 128; see also 'Future Shock: Comstock Goes Clip, Henry Scanlon Explains Why', *PDN*, 9/ 97: 60–8). Whatever the precise truth, the widely disseminated narrative of The Image Bank's foundation serves well as an archetypal account, strategically augmented by a few choice references to Comstock's version of events.

According to the special issue of *Zoom* magazine in honour of The Image Bank's 20th anniversary, its two founders

> shared a vision: to create a new type of stock image agency which serviced the advertising industry; an agency which was more sophisticated, truly international, which represented and commissioned top photographic talent, and which would utilize the most up-to-date technologies, merchandising and marketing techniques. (*Zoom* Special Issue, 1994: 4)

Michal Heron provides a breathless account of the changes wrought by The Image Bank, without once mentioning the agency's name:

> A dramatic change occurred when the first agency to serve the advertising market was founded. Entering the bastion of big money assignment photography, this agency introduced aggressive sales techniques and, novel to the stock industry, the concept of worldwide franchise agencies. (1996:13)

Notwithstanding Heron's claims and the hagiographic tone of the *Zoom* article, this emphasis on producing stock photographs for advertising was not at all new: Helen Wilkinson's (1997) study of the British agency Photographic Advertising Ltd in the 1930s makes it clear that stock companies were geared to advertising well before Kanney and Fried experienced their 'vision'. Miller, in turn, traces the historical evolution of stock back to companies producing and selling stereoscopic images in the nineteenth century, which mutated into news and documentary photo agencies, and later into advertising-oriented stock agencies. In fact, Miller gives credit for the establishment of the advertising-oriented stock *system* to large stereoscope companies, such as Underwood and Underwood, who were in business in the first two decades of the twentieth century: the 'industry's' first catalogue was published by the same firm in 1920 (1999: 128). Similarly, Michael Hiley's analysis of the dawn of advertising photography in late nineteenth-century England suggests that something similar to the stock system (even though he doesn't use the term) produced a thriving market in commercial images before commissioned assignments became the norm. Early advertising photographers were adept at producing 'telling scenes', stereotyped narrative images that 'might prove useful to advertisers' (Hiley 1983: 108–35) and which could be speedily supplied.

Yet the creation of The Image Bank *did* initiate a period of radical change within the stock industry. It reshaped several already-existing patterns of industry activity, articulating them within the terms of the visual regime of consumer culture and its governing discourses of marketing and advertising, and establishing what we can call the paradigmatic structures and outlook of stock photography in its 'classical' period:

The first transformation was the *institutional priority* given to advertising clients, the result of The Image Bank's almost exclusive dedication to the production of stock for the advertising industry. Most agencies prior to this combined any advertising orientation with an editorial one, and stock work with commissioned assignments: Wilkinson (1997) notes that the stock library probably took up less than half the time of the staff at Photographic Advertising Ltd, the rest being committed to commissioned projects and possibly advertising films. In contrast, The Image Bank was to immerse itself entirely in the advertising industry, was to become, as it were, the industry's image-producing arm: its mission was not simply to supply appropriate ready-made images, but to speak the industry's language, accept its practices and norms, adhere to its standards, and anticipate its needs – especially with respect to speed of delivery, image content and quality, and reduced costs. The timing of the new venture was crucial to the success of this effort: 'In the aftermath of the 1973 oil crisis, American business plunged into recession and the US communications industry suffered the fallout. Advertising agencies and their clients began to scrutinize the cost-effectiveness of expensive photographic assignments' (Zoom 1994: 4).

The second area of change concerned *production values*, transformed through The Image Bank's emphasis on technical excellence and photographic 'talent'. This was an attempt to counter the stigma levelled at its precursors as representing second-rate photographers or purveying 'out-takes' – the unwanted leftovers – from commissioned assignments. As Heron (1996: 14) notes, the prevailing opinion of the industry before the 1970s could be summed up by the phrase 'stock is schlock'. Promoting product quality was therefore an essential move if the company was to succeed in attracting the interest and maintaining the loyalty of influential art directors inured against stock and habituated to high-quality commissioned work.

In practice this involved a tripartite move: The Image Bank had to create a new type of market for stock images, a pool of high-quality images for selection that were produced specifically for stock, and a cadre of top photographers to create these images. Delivering product quality itself possessed two complementary dimensions, technical and aesthetic. The first required the perfection of conventional photographic duplication techniques: the development of superior 35mm duplicate transparencies that would 'banish the nightmare of the lost original' (*Zoom* 1994: 4) and enable The Image Bank to offer the same high-quality image via representatives across the globe. The second was more complex, the result of the mutual realignment of technical and production criteria, creative personnel and target market: the creation of a recognizable visual aesthetic based loosely on conventional advertising imagery, an authoritative and replicable fusion of formal and stylistic codes and preferred subjects, which would determine for photographers exactly 'how' the new, high-quality stock photographs should look. This, in effect, was to herald the birth of the generic stock image.

Attracting photographers capable of producing these images was, according to Comstock CEO Henry Scanlon, crucial:

> Some very talented people, all of whom had been making their living shooting assignments, began bringing the same level of talent to stock, to the point where the quality of the imagery rivalled or exceeded what buyers could expect to achieve if they hired a top-notch photographer for thousands of dollars a day out of New York or Chicago. (*PDN*, 9/97: 62)

This strategy, aimed ultimately at persuading influential cultural intermediaries of stock's quality, was not only designed to let the aesthetic characteristics of the images 'speak for themselves' to their target market. It also worked by promoting the images as the creative labour of well-known photographers: it guaranteed the images' *pedigree*, within a discourse of cultural production that stressed the transmission of 'quality' from source to product and the import- ance of source-recognition to the experience of cultural consumption. Thus it was 'essentially a brand extension process. How can you convince art directors who think only of assignment photographers to consider buying stock? Gather together a group of the most recognized names in assignment photography – and announce to the world that you sell their stock' (Scanlon quoted in *PDN*, 9/97: 64).

In order to achieve this, of course, the agency had to persuade photographers that stock was a viable and profitable career option. Once again, historical circumstances proved favourable, with the decline of the mass-circulation picture magazines over the 1960s and 1970s encouraging an overall reduction in the number of permanent, salaried staff photographers and an increase in freelance photographers. The latter both needed the sales opportunities pre- sented by stock, and were not contractually forbidden from selling out-takes or undertaking projects independently of their staff contracts (unlike most staff photographers, whose images were considered the property of their pub- lishers). The 1978 US Copyright Law, which asserted that an image is the property of its photographer, and that the client of a freelance photographer is only paying for the specified 'use' of that image, further augmented the appeal of stock: photographers could make profits from multiple sales secure in the knowledge that their copyright was legally protected (Miller 1999: 128).

Overall, the transformation in production values was to become the source of a central tension within stock photography between two imperatives: the necessity, on the one hand, to produce images sufficiently generic, polysemic and anonymous to tolerate multiple reuse in diverse promotional contexts, and the requirement, on the other hand, to promote images of a singular quality and apparent originality – the marketable works of prominent individual photographers – that would enable them to compete with the context-specificity and artistic pretensions of assignment photographs. As we shall see later on, this tension between the generic and the singular, the anonymous and the attributable, reappears in the digitized 'visual content industry'.

The third paradigmatic transformation was an inevitable expression of The Image Bank's symbiotic relationship with the advertising world and its promo- tion of a 'quality' aesthetic: the adoption of *professional marketing techniques*. The stock catalogue, introduced into the modern stock industry by The Image Bank in 1982 (following a prototype joint venture with another publisher in 1978), is the most obvious example of this strategy.[4] In part this was the result of financial necessity. Advertising 'creatives' needed to be convinced that stock images were a useful and valuable resource, and they could not be relied upon spontaneously to discover a company that did not promote itself. Financial necessity, however, should be seen as one, albeit determining, element of an overall discursive configuration that aimed to make the agency into a 'brand' in its own right. Hence the establishment of elegant corporate headquarters in a penthouse office in New York's Vanderbilt Avenue, and the creation of a distinctive mirror-image black and white brand logo and corporate identity which was immediately protected as an international trademark. As Rex Jobe, President and CEO of The Image Bank, argued when explaining the redesign of the corporate logo in 1994: 'When your customer base comprises the top creatives in the world, then it would be an insult to them not to pay close attention to your visual identity' (*Zoom* 1994: 14). The 'professionalism' and 'marketing orientation' of the company were as much about situating The Image Bank within the overall visual culture of the advertising industry, of placing it and its products within the corporate subconscious, so to speak, of its potential clients, as a natural extension of their professional identities and associations.

Comstock's Henry Scanlon describes these three elements – 'quality' production values, the recruitment of prestigious photographers, and the adoption of professional marketing techniques – as absolutely symbiotic, and he also emphasizes the ways in which The Image Bank and Comstock together shaped the industry through a division of labour in these areas, the former promoting 'talent' (well-known assignment photographers) and the latter pioneering the use of catalogues and other marketing techniques:

> So you had Comstock hammering away at the market with a tactic that tried to show art directors pictures, via catalogues, that would get the reaction, 'Wow, I didn't know you could get a picture like that in stock!', and Image Bank trying to get the reaction 'Wow! I didn't know that great photographer also sold stock!' – and the eventual result, after a long struggle, was the creation of a 'position' for stock in the minds of art directors and the development of a market for photography in general that dwarfed anything the industry had experienced during the days when assignment photography was the only 'cell' on the commercial photography block. (*PDN*, 9/97: 64)

The final transformational mutation that The Image Bank initiated was in its *global orientation*. Again, international connections were not new: Wilkinson describes the close working relationship of Photographic Advertising in the UK with agencies in Europe and the United States, and the reciprocal purchasing of one another's images. Such a system of reciprocal connections exists to this day, most typically in the form of 'representation', whereby a stock agency holds the catalogues of any number of foreign agencies and 'represents' them in its own home market, keeping 40–50 per cent of the revenues from any sales. In contrast to this rather loose network of reciprocal relations between separate agencies, each firmly established as an independent entity in its own particular locale, The Image Bank set up a global operation on the basis of mutually exclusive contracts with local licensees. The Image Bank could not sell its images on the licensee's territory except through the licensee itself; the licensee, in return, could only sell The Image Bank's products, and was, moreover, obliged to adopt the agency's administrative, archival and distribution systems, corporate design schemes, and of course the corporate logo.

The strategy behind this seemingly more restrictive and less lucrative operation (in comparison with the earning potential of multiple representation of other agencies) was to establish The Image Bank as an international presence, to 'position' it as a 'global brand', complete with global corporate headquarters (in the United States – first in New York, and since 1992 in Dallas). This exclusive, rigidly defined hierarchy of relations between a centre and its foreign branches, along with its daily performance (in integrated administrative routines), concrete symbolization (in design schemes and the corporate logo), uniform product and occasional ceremonial celebration (regular international licensee conferences at corporate headquarters, the first being held in New York in 1980), effectively added a global dimension to the construction of the stock agency as an 'imagined community' (Anderson 1983; Salaman 1997) for its employees and franchise holders.[5] It sustained and imposed a unified transnational identity that imparted a sense of extended belonging, loyalty and mission to the corporate culture in general, and to local licensees in particular, which could be called upon in dealing with customers, especially when the latter themselves came from similarly global advertising agencies or multinational corporations. These feelings, of participating in a greater whole whose reach transcends national boundaries and cultural differences, of collectively furthering the mission of that whole, could be said to establish the global stock agency not only as an imagined community, but as an 'imagined commonwealth', in all senses – including the most literal – of the last word of that phrase.[6]

So central was global expansion to The Image Bank's project that its first foreign licensee, The Image Bank, Canada, opened for business in July 1975 – a mere eight months after the company was founded. Licensees in Tokyo (1976), Brazil (1976) and France (1977) quickly followed: today the company's international network extends to 10 wholly owned offices and 62 franchisee offices in 40 countries – all of which have been taken over by the Getty empire. However, this model of rapid international expansion and consolidation as a global brand, unlike the other areas of the stock industry that The Image Bank transformed, was not widely adopted by other stock agencies. It made little sense for small and medium-sized agencies to emulate the grandiose formula of the The Image Bank at the expense of more immediately lucrative reciprocal relations with a diversity of agencies abroad. It did, however, become the dominant paradigm for the new breed of super-agencies in the late 1980s and especially through the 1990s, as each attempted to establish a corporate presence in a rapidly changing global market. Being a 'global' stock agency with multiple foreign branches, monumental corporate headquarters in the United States or Europe (usually the UK) and a unified sense of hierarchy, identity and mission is not simply about selling products, serving customers and making profits on an international scale. It is also about being able to *say* that one is 'global' to both clients and competitors in a culture – the culture of corporate marketing and advertising – where extension across space and national boundaries is a visible measure of consequence.[7] Thus being 'global' is a type of performance: a way of continually making manifest one's power. In this sense, while The Image Bank's global positioning constructed it as an imagined *commonwealth* to its own employees and licensees, it provided a model for competitors and clients on how to establish an 'imagined *empire*'.

The globalizing strategy of The Image Bank in the mid-1970s through to the present day ties in, of course, with far broader trends affecting American and European advertising, marketing and media corporations in general. Equally, it refracts a particular version of globalization as the transcendence of national and cultural boundaries for the good of all, a version which in the eyes of many critics masks the true structures of power within global media corporations and a globalized world, especially the hegemony of US capital and US cultural values (Schiller 1991; Herman and McChesney 1997). These issues will be addressed in later chapters, as they bear on the radical restructuring of the stock-photography business within an integrated and global visual content industry that is currently under way and that characterizes the latest, 'modern/postmodern' period in the sector's brief history.

While I have so far stressed the 'imperial' tendency set in motion by the transformations wrought by The Image Bank, I should, in all fairness, add that The Image Bank's formation consolidated an entire industry from disparate elements and galvanised a diverse range of professionals – commercial photographers, photographic agents – to identify with the stock business. This means that while The Image Bank made global marketing and advertising the key legitimating discourses of stock photography – the core of the industry's 'identity' – and provided an operational model for centralized organization, it also ushered in an era of massive expansion, in sales and profits, but also in the sheer quantity and diversity of agencies and photographers who defined themselves as part of the stock photography business. The Image Bank itself reports that the market 'tripled' from 1980 to the early 1990s, with today more than 2,500 stock agencies competing globally (*Zoom* 1994: 5).[8]

Comparing this period to the Californian gold-rush, Heron sums up the changes as primarily one of attitude or consciousness:

> With this opening of the previously untapped advertising market and the introduction of tough and sometimes glitzy marketing approaches, we saw, in the seventies, the rapid and irreversible move away from the small business mentality that had prevailed in the past. As a result, stock photography changed more in one decade than in the previous six. What was once a Mom-and-Pop, handshake business became irrevocably altered. (Heron 1996: 13)

Growth, however, did not necessarily mean uniformity, despite the dominance of the new marketing 'mentality'. While many of the growing number of stock agencies were influenced by The Image Bank, they also had to distinguish themselves from it in order to establish their own unique identities and selling points. Furthermore, many, such as FPG, emerged from the old popular photo libraries, news archives and private collections, and picture agencies, and some retained distinctive areas of specialization, operational habits, idiosyncratic archival procedures, and eclectic stocks of images, none of which were immediately or entirely subsumed by the new marketing and advertising ethos. Certainly, agencies shifted corporate resources and priorities ever more inexorably toward the advertising industries, but they did not, for example, necessarily lose their editorial clientele or their archives of nineteenth-century celebrity images.

Indeed, this diversity could accommodate a very small minority of companies that were (and still are) almost entirely editorial in orientation. One of these is the UK company Topham Picturepoint, which provides a good example of the incremental, seemingly haphazard and amateur, often serendipitous development typical of some agencies 'post-Image Bank'. Created from an initial purchase of an intact historical archive, which Topham Picturepoint's owner, Alan Smith, had discovered after he and his wife had applied to the archive for permission to reproduce one of its images in a book, it grew in a piecemeal fashion, acquiring other archives and integrating them partly from an intuitive sense of what could be sold, partly out of an overall desire to be as comprehensive as possible so as better to serve clients with 'multidisciplinary editorial projects' such as text-book and encyclopaedia publishers, and partly because of the owners' passionate curiosity and impressively broad range of personal interests. Its client base is overwhelmingly editorial (about 95 per cent), making it, according to Alan Smith, one of only three UK agencies with serious historical archives still specializing in this market: the other two, Popperfoto and especially Hulton Getty (formerly Hulton Deutsch, now part of the global Getty Images PLC group, one of the industry's super-agencies), have in recent years deliberately refocused, claims Smith, on the advertising market (interview with author: 26/8/98). Nevertheless, this almost exclusive editorial orientation does not mean that Topham Picturepoint is on the fringes of the industry. Smith has long been one of the key figures in trade organisations such as the British Association of Picture Libraries and Agencies (BAPLA), and more recently in the Co-ordination of European Picture Agencies Press and Stock (CEPIC).

The trade associations themselves provide further evidence of the interaction of elements of the stock industry that were both continuous and discontinuous with previous formations. BAPLA was founded in 1975, and its aims include promoting the industry, establishing a code of ethics for dealing with clients and photographers, providing guidelines on pricing, copyright and intellectual copyright, standard contracts, archive management and technological issues. It represents over 350 'libraries and agencies' in the UK. These include the big stock agencies, but also a wide variety of institutional archives (such as the British Library, The National History Museum, The National Portrait Gallery, the BBC and ITN) and specialist niche libraries. The sheer diversity of content offered by these agencies and archives is readily apparent from the BAPLA Directory for 1998/9, in which BAPLA members categorized themselves according to 97 different subjects, from Advertising and Aerial Photography to War and Weather. With the exception of Corbis, almost all of the big stock agencies appear in only one category – 'General' – (Getty Images PLC is actually represented twice here, by both Tony Stone Images and the Hulton Getty Picture Collection, neither of which appears in any other category[9]), a self-definitional modesty that belies the financial and institutional power of these corporations compared to that of most other agencies represented.

What the BAPLA directory really reveals, in fact, is a complex and somewhat contradictory industrial structure. On the one hand, this structure bespeaks the apparent marginality of the marketing-oriented stock-photography industry within a broader convocation of pictorial archives covering a far larger range of topics than is conventionally associated with advertising imagery. On the other hand, it also discloses the conscious self-regulation and self-promotion of institutional and organizational archives (galleries, museums, public libraries, media organizations, pressure groups), and their extensive commodification, along the lines laid down – and for the prices charged – by the hegemonic advertising-oriented stock industry.

Such a structure makes it imperative to recognize the intricate web of continuous and discontinuous processes, of relations of difference as well as similarity within the new advertising hegemony, that emerged from the overall transformation in the 1970s and 1980s. As Foucault observes:

> We must not imagine that rupture is a sort of great drift that carries with it all discursive formations at once: rupture is not an undifferentiated interval – even a momentary one – between two manifest phases . . . it is always a discontinuity specified by a number of distinct transformations, between two distinct positivities. (1972: 175)

The emergence of 'classic' stock photography in the mid-1970s, along with its unfinished project of self-definition, represents such a 'rupture' with the past: a new paradigm based on the specific transformations of key domains and the unremarkable perpetuation of others. Crucially, the four main defining principles of that paradigm described above – the institutional priority of advertising, 'quality' production values, marketing professionalism and global expansion – need to be understood not as isolated elements but as the integrated forces of a system of cultural production that impinge, non-uniformly and asymmetrically, upon the various moments of the production cycle, from the conception of the image to its sale. It is now time to analyse precisely how that system has traditionally created its definitive product – the stock photograph – within the broader framework of consumer and commercial culture.

Notes

1. Stock photography awaits its historian and its definitive written history. Aside from Abbott Miller's brief account, and the extremely vague descriptions that fill the introductions to the various 'How To Shoot Stock' guides (of which Michal Heron's book, quoted below, is a good example), the best the industry currently possesses issues from the volumes of Brian Seed's *Stock Photo Report*. The simple narrative told here cannot hope to do justice to the complexities of the industry's history and the richness of detail available both in archives and in the memories of key individuals, and is simply an important preamble to the main substance of the research.
2. Miller describes this reorientation as the formal separation of stock photography 'into two fields – photo agencies oriented towards advertising, and news agencies furnishing documentary images' (1999: 128).
3. In February 2000, however, United News and Media announced plans to sell VCG to Getty Images PLC. See Chapter 5.
4. Henry Scanlon claims that Comstock pioneered the modern stock catalogue.
5. Benedict Anderson employs the phrase 'imagined community' to describe the nation as the construct of specific discourses. The phrase has since been extended and applied to a variety of entities which are constructed to

provide a sense of purpose, meaning and identity for those they include. I follow Salaman (1997) in arguing that corporations can also be described as imagined communities.

6. The wealth generated by this system was far from imaginary, however.
7. Leiss, Klein and Jhally (1997: 166) make a similar point about the emergence of global advertising 'mega-agencies' in the late 1980s: it gave the agencies 'clout' when dealing with global corporate clients, and especially 'critical mass' and 'buying power' in negotiations with the new transnational media giants.
8. This rough estimate of the number of stock agencies worldwide is still considered reasonably accurate today.
9. At the time of the Directory's publication, The Image Bank, which is also only listed in the 'General' category, was still owned by Eastman Kodak.

3

Shooting for Success: Stock Photography and the Production of Culture

Commercial Photography as Cultural Production

Echoing the public's general unawareness of stock photography is the overwhelming scholarly and critical silence of media and cultural analysts. Despite its obvious significance as a principal producer of photographic images, as a major force in contemporary visual and consumer culture, and as an important section of the culture industries, the stock photography business has never been the subject of serious academic research. As I mentioned earlier, there are two important exceptions to this rule: Helen Wilkinson's (1997) investigation of stock photography in 1930s Britain, and Abbott Miller's (1999 [1994]) analysis of the contemporary stock industry. These are pioneering but all too brief pieces, and they virtually beg for theoretical elaboration and critical dialogue: Miller's paper actually ends with such an appeal (1999 [1994]: 133). Given the context of overall academic disregard, it is edifying to note that both articles originally appeared in journals associated with design research (Wilkinson's was published in *The Journal of Design History*, and Miller's initially appeared in *Eye*), a field which is still, and to my mind unjustly, largely confined to the fringes of media and cultural studies.

Unfortunately, just as there are no specific studies of stock photography as a mode of cultural production, there are all too few 'sociological' studies of the contemporary production process of professional photography in general – with the exception of photojournalism – and of commercial images in particular. This dearth is strangely at odds both with the increased scope, sophistication and vigour of historical research on photographic production in earlier periods, and with the perceived dominance of 'the image' – especially the commercial image – in contemporary culture.

49

As the principal voice in this scholarly void, Barbara Rosenblum's *Photographers at Work: A Sociology of Photographic Styles* (1978) offers a useful framework for analysis, even if its empirical findings are somewhat dated (though there are a surprising number that still ring true). Aspiring to explain 'why things look the way they do', Rosenblum argues that sociological accounts of the conditions under which photographs (and other material objects) are produced and distributed can help us to understand their distinctive visual characteristics, their 'styles'. Using ethnographic research methods, particularly participant observation, she analyses three photographic styles – news, advertising and art photography – from three points of view: (1) the organization of work; (2) the impact of institutional features and shared understandings; and (3) the effect of photographers' conceptions of what they do.

These three perspectives, with the emphasis placed firmly on the first, attest to a thorough acquaintance with contemporary (for Rosenblum) sociological research on the production of culture (especially DiMaggio and Hirsch 1976; Peterson 1976). They yield a comprehensive examination and explication of the photographic production process in terms of the power relations between photographers and others (editors, designers, clients) regarding control over work, the economic and social constraints on production, the social organization of distribution, and the various conceptions of 'creativity' among photographers.

Rosenblum's investigation of advertising photography seems particularly promising. She observes that the photographer's position of present and future financial dependence upon the art director and his or her client severely limits the photographer's role: 'For most advertising photographers, the social organization of advertising has the net effect of chiselling away at the broad range of knowledge and expertise that the photographer brings with him. The photographer's contribution is virtually reduced to technical labor' (1978: 80). With the exception of top industry practitioners, photographers do not make any contribution to the 'concept' behind the image, this being the preserve of the art director, usually with the approval of the client: rather, 'the photographer is called upon to supply his skill to turn a graphic design into a photograph' (81). Such technical virtuosity is then constituted as the entire space of creativity itself, there being little else available, in that creativity becomes, in the discourse of typical advertising photographers, the innovative solution of technical challenges – how to shoot underwater, in poor light conditions, etc. – for which standard technical solutions are, for whatever reason, inappropriate. Furthermore, deprived of creative control over the conception of the image, the photographer often turns 'creativity' into a performance, inviting the art-director and client into the studio during shoots and effectively transforming the site of production itself into an arena of spectacular play.

Thus far the analysis, though acute, seems not to be wholly relevant to the production process of stock images. Rosenblum's account is exclusively focused on commissioned assignment photography, still the dominant system of advertising photography at the time of her research. In stock photography, however, photographers are not expected to produce a photographic transcript of an art director's sketch but to produce an image for which they are usually – in theory at least – entirely responsible, both conceptually and in terms of technical execution. Indeed, Rosenblum argues, for assignment advertising photographers, the separation of conception from execution, the norm of illustrating a concept not of their own choosing, is a key factor in distinguishing between their world of work and its products and that of art photographers, for whom the unity of conception and execution is paramount. Tentatively, at least, it could be hypothesized that stock photographers should also enjoy the kind of autonomy, and integration of conception and execution, often associated with the production of art.

As we shall see later on, this hypothesis is deeply flawed, but it does suggest that assignment photography imposes direct constraints that are either absent or highly mediated in stock photography. Other constraints noted by Rosenblum do, however, seem more obviously to apply:

> The institution of advertising is similar to journalism in that there are basic stories. Many themes found in advertising – what may be called advertising stories – are institutionalized. A family breakfasting together or the 'boys' having a beer after a game are examples of advertising stories. Even a close-up shot of a bottle of beer is a type of standard advertising picture. In short, advertising photography relies heavily on typical situations, typical themes and typical arrangements of people and/or products. (81)

These standardized scenarios dominate the expectations of advertisers regarding the final image, with the proviso that while the image is to be 'retrieved from the institutional stockpile of advertising stories' it is also to provide, in some way, an original 'twist' that will differentiate both the advertisement and the product from other advertisements and products: 'in short, the advertiser wants an "original standard picture"' (81). Such originality usually, according to Rosenblum, takes the form of technical variation – manipulating focus, lighting, colour, scale, etc. – performed within the narrow confines of an overriding preference for photographic realism: 'art directors seem to believe that advertisers will most readily approve of a straightforward pictorial rendition of their product' (81).

This dialectic of standardization and variation, or 'pseudo-individuality' as Adorno and Horkheimer called it (1979: 154), is a key theme in accounts of advertising and cultural production in general. It is also at the heart of the rights-protected stock industry and its definitive product, the 'generic image', and as such will be given more considered attention later in this chapter. For the moment I refer to it in order to show how Rosenblum's account, though devoted to a process of image production which was in significant ways supplanted by stock photography, provides powerful tools for understanding how the web of institutional relationships, expectations and conceptions impact upon photographic style.

There is, however, a central problem with Rosenblum's analysis. In a key passage at the end of her introduction she states:

> One final note: the analysis of styles here rests on the association or correlation between two types of data. On the one hand, there are descriptions of three categories of photographs. On the other, we have descriptions of the social worlds in which these pictures are made. I am making a connection between the two sets of data . . . This analysis does not intend to assert that one specific thing in the work setting, let us say, technology, 'causes' one particular aesthetic feature in the photograph . . . Rather, I treat one particular style of photography as a totality and treat a socio-economic system as a totality of patterns. In short, the analysis rests on the association between totalities (1978: 8–9).

The problem has two related aspects. First, Rosenblum doesn't really keep her promise to analyse the categories of photographs. The descriptions of the three styles are restrictively brief, confined to a six-page chapter at the beginning of the book, while the data on the social and economic environments in which these styles are produced occupies the rest of the research (129 pages in total). This quantitative imbalance reflects a qualitative one. The discussion of the styles is superficial, to say the least, consisting largely of generalizations and abstractions bereft of either historical, cultural or textual specificity: of the few photographs that are reproduced, none is subjected to any kind of thorough description or analysis in the main body of the argument. Brevity combined with superficiality allows Rosenblum to comprehend each style as a 'totality', with no room for complexity or contradiction. Their distinctiveness and cohesiveness is taken to be 'empirically unproblematic' (ibid.: 13), the justification for this claim being an ad hoc classroom experiment in which Rosenblum's students classified twenty images.

This failure to deliver the goods is really a manifestation of a deeper theoretical and methodological problem: the implicit assumption that the relationship between work organization and style is causal, one-way and exclusive. Rosenblum's pioneering but problematic account in effect rehearses a key controversy within the study of culture in general, the thesis that cultural products are determined by the 'underlying' socio-economic forces manifested in the organizational environments and processes which materially produce them.[1] Thanks to an applied version of the 'production of culture' perspective (Peterson 1976) that became prominent in American sociology in the mid- and late 1970s, Rosenblum can define news, advertising and fine-art 'styles' as self-evident, separable and self-sufficient categories because they are perceived solely as the products of three distinctive forms of work organization. This assumption, as Simon Watney observes, causes her to 'fall back into a kind of latent functionalism, as if the demands of a particular branch of production such as photojournalism always secure an inflexible uniformity of appearance' (1999: 149).[2] It sanctions the lack of historical or cultural explication of the styles and their development, the insensitivity to nuance and complexity, indeed the very brevity of the formal analysis: as Kreiling (1978), writing at about the same time as Rosenblum, noted, 'symbols are not real or consequential to most sociologists, who try to explain their manifest forms and intrinsic meanings into some "real" world of forces behind them'. In order for this more 'real' world of forces to be truly determining, Rosenblum's styles have to map onto the work environments in which they are produced, if not in terms of a one-to-one correspondence of dependent formal characteristic and independent socio-economic variable, then as self-contained and ahistorical totalities. They cannot be wholly or partially produced elsewhere in the dynamic weave of symbolic forms and practices we call 'culture'.

The assumption also leads to a conscious evasion of the question of 'meaning': 'This chapter is a formalistic analysis,' Rosenblum declares, 'that is, I look primarily at the subject matter and its rendition. An analysis of meanings, in the tradition of Gombrich or Panofsky, is beyond the scope of this inquiry and would lead to other questions' (1978: 13). Assuming that such a separation is even possible (Panofsky was not at all sure[3]), what are these 'other questions' that make the eviction of meaning so necessary? Presumably, why given types of subject matter and their various renditions produce particular kinds of meanings, why certain meanings invoke or require the particular rendition of specific subject matter, and *why these selected meanings should be produced by these work environments*? In other words, questions that concern the relationship between production processes, symbolic forms and ideologies; questions which point, yet again, to the broader realm of culture, and whose avoidance makes it impossible for Rosenblum to address the overall social, ideological and cultural functions of news, advertising and art photography. Questions, in short, that would radically politicize her project.

Perhaps predictably, the excluded term – 'meaning' – returns to haunt the research, in true deconstructive style. Hence Rosenblum's analysis of an institutional stockpile of visual 'advertising stories' that the photographer draws upon (mentioned above), begs the question 'but why *these* stories?', which leads inexorably to a consideration of their cultural significance. This is not a question that can be answered formalistically with any satisfaction, just as the preference for photographic realism is only tautologically explained by stating that it issues from art directors and advertisers ('so why do *they* prefer it?'): a more penetrating analysis would require the investigation of the 'meaning' of photographic realism as a set of constructed beliefs and conventions, and of its relevance to the institution and aims of advertising; in other words, a critical account of advertising's relationship with the social experience of consumers and the forms in which that experience is visually represented elsewhere in the culture.

Similarly, the broader cultural context of style formation cannot be repressed absolutely. In her concluding discussion, Rosenblum herself acknowledges that the three chosen styles are by no means self-contained categories, 'that there is borrowing and exchange between them' (ibid.: 112). Rejecting the mobility of photographers as an explanation for such exchange, she opts for the notion of 'diffusion': 'The stylistic conventions become part of the larger culture, accessible to everyone . . . Some photographers in one field might utilize the conventions usually associated with another type of photography, and if the conditions permit, the borrowed convention will enter another specialized photographic vocabulary' (ibid.). This admission effectively undercuts Rosenblum's core assumption, that there is a determinate and determining correspondence of socio-economic and aesthetic totalities, free from the intrusion of the network of symbolic forms, discourses and actions beyond.

Rosenblum's study, then, while integrating a wealth of original data on the photographic production process, is, in both theoretical and methodological terms, a prisoner of a particular conception of cultural production that was influential in the United States in the mid- to late 1970s.[4] In contrast, more recent studies of photographic production – specifically applied to popular photojournalism – have been based on notions of cultural production that address both the organization of production processes (albeit in a more limited framework than Rosenblum's) and the meanings of the images within their specific historical and cultural contexts. The most pertinent, both for the contemporary currency of its subject matter but also for the rigour with which the organization of production and the meaning of the images are analysed, is Lutz and Collins' *Reading National Geographic* (1993).

'Cultural products have complex production sites;' note Lutz and Collins, 'they often code ambiguity; they are rarely accepted at face value but are read in complicated and often unanticipated ways' (11). This complexity leads Lutz and Collins to analyse the photographs of non-Western 'others' appearing in

National Geographic from three perspectives: (1) *the process of image produc-tion*, including an historical exposition of the development of *National Geographic* as an institution, its relationship to broader cultural trends, the construction of its identity and its audience, plus an analysis of the organization of work at the magazine; (2) *the structure and content of a sample of images*, analysed in terms of their content and their immediate textual/graphic environ-ment, their relationship to photographic genres and socio-cultural contexts, and the 'looking practices' of magazine staff and readers; and (3) *the responses of readers to the photographs*, paying attention to questions of conformity or resistance to the 'communicative intent' of the magazine, interpretations based on the recognition of cultural difference, plus possibilities of empathy and identification with those photographed.

This tripartite approach, involving a mix of research methods (archival research, interviews with staff and readers, quantitative and qualitative content analysis of images, captions and layout), produces a sophisticated, compre-hensive and authoritative account of the significance and power of *National Geographic* photography. As a model for investigating stock photography and the visual content industry it is extremely suggestive, yielding a number of very useful approaches which will be explored more thoroughly at the relevant junctures. And yet its applicability to the current case is subject to important limitations. These stem mainly from the difference in research subject: *National Geographic* is a single, albeit very prominent, organization creating limited types of images, in a unified and largely uniform framework of production and distribution, that directly addresses an identifiable readership in a highly specific context of consumption (magazine reading). It operates in the immedi-ate discursive frameworks of photojournalism and popular science, and in the wider context of Western representations of cultural (especially 'Third World') otherness. The stock-photography/visual-content industry is a large, somewhat amorphous, business constituted of competing elements, with a paradigmatic but not absolutely dominant mode of production, a wide and increasing variety of image styles and content, a primary audience of professional cultural intermediaries within the advertising and design industries, and a secondary mass audience of viewers who encounter images (usually after radical altera-tion) in the diverse material contexts of consumer culture (magazine advertise-ments, billboards, direct-mail shots, corporate brochures, editorial content, product packaging, websites, etc.).

These differences mainly affect the appropriateness of employing in one project all of Lutz and Collins's methods, and for reasons that I have already set out, I do not follow through the research on production with an investiga-tion of the final reception of stock images by actual consumers – the equivalent of Lutz and Collins's analysis of readers' responses to *National Geographic*.

In addition, a partial concomitant of the more unified and homogenous world of *National Geographic* is that the account of image-production privileges the notion of a *linear process*: Lutz and Collins organize their extremely illuminating narrative around distinct sequential *stages* of production – story-initiation, the field-work of photographers, image-selection, layout, captions and printing. Given that one has to start somewhere, it seems petty to reprove Lutz and Collins for treating production as a 'process', especially since it is institutionalized as such within *National Geographic* itself.[5] In fact, the notion of production as a process in which raw material (in this case initially conceptual rather than material: the 'story idea') is worked upon in a chronologically arranged series of separate stages until it reaches its final form, is both commonplace in Western society and axiomatic to some of the sociological models of cultural production already discussed. It is, essentially, an industrial 'production-line' conception of production, and it is still a powerful – if not, arguably, the pre-eminent – tool for rationalizing and controlling the diverse elements of productive activity. What is slightly troubling about Lutz and Collins's account, therefore, is not that it mirrors the industrial organization of production at *National Geographic* – given the research subject that seems reasonable – but that it does so uncritically. There is no discussion of what gets left out by such an account. The convergence of the parallel orders of narrative sequence and industrial process naturalizes them both, renders them self-evident, and makes unaskable the ultimate question: why is production so organized? In particular, marketing and advertising considerations, which are, according to Lutz and Collins, responsible for some of the major trends in (and conflicts over) editorial direction and photographic content, are relegated to a brief discussion at the end of the chapter that seems to do little justice to their impact upon all stages of production. This is something that could possibly have been avoided in an account that worked 'vertically' as well as 'horizontally', tracing the interaction of specific forces at different moments in the production chain.

It is difficult to avoid such a linear, horizontal bias, especially in cases where separate moments of the cultural process are concretely manifested in discrete forms of technical administration. To focus on these stages alone would miss, however, the ways in which they carry traces of one another and are inflected, unevenly, by 'external' (to the linear process) socio-economic and cultural forces, as well as the forms and powers through which they cohere and are articulated together as a complex whole. It would also miss the problem of beginnings: that the symbolic nature of cultural material tends to make it prefabricated elsewhere, perpetually deferring any product's point of origin. That is why culture is a circuit, not a conveyor belt: it comes back to us transformed. To conceive of stock photography as a process of production, then, requires an analytical starting point that is as arbitrary as the intersection of a circle.

The Production of the Stock Image

Hence I would like to begin my analysis of the 'production process' of stock photography by proposing a slightly unorthodox approach. Rather than structuring the account 'horizontally' according to the discrete stages of a linear sequence (like Lutz and Collins), or according to such predetermined (and admittedly useful) concepts as 'control over work', 'the economic and social constraints on production', 'the social organisation of distribution' (Rosenblum 1978), I want to explore the configuration of a number of key terms that emerge from within the industry itself – from the discourses of professionals – but that resonate far beyond it: 'success', 'creativity', 'meaning', 'genre', 'concept' and 'the catalogue'. In so doing I hope to be able to distinguish 'moments' in the circuit of culture without stripping them of their multiple practical and discursive interconnections, putting into play the dual (sociological and semiotic) focus on stock photography's 'cultural economy' and its 'mode of signification'.

Success

'Success' in stock photography almost invariably refers to the income earned by an image and its photographer: both the amount of income and its stability over time. Given that the rights-protected stock system is based on independent freelance photographers competing for the attention of stock agencies (which compete for the budgets of other cultural intermediaries), such a definition is hardly surprising. Neither is its centrality to the discourse of professional stock photographers. Not only is the term itself frequently used in trade journals and conferences, but there is a constant search for role-models ('master' photographers) and examples ('best-selling' images) which can be mined for guidance, as in the following popular sessions at *Photo Expo East '98*: 'Secrets to Success in Stock Production', 'How Great Ads Got That Way', 'Stock Photography: Best Sellers and Why', 'How to Become a Master Photographer', 'The Masters of Stock Photography'. In turn, 'How To' guides such as Michal Heron's (1996), which are aimed primarily at younger, less-established photographers, generally prioritize commercial sales over other potential indicators (though see the section on 'creativity', p. 62).

More specifically, 'best-sellers' or 'successful' photographs are those that are used, over a period of time, by a number of advertising or design professionals in multiple formal, commercial and social contexts. Since stock agencies normally grant their clients only limited exclusivity (if any) on the images they hold in stock, this capacity for multiple usage is one of the fundamental commercial premises of stock photography, allowing photographers and agencies to make money while charging lower prices than for assignment photographs. It is, therefore, the extent of resale to cultural intermediaries such as art directors, picture editors and designers, rather than the response of consumers to the advertisement or brochure in which the image appears, that most directly mediates the criteria of 'success', feeding them back into the production process. Indeed, the consumer's impact upon the image is made thoroughly circuitous by the fact that once purchased by the cultural intermediary the image then goes through a stage of recontextualization – combination with texts and other images and graphic elements – during which it is often substantially altered for the final advertisement or marketing brochure.[6] In other words, there is no self-sufficient moment of production that precedes and is directly influenced by a reciprocal moment of consumption which magically feeds back into it, with distribution as a mere bridging stage. Instead, we find the complex and highly organized articulation of interlinked stages and actors: *production* of images (photographers), *selection* of images submitted by photographers for inclusion in the agency archive (stock agencies), *promotion* of a limited number of images and the *distribution* of those sold (stock agencies), *recontextualization* of the purchased image in the final 'text' by other cultural intermediaries – advertising agencies, marketing departments, graphic designers, etc. These stages almost, *but not quite*, constitute a self-enclosed circuit before the image is encountered by the consumer.

There are two main reasons why the circuit is not entirely self-enclosed. The first is that cultural intermediaries select a photograph according to technical, administrative and financial criteria (colour, detail and styling, proportions, availability, exclusivity, price) as well as on the basis of their conceptions of its impact upon consumers. Judging this impact also involves assessing the range of potential cultural references for the target audience and their relative potency (see the discussion of 'targeting' and 'lifestyle' in Chapter 4, pp. 102– 105). These cultural references will change from audience to audience and over time, and the selection of the cultural intermediary will (ideally) change accordingly. What this means is that the unstable and dynamic realm of consumer taste and symbolic decoding *does* impact upon production, but through a form of double mediation that usually involves a time-lag: it is relayed by clients back to agencies through their purchases, and relayed by agencies back to photographers either as direct guidance ('this stuff just won't sell') or simply because their images are no longer being selected or promoted by the agency.

The second reason is that photographers and agencies are themselves responsive to changes in cultural trends. However, according to industry insiders most photographers tend to be conservative and oriented to short-term revenue generation, milking the success of a particular type of image for as long as possible.

This conservatism is, according to Becker, typical of most creative personnel in any 'organized art world' who are thoroughly at ease with the resources, norms, constraints and expectations of their work environment. Becker labels them 'integrated professionals', capable of producing popular, standard products efficiently and repeatedly, but also to the extent that 'a fully professionalized art world may become enslaved by the conventions through which it exists, producing what we would call (if we took the results seriously) hack work' (Becker 1976: 45). In the case of stock photography, this conservatism is built in to the very structure of photographer–agency relations. As contracted freelancers, photographers are only paid when their images are sold. Without the benefit of an income unrelated to immediate sales, they are therefore discouraged from undue experimentation, it being far less risky to produce technically competent variations of an already successful formula. The iconographic features of successful formulae are not, however, simply determined by the actual sales of each photographer's own work. Rather, they are fixed most effectively and concretely through the work of *other* photographers, manifested in the agency catalogue.

Agency catalogues represent a selection of those images that are seen as having the greatest sales potential. As a criterion for inclusion, this is effectively self-fulfilling: according to Robyn Selman, Director of Acquisitions at Direct Stock, approximately 80 per cent of all images sold by a stock agency are sold through the catalogue (*Photo Expo East '98*: 30/10/98). Thus the catalogue not only reflects the agency's perception of an image's sales potential; it virtually guarantees its commercial success relative to non-catalogue images, however similar they may be. For photographers without access to actual sales figures (i.e. almost all of them), catalogue selection has become the most common indicator of an image's success. As Jon Feingersh, a prominent US stock photographer, has noted, scanning catalogues for images means that 'you will copy those images from the catalogues – unconsciously probably, even though the images in catalogues are usually at least two years old' (*Photo Expo East '98*, 29/10/98).[7] Comstock's Henry Scanlon describes the practice scathingly:

Lacking an art director's layout, they [stock photographers] turned to a simulacrum: other photographers' work, primarily as seen in stock agency catalogues, and shot pretty much the same thing. This has been done by photographers by the hundreds, with the active encouragement of certain photo agencies (*PDN 9/97*: 62).

Hence if the successful image is defined as that which is maximally resold, it is also that which is maximally imitated. The systematic imitation of successful photographs creates image types that function as visual correlates to general categories ('The Family', 'Business', etc.), thereby reproducing and reinforcing the classificatory schemes of stock agency archives and catalogues and their connection to cultural stereotypes.[8] Furthermore, the process of imitation is also generative, since each image type also acts as a template for the creation of other similar images, becoming, in the words of Roland Barthes, a 'unary photograph': 'a transformation is unary if, through it, a single series is generated by the base' (1984: 40). Through imitation, therefore, classification itself is not simply an organizing principle imposed upon an already-created ensemble of disparate images; rather, it is instituted as a generative matrix which fundamentally determines and orders the production of new images, each of which must be slightly different in its recognizable fidelity to a unary base and its generic iconography.

The result is similar to that described by the concept of 'formatting' used by Bill Ryan (1992) in his analysis of the popular-music business. Formatting is a process of creative control based on corporate attempts to confront the uncertainties of the market for cultural commodities. It is a system that aims at predictable, marketable results. Instead of regulating cultural production according to creative ideas or authorial dictates, manufacturers take as their starting points potential areas of demand and the propensities of the target audience, usually identified through market research and the commercial success of previous cultural products. Translated into creative policy, this version of product planning is built around the marketability of familiar and recognizable product types or genres. While these represent the structured conventions that link audiences and producers in a common framework of meaning (see the discussion of 'genre', p. 76ff), they also minimize the role of guesswork, intuition and arbitrary inspiration in cultural production: in short, they repress all those stubborn – ethereal and corporeal – elements of the creative process that cannot be planned in advance. This does not rule out 'originality'; indeed, originality itself – important to the appeal of a new product – is formalized and standardized as a strategic and calculable deviance from a recognizable type. As a result of this process, Ryan argues 'form has been transformed into format. Art is made subject to administration. Conventions drawn from the past are imposed in the present as a rule which dictates endless repetitions of itself and the conditions of its making' (1992: 162).

Like the notion of formatting, then, the discourse of 'success' in the stock industry articulates, authorizes and executes the twin attributes of Adorno and Horkheimer's culture industry (1979): *standardization* and *pseudo-individuality*:

What is individual is no more than the generality's power to stamp the accidental detail so firmly that it is accepted as such. The defiant reserve or elegant appearance of the individual on show is mass-produced like Yale locks, whose only difference can be measured in fractions of millimetres (1979: 154).[9]

Unlike formatting, however, in stock photography these attributes are not the result of a deliberate corporate strategy executed from above. Rather, they are imbricated within the contractual and financial relations between producers and distributors, photographers and agents, that frame the production process, and in the sanctified status of the catalogue as the touchstone of saleability.

However, this generative power of 'success', along with its exclusively commercial definition, represents a *dominant* deployment of the term, one that suits the stock system as operated by stock agencies. What is elided in this account is the fact that the meanings and powers of 'success' are not fixed in perpetuity but need to be constantly reiterated because they are open to contestation by other actors, and other discourses, at work in the stock system and in the general culture. 'Success', then, is the subject of what Bourdieu calls a 'classification struggle' between conflicting social positions, occupational interests, cultural values, interpretations and world-views (1986: 309–10). To be precise, the continued employment and reiteration of 'success' makes manifest the discursive intersection of *two* primary 'cultures of production' – corporate and artisanal – each proposing, with unequal strength, its own definition of the term.

The corporate culture of production is based on the values and interests of stock agencies, in particular the centrality of marketing discourse and the use of formatting as an attempt to anticipate (those who anticipate) the vicissitudes of consumer taste. The artisanal culture of production is based on relatively autonomous practitioners (photographers) who understand themselves as professionals with acquired skills (usually the result of institutionalized forms of training and apprenticeship) and who practice a 'craft' or an 'art'. These individuals themselves constitute the business enterprise (occasionally with minimal additional staff), and they are in a relationship of commercial competition with their peers. At the same time, however, the peer group acts as an 'occupational community' (Gregory 1983), creating a culture of mutual assistance and collective judgement that both establishes and deploys the criteria by which photographers evaluate the worth of each other's work: these are the non-commercial consequences of such activities as the selection of role models, the distribution of advice and encouragement, the polling of peers in trade journals, and the exhibitions and competitions held by magazines and at trade conferences. Some of the motivation for this culture of mutual assistance is the sense that as independent artisans photographers are at a disadvantage when pitted against the resources of corporate stock agencies. It derives more fundament-ally, however, from a shared professional identity which itself reproduces (from other cultural fields) and proposes diverse definitions for 'success' – technical and aesthetic as well as commercial – that emerge from what Bourdieu calls 'the space of possibles' (1993: 176), the system of common (conscious and unconscious) references that situates the individual participants in a specific field of cultural production in relation to one another. While these definitions are very frequently at one with the dominant corporate definition, or are at least easily incorporated by it, they can act as sources of friction. For a clearer view of the potential for friction, as well as for incorporation, it is time to turn to the relationship between 'success' and another term: 'creativity'.

Creativity

In *How to Shoot Stock Photos that Sell* (1996) Michal Heron – who is a veteran freelance photographer and also runs her own stock business – makes the following observations:

> The dizzying changes of the past few years have given rise to an important debate among professionals regarding the effect on photography of the new marketing approach to stock. One of the hottest current disputes is how to reconcile the demand from agencies for saleable images with the desire of photographers to shoot creative, innovative, personally satisfying photographs . . .
>
> In today's competitive market, only agencies with an aggressive approach to the business and a thorough understanding of it will survive. Likewise, those photo-graphers who move with such agencies will benefit. Photographers and agencies who stay with horse and buggy methods of production will be left behind. According to the new breed of agencies, photographers who want to make it in stock must follow their guidance almost in lock step – and do this to make money.
>
> On the other hand, shooting exactly what the stock agent wants or says the market needs, especially if it doesn't appeal to you, can result in sterile, mechanical, lifeless – usable, but certainly joyless – photography.
>
> The dilemma is a familiar one. The issue of a photographer's creativity versus someone else's needs has always plagued photographers in assignment work. Until recently it was not a problem for stock photographers. Now they, too, face these questions: first, how does this pressure to create saleable product affect the creative satisfaction of a photographer? At what point do creativity and innovation become deadened by production of the predictable image? Where is spontaneity in seeing, in personal vision, in the excitement of experimentation?
>
> Second, what will this tension do to the appearance of stock? Will stock become only a more technically polished version of the stock of 30 years ago – the aesthetic cliché? By a slavish devotion to marketing are we creating a body of facile, sterile work? However sophisticated the technique of such photography, I suggest that an abundance of lifeless, predictable work cannot be good for the industry (1996: 15).

I have quoted at length because Heron's comments, although apparently simple, reveal the complexity of the 'artisanal' discourse around creativity and success in the stock industry, its weave (or 'braid', as Barthes would call it (1974: 160)) of codes of history, culture and vocation. To begin with, Heron discusses the relationship between saleable images (which she also calls 'product') and creatively satisfying images ('photographs') as symptomatic of a historical turning point in stock photography, marked principally by the near-total dominance of marketing considerations and techniques in determining how stock agencies select images for promotion, and a shift in power relations between agencies and photographers (based on the former's superior 'business understanding'). Interestingly, although Heron does not specify the nature of the relationship for assignment work, her discussion reminds us of Rosenblum's description of the relative lack of creative control enjoyed by advertising assignment photographers due to the separation of image-conception and execution. Heron implies a similar loss of control over conception for the stock photographer.

Furthermore, Heron presents the relationship between marketability and creativity almost exclusively in terms of a conflict, and this conflict is rendered symbolically across two parallel dimensions, which we can call the dimensions of *character* and *appearance*. The dimension of character acts as a localized version of what Barthes, in *S/Z*, terms the 'semic code': 'the seme (or the signified of connotation, strictly speaking), is a connotator of persons, places, objects, of which the signified is a *character*. Character is an adjective, an attribute, a predicate' (1974: 190, Barthes's emphasis). Heron's text connotes the attributes and (thereby) the existence of two such characters: it establishes the traits of a primary character – 'the photographer' – defined as an active, self-motivating individual in opposition to a secondary character – 'the stock agency', defined collectively (the text refers primarily to 'agencies' in the plural), organizationally and even as a kind of species (there is a 'new breed'). The dimension of *appearance* is a cultural or 'referential' code; it refers to bodies of cultural knowledge (professional, aesthetic, anthropological), formulating them into two opposed categories of criteria (one positive, one negative) for evaluating the appearance of stock photographs. Crucially, the connection between these two dimensions or codes is based on metonymy: attributes of the character (the photographer or the corporation) are projected onto the photograph's appearance, establishing principles of aesthetic value through the transmission of traits from author to text, from artist to work (Bal and Bryson 1991: 180). (The relation is reversible as biography, allowing for the qualities of the image to be traced back to the traits of its creator.)[10] The connection, however, is also one of cohabitation within a common symbolic space, created by Heron's text and the discourse that runs through it, that gives an elemental or epic form to the antithesis of photographic creativity and saleability: character and appearance share nothing less than the space of *life* and *death*; the forces of fertility, spontaneity, animation and innovation do battle against the impersonal agents of lifelessness, slavishness, sterility and predictability.

This discourse on creativity very clearly endorses and reproduces a popular, 'romantic' account of artistic and literary creativity which privileges the authenticity of the artist's individual personality. More precisely, it derives the creativity of the image from a particular fusion of qualities: the photographer's 'objective' sensory capacity with regard to the external visual world, and his or her interior imaginative energies. This fusion is achieved, in part, by mobilizing the *optical* and *prophetic* connotations of the word 'vision', such that quasi-religious/imaginative fantasy and optical or perceptual truth are mutually dignified and transferred (mysteriously, miraculously) to the photograph, which becomes the material re-presentation before the viewer of the founding ecstasy/perception. Such a strategy not only pays homage to a distinguished tradition within writing on art, and painting in particular, as being about the pristine transmission of perception from the consciousness of the artist to that of the viewer (Bryson 1983), it also neatly holds in balance what Sekula calls the two 'chattering ghosts' that haunt photography – bourgeois science and bourgeois art (1981: 15), resolving, or at least repressing, all that might be troubling about connecting photography – an automated, mechanized technology – with human spontaneity and creativity.

Not all anxieties are so easily kept at bay, however. As the manifestation of 'spontaneity in seeing, in personal vision, in the excitement of experimentation', creativity is defined precisely through its opposition to highly regulated systems of collective cultural production: in other words, to the stock-photography industry as we know it. The logical consequence of this opposition, however, must be disavowed for stock photographers to retain their self-respect while also retaining their livelihoods. Hence the fully ideological nature of the closure of Heron's text – 'an *abundance* of lifeless, predictable work cannot be *good for the industry*' (my italics) – which implies that there could be *just the right amount* (for the good of the industry) of lifeless, predictable work. This closure effectively substitutes the potentially explicit antagonism between corporate and artisanal cultures of production in the present with an appeal (through negation) to a utopian ideal: a stock industry that is not based on an excess of image-predictability.

Thus the artisanal discourse of creativity contains a central paradox, which it attempts to resolve *quantitatively*. On the one hand it is based on a romantic aesthetic that privileges spontaneity and the personal vision of the artist, and on the other it must work within a stock system dominated by marketing and product formatting. The discourse enacts a precarious resolution by tempering spontaneous creativity with just the right measure of saleable predictability. Indeed, the paradox and its resolution run through Heron's entire book. While its title stresses saleability (*How to Shoot Stock Photos That Sell*), several of its chapters provide step-by-step guidance on how to attune a photographic 'style' (comprising shape, space, focal point, backgrounds, colour) that is assumed to be highly personal to the planned usefulness and deliberate market-ability required by stock (Heron 1996: 17–24).[11] This fusion reaches its theoretical apotheosis in Heron's book in the section on the 'concept', which will be dealt with more fully later (see p. 78ff), and achieves its ultimate practical manifestation in the thirty-five pre-prepared stock assignments she suggests to her readers, specified to the last detail (outlining the preferred type of shots, framing, type of lighting, models, ethnicity of models, props, locale, etc.). In other words, while the artisanal discourse defines creativity in terms of spontaneity and personal vision, it is no less concerned with discipline and strategic planning based on carefully selected criteria and formulae. It is devoted, at least in part, to the systematic control of the creativity it extols.

Similar tensions appear in stock photographer Jon Feingersh's advice to others. In his session at *Photo Expo East '98*, 'Secrets to Success in Stock Production' (29/10/98), Feingersh trod a thin line between 'creativity' and 'saleability'. He praised the virtues of the former while propounding a method-ology for attaining the latter, based largely around 'identifying images with one-word concepts' (again, see the section on the 'concept', p. 78ff). An accompanying printed handout called 'Keys to Success in Production Stock Photography' was equally ambivalent. Propounding twenty-three keys to success such as 'Invest in Yourself', 'Read Contracts Carefully' and 'Choose the Right Agency', Feingersh continually stressed the need for good stock photographs to reflect visual trends in advertising and marketing imagery without them becoming copies of other images:

6) START A CONCEPT FILE. Clip magazine ads religiously, and add to your files constantly. On those slow days when you can't get jump started, go to our file and find inspiration. Look at the ads for clues as to trends, stylistic changes, gesture, cultural movements which should be mirrored in your stock photography. Again, don't copy! . . .

7) OBSERVE CURRENT MEDIA FOR TRENDS AND THEMES. Study the ads which are on blockbuster TV shows, major golf tournaments etc., as these have the highest production values and should indicate what the print advertising market also needs. Become aware of gesture, proxemics, and symbols. Watch TV and movies with special attention to how people relate and interact . . .

9) DON'T COPY OTHER PHOTOGRAPHERS' WORK. Be true to yourself and your own vision. Don't try to obtain every stock agency catalog and use them as shooting scripts. Those photos have been in the file for years, and the researchers

and clients are already tired of them. The stock photography market and the country's demographics change so rapidly that those photos are *way out of date*. The best way to be successful is to BE ORIGINAL . . .

18) FORGET MONEY. After taking a businesslike approach, remember that being concerned with *MONEY ONLY* will stultify your images. Think about your hopes, your craft, your vision, your particular viewpoint on our culture. Try to remember those creative impulses which made you wish to enter photography in the first place, and photograph accordingly. (Feingersh's emphasis)

This last section provides yet another example of the way in which the artisanal discourse designates personal artistic authenticity as the source of creativity (and also as the best path to ultimate financial success). By urging the photographer to 'forget money', it also reproduces the ideology of the economic disinterestedness of art, what Baudrillard calls art's 'aristocratic measure of value' (1981: 113). This ideology supports the paradoxical logic of the traditional art market, ensuring that the greater an art object's 'spiritual value' – its perceived distance from the vulgar world of monetary exchange – the higher its monetary worth (hence the double meaning of the word 'priceless' when attached to an artwork: it is above mere monetary calculation and thus very expensive). As Bourdieu ironically characterizes it: 'The world of art, a sacred island systematically and ostentatiously opposed to the profane world of production, a sanctuary for gratuitous, disinterested activity in a world given over to money and self-interest' (1993: 197; see also Berger 1972: 135; Baudrillard 1981: 113–22). Here, however, the ideology is not associated with the consumption of art, but with the very process of producing stock photographs. It is not the commercial nature of *art* that is being disavowed, but the commercial nature of *commercial photography*, in what might be described as the opening statement in a rhetoric of legitimation that will eventually extend beyond the artisanal field and be employed by corporate culture to justify advertising in toto (advertising is art because artists create it). And Feingersh's last sentence is particularly interesting, for it suggests a reverse-developmental scheme for the success of the 'creative' stock photographer that can be traced psychoanalytically ('Try to remember . . .'). The denial of economic interest is lodged in the recovered image of the photographer's self-generated birth *as a photographer*, that primary moment of vocational self-identification which (mythically) precedes the photographer's entry into the commercial profession. The latter acts here as an Oedipal 'Law of the Father' which imposes upon the fledgling artist the reality of external constraint, made manifest in the ultimate form of the symbolic: money itself, the symbol of endless exchange. Feingersh urges the photographer to 'forget money' (the symbolic order) so that the photographer can 'remember' her or his imaginary self as an 'artist'.

The opening sections of Feingersh's handout are less extreme in their support for the artisanal discourse of romantic creativity and its disavowal of commercial interest or formatting. As in Heron's book, they urge photographers to subsume themselves in other images and to find inspiration in them, while always stopping short of 'copying'. In fact, the repeated mantra 'don't copy!' comes to indicate the main anxiety (and insoluble problem) besetting the artisanal culture of stock-photographic production: how can one avoid 'copying' in an industry whose *raison d'être* is the systematic recycling of images for multiple use? In other words, while Feingersh implies the need strategically to control 'visionary' creativity through immersion in other images and the collective tastes and proclivities they embody, he also emphasizes the need to arrest that immersion before it degenerates into formulaic calculation and impersonal simulation. How this is to be achieved is not spelled out in any detail.

The corporate culture of the stock industry has many things to say about creativity that are similar to the discourse of its artisanal counterpart. Jonathan Klein, CEO of Getty Images PLC, opened his key-note speech at *Photo Expo East '98* with the words: 'Photography is not a job – it is an art.'[12] He quickly added, however, 'Photography must also be commercial – i.e. relevant. It must be capable of being licensed to a third party, even to a high priest of consumerism, or at the other end, to a high priest of culture.' (31/10/08). This brief quote mirrors, to a certain extent, the antithetical structure of Heron's and Feingersh's arguments: 'job' is opposed to 'art', 'consumerism' to 'culture'. Except that instead of the photographer's anxious and interminable tight-rope walk between these poles, Klein boldly fixes the term which subsumes these opposites and allows them to function within a single coherent system: commercialism.

Note the rhetorical sleight of hand employed here. 'Consumerism', which one would ordinarily assume enjoys considerable semantic overlap with the word 'commercial', is made into one of a pair of equal and opposed alternatives (the other is 'culture') that are then subsumed within the seemingly impartial embrace of 'commercial relevance'. This establishes a set of spatial and ideological relations between the three terms, that, in its equidistant positioning of the antithesis of 'consumerism' and 'culture', both neutralizes and naturalizes the 'commercial' field in which they are said to operate. Moreover, 'commercial' initially appears to be defined by term 'relevant'. But in the explication that follows the reverse is actually true: relevance is defined both commercially and in terms of mediation. Thus a photograph is relevant not when it speaks to the experience, emotions or understanding of a viewer, but when it is capable of *being sold* to a 'high priest' – a sanctified expert – who is also a 'third party' (on the assumption that the omitted 'second party' is the viewer, this epithet designates, if it does not necessarily dignify, the role of cultural intermediaries in making images 'relevant').[13] 'Relevance' is given a specifically charged ideological meaning within the discourse of the stock industry's corporate culture, one that supports the industry's mediating function between producers of images and their viewers.

This corporate harmonization of 'art' and 'sales', of creativity and market-ability, is not always so simple, however. Interviewed by *Photo District News* in September 1997, Comstock CEO Henry Scanlon framed the distinctions between assignment, stock and royalty-free photography (which he calls the 'three tiers' of commercial photography) in terms of a radical realignment of 'creative' photographers and merely competent 'technicians':

> My definition of 'photographer' is very different from that of a lot of people who call themselves photographers – but who are really just technicians. Now sometimes they are extremely skilled technicians, but they are mere technicians nonetheless. And the technicians have been predominating, overwhelmingly, in the stock photo-graphy industry – to the point where the real 'photographers' have been buried under the technicians' avalanche of pseudo-photography.
>
> And these photo-technicians, doing nothing more than copying the work of others who went before them, some of them making tons and tons of money in stock, should not only be worried [about royalty-free photographs], they should be going to night school to seek an alternative career . . .
>
> Once 90 percent of the pictures currently being sold by 'traditional' stock agencies – the copies of copies of copies – get pushed down into royalty-free (and that is exactly what's happening as we speak), what's left?
>
> Photographers. Not technicians – photographers. The hardy few who have been lurking out there, waiting for the 'noise' to abate so that they can bring some real creativity, some real vision and unique sensibility to the 'traditional' stock tier of our three tiered model (62–4).

I will deal with the organizational, financial and technological implications of this discourse in later chapters. For the moment, suffice to say that we are once again confronted with the antithesis of, on the one hand, image-produc-tion based on the imitation of other successful images, and on the other a creative power lodged in the visionary capacity of the gifted elite (here estab-lished as a type of avant-garde, pioneering but also lonely and somewhat ominous, outsiders lurking in the wings). However, rather than harmonization or cohabitation within the terms of the traditional stock industry, Scanlon proposes an overall transformation based on the realignment of fields of photographic production: 90 per cent of the images produced by traditional stock are to be 'pushed down' into another system of production and distribu-tion, royalty-free. Such extreme valorization of the 'creative' photograph and demonization of the standardized image is not typical of the stock industry's corporate culture (though it is becoming more so), but it does tie in with one of the four paradigmatic transformations wrought by Comstock and The Image Bank in the late 1970s and early 1980s: the emphasis on *production values*, meaning both technical excellence and creative photographic 'talent'. Stock photography, if it is to compete with the artistic pretensions of assignment images 'tailor-made' to the needs of clients, has to promote images of a singular quality and apparent originality – the marketable works of prominent and recognized individual photographers. Paradoxically, therefore, while it plays safe with standardized, predictable and formatted photographs, the corporate culture needs to augment the marketability of its images by promoting the name-recognition and distinctive signature styles of 'creative' commercial photographers.

This investment in the notion of creativity represents the discursive 'hinge' between the two cultures of production, corporate and artisanal, and more broadly between the visual regimes of consumer culture and high art. It brings together the marketing and promotional logic of the former with the collective 'imaginary' of the latter, conjoining commercial strategy with personal identity and cultural (artistic) aspiration (I use the term 'hinge' advisedly: the hinged planes may become uncoupled; the hinge may encounter friction). Moreover, through the promotion of personal 'vision' alongside the actual production of generic sameness, the corporate culture aspires to *incorporate* the artisanal definition of creativity, making it the prize for which photographers compete to innovate, despite the financial risks that such experimentation might entail for them. 'Creativity' is thereby made an engine of stylistic variation and transformation which nevertheless works *against the grain* of photographers' economic dependence on stock agencies (as outlined in the section on 'Success', p. 57ff.). That is why it needs to draw, for its motivating power, upon some of the most venerable and powerful discourses: discourses that not only pertain to artistic and cultural value, but to the very autonomy and authenticity of the (creative) self. And it is this power at the root of the incorporated discourse that always threatens to break it free, and that makes 'creativity' one of the key sites in which the integrity of the stock system – the unity of the same and the new, the formulaic and the innovative, the 'false identity of the general and the particular' (Adorno and Horkheimer 1979: 121) – is both performed and put perpetually at risk.

Meaning

The success of the stock image is anchored in its apparent social significance to advertising consumers as interpreted by professional cultural intermediaries. The way in which such anchoring works, and its problems, can be approached by analysing the vexed question of photographic meaning, both in the context of stock photography and more broadly in photography theory.

Two kinds of *fixed* photographic meaning are firmly established within theoretical writing on photography: we can call them 'intentional' and 'indexical'. The first derives most of its force from traditional art theory, promulgating a transmission model of visual communication that is frequently associated with Albertian perspective in painting and is interpreted as culminating historically in the photographic camera.[14] It stresses the photographer's artistic vision as a kind of 'purely mental, imaginative command over the camera' (Sekula 1981) which conveys a specific message to a receptive viewer.[15] It places the burden of meaning-creation upon the intentionality of the photographer, with the photograph itself acting as a perfect conduit for the unimpeded transfer of this message to the viewer's susceptible eye and consciousness.

John Berger, for instance, makes the following claim: 'a photograph is a result of the photographer's decision that it is worth recording that this particular event or this particular object has been seen', with the defining line between memorable and banal images being 'the degree to which the photograph makes the photographer's decision transparent and comprehensible' (1972: 179). In a later essay, Berger limits the photographer's intentionality to '*a single constitutive choice*: the choice of the instant to be photographed. The photograph, compared with other means of communication, is therefore weak in intentionality' (1982: 89–90, Berger's italics). In fact, photographers have much more control than this over the images they create, unless they spontaneously take automated snapshots (which they do not develop) of external events that they merely observe – a situation which is far from the case with stock and other types of professional photography (and much amateur photography). This does not mean, however, that photographers therefore have control over the image's *meaning*: for this to follow we would need to accept the transmission model of photographic communication. As Simon Watney has astutely observed of this account of photographic meaning: 'Photography thus emerges as an agency for meanings which pass through its 'transparent' space, rather than being constituted by it . . . The image itself is not a problem' (1999: 148). The 'intentional' account of meaning-creation has, of course, to elide one of photography's distinctive features as a medium, since its automated, mechanical and chemical nature might suggest that, as opposed to painting, the photograph would perfectly record an external reality rather than an artistic or communicative intention: nature, as Daguerre suggested in 1839, *reproduces itself* through the seemingly neutral agency of a chemical process (Trachtenberg 1980: 13). The elision is attempted not only by stressing the 'photographer's decision', but, perhaps ironically, by emphasizing the craft techniques of darkroom development processes as an artistic performance that complements and realizes the original intention, endowing photography with the virtues of manual dexterity associated with painting. (It also, as Rosalind Krauss argues, confers upon the resulting photographs 'the combined aspect of rarity and uniqueness that a pictorial original is thought to possess in the first degree and a print made after the original would possess only in the second degree' (1984: 63).) Like much else in both photographic theory and practice, the attempt to base meaning on intentionality returns to the tap root of artistic discourse.

The second account of fixed photographic meaning, most powerfully argued by Roland Barthes in *Camera Lucida* (1984), privileges the indexical relationship of the photograph to the photographed. It refutes intentionality by insisting on photography's chemical, even magical (Barthes 1984: 88), connection to the (past) reality it depicts: 'in any photograph, the object depicted has impressed itself through the agency of light and chemicals alone, inscribing a referential excess beyond the control of the creator of any given image' (Baker 1996: 75). This makes the image a unique material trace of the referent, like a fingerprint or a death mask (Peirce 1931–58; Sontag 1977; Bryson 1983; Barthes 1977a; Metz 1985; Pinney 1992). Although the photograph may be mechanically reproduced almost to infinity, the spatial and temporal field of its object, and thus of its own becoming, is singular and irredeemable: this is what allows photographs to claim a legal, evidentiary capacity regarding the existence of the referent at a particular moment (Sekula 1989), and also a simultaneously redemptive and tragic relationship to the passage of time (Benjamin 1980 [1931]: 202; Barthes 1984). Hence 'the Photograph mechanically repeats what could never be repeated existentially . . . it is the absolute Particular, the sovereign Contingency, matte and somehow stupid, the *This*' (Barthes 1984: 4).

Significantly, this indexical account does not deny the potential of a photograph to elicit multiple meanings according to the cultural codes employed by viewers: rather, it establishes a hierarchy of values that sets the pure and singular referentiality of the photograph (its 'denotation' (Barthes 1977a)) above such secondary, cultural 'connotations'. Referentiality and indexicality are privileged ontologically. Connected, in *Camera Lucida*, to the mode of viewing called *punctum* (whereby an accidental element of the image 'pricks' or 'pierces' the viewer: this is opposed to *studium*, the average, cultural field of interpretation), they are understood as emanating from the unique (chemical, magical) essence of photography, an essence which allows it to transmit reality to the viewer without the use of a code ('the *studium* is ultimately always coded, the *punctum* is not' (Barthes 1984: 51)). Cultural codes of meaning are therefore, in a sense, an imposition and an unavoidable supplement.[16] This ontological primacy of indexicality over codification means that for Barthes the photograph is *in essence* unclassifiable, for it is involved 'in the vast disorder of objects, all the objects of the world' (1984: 6): it can only be classified through the supplemental imposition of a code, a crude cultural typology. The existence, then, of a 'generic photograph' – a photograph *designed in advance* to generalize its unique referent into a type – may be at best a philosophical contradiction, and at worst a betrayal of self.

In opposition to the fixity of meaning in intentional and indexical accounts, the converse idea of photographic ambiguity or, better still (in that it implies a readiness for the transaction of meaning that is immanent to the making of every photograph), photographic *promiscuity* (McQuire 1998), is also well entrenched in photography theory, particularly within a 'materialist' or 'constructivist' school of thought which disputes Barthes's 'realist' approach while borrowing from his earlier semiotic writings.[17] This approach emphasizes that meaning is generated in the encounter between an image and a historically and socially situated context of viewing (for example Sekula 1981; Sekula 1982; Tagg 1988). It disputes intentionality by transferring the determination of meaning away from authorial intent and into the field of relations between production, distribution and reception. It counters indexicality both by emphasizing the culturally coded character of the photograph and by reiterating and extending Walter Benjamin's (1992) argument that photography decontextualizes the referent from its unique spatial and temporal existence, turning it into a classifiable and exchangeable 'sight' within the vast catalogue of the world-as-image, a process he famously described as the loss of the (art) object's aura in the age of mechanical reproduction.

In the context of these theoretical approaches, the immediately striking thing about the stock photograph is that any fixity of meaning is in tension with its commercial success. In order to achieve maximum sales, the image must be open to use, interpretation and alteration in a variety of different contexts for a diversity of purposes and products, many which are unanticipated by either the photographer or the stock agency. According to Andrew Saunders, VP of Getty Images PLC and Director of Imagery at Gettyone:

> A licensed image is made for licensing and therefore it has to be able to be sold multiply. The most successful stock images are images which can straddle more than one concept. So you can have 'communication', 'teamwork', 'togetherness', 'global business'. So in some ways I would say that to make a really successful stock image is, bizarrely, more difficult [than making a commissioned image], because it has to function on many different levels'. (Interview 18/1/2001)

The stock photograph is premised upon polysemy. Its meaning can be neither stable nor totally explicable through reference to the 'intention' behind the image, the object it depicts, or its style or formal structure; rather, its meaning has to be contextual, emerging in the relationship with other images, the texts that appear alongside it, the product or purposes with which it is associated, the socially situated media and environments in which it is displayed, and the cultural proclivities and interpretative strategies of different viewers. This openness, it should be stressed, is material as well as semantic: it can involve radical image manipulation, including the use of one image as the background to another. The commercial importance of this openness and instability is absolutely understood by photographers and stock agents: it is therefore the result of planning, or more commonly the fruit of 'experience' (Saunders, 18/1/2001), on the part of photographers. The stock photograph is polysemic and formally malleable *by design*.

Furthermore, this openness is not simply essential to the stock image as it is viewed by different cultural intermediaries with diverse marketing and design needs, but is, according to some commentators, central to the success of each advertising image. Leiss, Kline and Jhally make the following observations about 'ambiguity':

> the ambiguity that can be supported by visual imagery is significant, both for the ease with which symbolic qualities can be dispersed over a wide variety of product categories and types, and for the resultant indeterminacy of the associations . . . The openness of the product image to varying permutations and interpretations means that both advertisers and consumers can experiment freely with the meanings – which many be constructed differently by each, to be sure – in a particular ad campaign. (1997: 293-4)

Thus far the stock image entirely endorses the model of photographic promiscuity: meaning is not determined through intention nor is it identical with the image's referent. Such semantic and formal openness, however, does not imply an unlimited plurality of potential meanings and appearances, but rather a flexibly restrictive 'field of possibilities' (Eco 1989: 14): the image is *parsimoniously* polysemic. Moreover, as Andrew Saunders further notes:

> The people who commission (images) for products and services have the freedom of being able to be specific, and that's the difficult thing about stock – the genericism of stock is its downfall. The genericism is the thing you have to overcome, but you still have to keep it generic. So you have to make an advertiser feel that that picture suits their purpose perfectly but then you also have to ensure that someone else is going to feel the same way. (Interview 18/1/2001)

Thus the stock image must be capable of a multiplicity of appearances, whose multifarious and precise permutations are, for the photographer, beyond calculation: yet it must also encourage a *specifically* appropriate and relevant meaning when encountered – in catalogues or on CD-ROMs and websites – by the cultural intermediaries who are its potential buyers. *Crucially, these qualities of generality and particularity are split between the sites of distribution and circulation.* The image must seem obviously generic to stock agencies (who will select it for distribution because of its multiple sales potential), and singularly specific to potential advertisers (who will buy it and put it into circulation because it perfectly serves their particular purpose).

These paradoxes – planned unpredictability and generic specificity – can be restated with a rhetorical flourish by reversing what is probably Barthes's (and possibly anyone's) most famous dictum about photography: that the photograph represents 'a message without a code' (1977a: 17). For the stock photograph, in the 'raw' state of production and promotion in which it appears before the cultural intermediary, imparts *a code without a message*. It offers up an ensemble of possible references to pre-formed systems of cultural meaning, yet since – unlike commissioned advertising images – it is produced with no final purpose or addressee in mind (a decision which is left to a later stage), it proposes no definite destination but only multiple trajectories. Rather, the codes which it invokes themselves suggest ideal addressees who can never be more than distant points of calculation, and it is this act of *suggestion/calculation* which the image performs before the cultural intermediary. This is what makes stock photographs so fascinating and, in a sense, so brazen: certain viewers, at predetermined points in the production–distribution–circulation system, can see the arcs of their trajectories intersect. In this they conform, surprisingly perhaps, to a pattern Barthes discerned in a different medium: the literary writing of the classic realist text:

> Idyllic communication denies all theater, it refuses any presence *in front of* which the destination can be achieved, it suppresses everything *other*, every subject. Narrative communication is the opposite: each destination is at one moment or another a spectacle for the other participants in the game . . . Thus, in contrast to idyllic communication, to pure communication (which would be, for example, that of the formalized sciences), readerly writing stages a certain 'noise' (1974: 132).

The (limited) similarity between the readerly text (in this case Balzac's *Sarrasine*) and the stock photograph is not a matter of mere serendipity. The stock photograph is designed to turn the trajectories of its multiple potentialities and their ideal addressees into a *spectacle of rhetorical potential* before a very real, and very powerful, 'participant in the game' – the cultural intermediary who will decide exactly which potentiality to actualize. It is this spectacular characteristic of the stock image that allowed Jon Feingersh, in his session at *Photo*

Expo East '98 (29/10/98), to turn the audience into participants in a game that required them to guess the potential uses (type of product and advertisement), meanings and target consumers of a number of his photographs. Such theatricality, the spectacular performance of cultural codification before the gaze of the cultural intermediary, is the form taken by the stock image's own self-promotional rhetoric (see Chapter 4), a rhetoric which is intimately tied to the pivotal position of the cultural intermediary in the production system, the power relations between photographers, agencies and clients, and the core discourses of marketing and advertising.

Theatricality, however, is not limited to the relation between the completed image and the cultural intermediary expressed in a kind of preview of potential meaning. It also intervenes in the material processes of image production, defining the relation of the stock image to the objects and scenes it depicts. For these are almost always *staged*: the stock photograph creates its 'real' by constructing it through the active selection and deployment of a host of techniques and objects: scenery, lighting, props and professional models or actors. Hence the theatricality of the stock image fuses, in precise ways, indexicality (the image is the trace of a scene that was enacted before the camera), intentionality (the photographer decides what to shoot, how and why) and strategic, manifest polysemy (the actually staged scene, intentionally constructed, mobilizes an array of cultural references in such a way that they are visible to the cultural intermediary). The relation between these three types of meaning creation can be described as follows. Rather than the message beginning with the artist's visionary intention or with the depicted reality itself, with secondary layers of meaning added post facto through viewer interpretation, it begins with the projection (by the photographer or agency) and calculation of probable cultural associations and instrumental uses that are relevant to an imagined cultural intermediary (who herself is understood to be anticipating the associations of consumers); this projection then leads to the formation of an intent to photograph a parsimoniously pluralistic connotative scene; this scene is then staged and performed in the material reality present before the camera. The resulting image, however, usually naturalizes this process of projection, calculation and theatrical performance as the appearance of the 'real' (this is necessitated by the use advertising discourse makes of social experience – see the section on 'the concept' p. 78ff.), but without losing its ability to 'stage' connotations before the cultural intermediary.[18] It is, in part, this combination of realistic mimesis and conspicuous connotative potential that gives generic stock images their simultaneously 'real' and 'staged' look.

Exactly what mechanisms enable the production of these kinds of images, and how do they both enable and limit polysemy? The three most prominent are the notion of 'genre', the 'concept' of the image, and the instrument of the catalogue, working in concert as key elements in stock photography's mode of signification.

Genre

'Genre' has been the subject of extensive analysis in literary and film studies, as well as in research on the popular music industry. For reasons of space I will simply define it as representing the structured conventions and classificatory regimes that link viewers, images and producers in a common framework of meaning, and that it designates, from the point of view of the formal structure of the image, what the term 'formatting' explained with regard to the production process. To paraphrase Steve Neale's (1990) important essay on genre and the cinema, genres consist both of categories of images with shared formal attributes and similar referents and of 'specific systems of hypothesis and expectation' among viewers, whose interaction in the viewing process helps to render the images intelligible. As classifications based on shared cultural assumptions that allow meaning to be created non-specifically but typologically, genre frees the photograph from the prison of its indexical singularity, from the derivation of meaning through the unique causal connection to a singular referent, enabling instead the production of meaning through the image's iconic resemblance to *other images* (usually with similar referents): we know what a soft-focus picture of a couple kissing might mean in part because we have seen other images that we judge to be similar. These other images may be stock photographs (and the grouping of similar images together in stock catalogues reinforces the sense of generic identity), but they may equally originate elsewhere, including, of course, in the mass media. This means that each image becomes part of an 'inter-textual relay' (Neale 1990: 49) and reproduces, calls forth and adds to an ensemble of recognizable formal, iconographic and referential features to produce an image type. Each image can then act as the representative of this image type, as its appropriate incarnation in particular circumstances, such as this or that advertisement.

Thus far the theory. But what of the connection between the critical term 'genre' and the professional designation 'generic image'? The latter is widely used in the stock industry, providing stock photographers, agency management and clients with an associative short cut to a discrete visual aesthetic. To begin with, the word 'generic' suggests 'general', 'non-specific', 'universal' and, in the commercial sphere, 'without brand name': this is the kind of meaning intended by Getty's Andrew Saunders, quoted above. In the last sense ('without brand name'), of course, all stock images are necessarily generic, and photographers are constantly at pains to eliminate identifiable labelling and brand names from their images: this is a basic rule which sets stock photographs apart from commissioned advertising images, facilitating their resale and redeployment for the promotion of different products. However, following the sense of 'general' and 'universal' the generic photograph seems to be at odds with the 'specific systems of hypothesis and expectation' that underpin classification according to this or that genre. Rather, the term marks out an identification with *the very possibility and foundation of genre* as a typological abstraction from the specificity of the individual image: generic images are *designed* as taxonomic units rather than as singular productions, they are constructed typologically and archivally – in order to be classified (in agency archives) and in order to classify (social reality) – a feature I will address more thoroughly in Chapters 4 and 5. This generative functioning of classification as the framework in which stock photographs become possible (described in the section on 'Success', see p. 57), in which they emerge as intelligible objects, is matched by the classification of depicted social groups and realities that stock images perform, and the specific targeting of audiences and meanings which is their end.[19]

Yet this is not all. Direct Stock's Robyn Selman, discussing a shoot which had cost $5000 and whose images had earned $80,000 in their first year, offered the following description of a generic image of a family at the beach:

a) no one model stands out too much.
b) the styling is perfect.
c) it's happy, glad.
d) there's an age-range of 10–15 years.
e) most importantly, it has a wide variety of applications.
f) use the same models but change the clothes and you've got multiple images with low-production costs. Using 35mm film post-production costs are low too. (*Photo Expo East* '98: 30/10/98)

Given this description, more seems to be implied by the term 'generic image' than that the image can be assigned to a particular genre, or even that it is created for easy and simple abstraction into a general taxonomy. It is, as we have already said, designed for multiple use, a quality which is reflected by the assurance of an age-range: the differing ages of the models (none of whom stand out) allows for a range of identifications by diversely aged audiences. It also maximizes the potential of the shoot in the production of several slightly different images. By varying minor, easily adjusted and inexpensive elements of the scene (clothes rather than setting or models), one can suggest different referential codes and audiences: this is the photographic equivalent of marketing-led 'flexible' or 'small-batch' production that allows different market segments to be addressed through the alteration of minor details in the product or its packaging. Finally the image is 'perfect' and 'happy', a feature that will be discussed in the next section and in subsequent chapters.

Overall, then, genre explains the creation of a predictable field of potential meanings through the judgement of pertinent referential, stylistic or iconographic similarity on the part of photographers, agents, cultural intermediaries and viewers. The 'generic image', as understood within the industry, is designed for abstraction and classification within such a general taxonomy, but it also rationalizes the image-production process to address segmented audiences through the minute adjustment of signifiers: it necessarily aims to control difference and divergence as much as similarity. What fills out both the iconic similarity between generic images and their minuscule but significant differentiation, what matches generic signifiers with distinctive socially significant signifieds, thereby providing them with predictable 'content', so to speak, is the 'concept.'

Concept

According to Michal Heron:

> the most successful stock today is that which conveys an immediate message to the viewer: it will communicate a thought or a concept. If concepts are the ideas or emotions conveyed in a photograph, then it is through the concept that the idea is conveyed. Find the right symbol and there's your subject matter. For example, the concept of winning can be conveyed by a photograph of a runner breaking a tape in a race. (1996: 26)

Heron goes on to give a list of 30 visual symbols matched with basic concepts.

The 'concept' of an image is a postulated metaphorical meaning that directs and simplifies the task of interpretation.[20] Most successful stock agents and photographers insist that a clear 'concept' is central to a photograph's commercial success: 'unsuccessful stock images,' claims still-life stock photographer David Arky, 'usually do not have a clear metaphorical application . . . they are more complex and challenging' (*Photo Expo East* '98: 30/10/98). The centrality of the 'concept' helps the stock industry to reproduce a reified and abstracted (and thus apparently enduring) core of cultural meanings through restylization: 'find the metaphors that are deep in the culture,' advises Robyn Selman, 'and understand how to do them in a new way: chess photographs will continue to be metaphors for business strategy, but they need to be photographed creatively, in line with changing stylistic tastes' (*Photo Expo East* '98: 30/10/98). Significantly, it also provides it with a legitimating sense of historical mission: 'Like the icons throughout the history of art, visual symbols are used to evoke certain emotions and associations. In stock they are commonly used to convey a series of basic concepts' (Heron 1996: 27). Or as stock agent Bob Roberts put it: 'we are telling stories, story tellers, telling the same stories again for a modern audience' (*Photo Expo East* '98: 30/10/98).

There is, of course, a sense in which by reproducing 'the world of specific themes or concepts manifested in images, stories and allegories' (Panofsky 1955: 29) stock photographers are indeed engaged in what we could term 'practical iconography'. Yet notwithstanding the venerable ancestral veneer and philosophical connotations of 'concept', the stock industry's use of the term is actually adapted from conventional usage in the contemporary advertising industry, in which it refers to the universe of meanings to be associated with a product.[21] This borrowing reveals the essence of the concept-based stock image: it constitutes a pre-formed, generically familiar visual symbol that calls forth relevant connotations from the social experience of viewers which are then metaphorically projected onto products. As Judith Williamson long ago observed, in modern advertisements 'two systems of meaning are always involved: the 'referent system' and the 'product system' (1978: 43). A 'referent system' refers to those characteristics and affective values associated with an already-structured area of social experience and the visible objects within it. These values are then metaphorically transferred into the 'product system': 'This is the essence of all advertising', Williamson writes, 'components of "real" life, our life, are used to speak a new language, the advertisements' (1978: 23).[22]

These 'components' are selected with the utmost care, however, according to the needs and purposes of product marketing and the advertising industry. Leiss, Kline and Jhally describe advertising's primary social function as 'the selling of well-being and happiness through the selling of goods' (1997: 294), achieved through the systematic and selective redescription of reality. In practice, then, there are clear although fluctuating limitations on those concepts that are signified within stock images, and on their generic visual signifiers: social reality is represented only by certain types of photographed scenes and objects and not by others. This does not rule out 'unhappy' concepts – such as struggle or exertion – connected to the ultimate achievement of well-being, but it does mitigate against signifieds that represent its absolute negation: despair, futility. In terms of generic signifiers, the overwhelming emphasis is on those with predominantly 'positive' connotations: it is unusual to find coffins, guns or dirty hypodermic needles in stock catalogues – except in rare cases that are usually a residue of stock photography's origins in the editorial market – or even to find rain in a scene depicting a family holiday. Moreover, photographers repeatedly emphasize that popular concepts remain constant: 'Best selling images are those that very quickly convey a message. It's safe to say that the same concepts are always going to be popular: love, family, strength, success' (Paul Henning, stock consultant, formerly of Comstock, in *PDN Photo Expo East '99 Supplement*, October 1999: 25).

I will deal with the cultural significance of stock images in detail later on. Ultimately, however, the limits on both concepts and generic signifiers are determined by the overall need for advertising to address what Robyn Selman calls the 5 per cent of the US population which controls 55 per cent of the discretionary income – that is, that has an income of more than $100,000 a year' (*Photo Expo East '98*: 30/10/98). This involves creating generic images that speak to and about a specific generation of the American middle class and that increasingly equate success, and the spending which demonstrates it, with leisure time and family. This hegemonic limitation was until fairly recently compounded with ethnocentrism: scenes other than those imaginable in white middle-class lives were unlikely to appear in catalogues. However, as I briefly mentioned in the Introduction, shifts in advertising and marketing practices have led to the appearance of less obviously stereotyped and more diverse image styles and content, including 'artistic' images, more 'realistic' (i.e. grainy and black and white) images and images of 'ethnic' and 'minority' subjects.

The willingness to include more 'ethnic' images is specifically due to the recognition among advertisers of a growing Black, Asian and Hispanic middle class (Turow 1997; Heron 1996), although contradictions still abound due to the whiteness of many photographers and most senior agency executives. One top stock photographer, for example, described his new-found sensitivity when he noted that among the ethnically appropriate props he used in the background of a shot of a young Korean woman was a 'Japanese screen', Korean and Japanese cultures being in his mind conveniently identical (*Photo Expo East '98*: 29/10/98). Another example is The Image Bank Catalogue 18 (1996), which shows images of ethnic minorities, disabled people and the elderly in the exotic category 'One World', but whose category 'People' is almost exclusively white: this illustrates Richard Dyer's argument that the representational dominance of source of whiteness is its ability to be everything and nothing, to 'colonise the definition of normal . . . the colourless multicolouredness of whiteness secures white power by making it hard, especially for white people, to "see" whiteness' (1988: 45–6). Finally, stock's new-found multiculturalism may have resulted in more images of the Black and Hispanic middle class at home and abroad, but its consumer-driven need for disposable income still means that there are hardly any Native Americans, and almost no single-parent families of any ethnic group.

Finally, the notion of the 'concept' foregrounds the semiotic and industrial centrality of ekphrasis, broadly defined as the verbal representation of visual representation, as a mode of cultural production. For 'concepts', despite the mentalistic connotations of the term, are not deployed as disembodied, ethereal entities. Rather, they take the form of words: David Arky and Robyn Selman concluded their session on stock photography bestsellers by distributing a copy of Barron's *Handbook of Commonly Used American Idioms* to all participants (*Photo Expo East* '98: 30/10/98); Jon Feingersh, as noted above, promoted the use of 'one-word' concepts; while Michal Heron asks her readers to match visual symbols to a further list of thirty or so concepts, almost all of which are rendered as single words: togetherness, tenderness, romance, teamwork, competition, sharing, fun, independence, achievement, security, tradition, freedom, courage, among others (1996: 28). This movement between verbal and visual media is crucial to the process of projecting potential cultural references that drives the production process, and it can work either by photographers first selecting a concept-word and then matching it to visual correlates, or by the reverse procedure – deriving the concept from available visual subject-matter: 'As stock photographers', Heron observes, 'we can become *visual translators* – from concept to icon to subject matter or the reverse – finding the symbols inherent in the subject and finally ending up with the expression of a concept' (1996: 28, my emphasis). In this relationship, however, words are used to guide and control meaning, while the image is treated as the expressive material from which the significant verbal kernel can be derived: it is the conduit for the verbal message. This dominance of the verbal over the visual is closely linked – with two major exceptions – to what Barthes calls 'anchorage':

> The denominative function [of the verbal text that accompanies advertising images] corresponds exactly to an *anchorage* of all the possible (denoted) meanings of the object by recourse to a nomenclature . . . When it comes to the 'symbolic message', the linguistic message no longer guides identification but interpretation, constituting a kind of vice which holds the connoted meanings from proliferating, whether towards excessively individual regions (it limits, that is to say, the projective power of the image) or towards dysphoric values. (1977a: 39, Barthes's italics)

The first exception is as follows: Barthes is referring to the relationship between an image and accompanying written texts (advertising copy, captions, headlines) *as it affects the image's reading*. But the 'concept' situates anchorage at the beginning, rather than at the end, of production, as a systematically planned objective. Through concepts, words not only enable the anticipation and channelling of interpretation, they directly impinge upon the decisions that photographers take at the very earliest stages of production, and that other agents (stock agencies, cultural intermediaries) make later on. The second exception exemplifies the difference between the anchoring text of the advertisement and the verbal concept of the stock image. For concept-words are normally of a certain kind. The vast majority of them are the names of emotions or values rather than of objects, and they connect to broad psychological, social and ideological domains while at the same time, as single nouns, enjoying a radical isolation from specific contexts that suggests pure denomination: 'courage' names a quality (that connects to others), but courage to do what, in the face of what? To borrow Barthes's seafaring imagery, concept-words are anchored paradigmatically but cast adrift syntagmatically. Hence, they are both the particular keys to highly charged connotative domains and yet felicitously vague, making possible stock photography's potentially antithetical objectives of context-specific metaphorical projection and the polysemy necessary to multiple reuse. Their effect is almost mythical, certainly ideological: concept-words, as elements of image production, correspond quite precisely to what Barthes calls the 'semes' of connotation which are generated when the image is read. To adapt Barthes's analysis of one such 'seme', the connotation of 'plenty' in an advertising image (1977b: 48), we can understand the concept-word 'courage' as being 'like the essential cipher of all possible instances of courage, the purest idea of courage . . . The seme "courage" is a concept in a pure state, cut off from any syntagm, deprived of any context and corresponding to a sort of theatrical state of meaning'.[23] In other words, concepts make up a peculiar kind of rhetoric employed at the very heart of stock photography as a system of cultural production premised on image-recycling, a rhetoric which disavows – *as a commercial and semiotic imperative* – the specificity of its persuasive metaphorical power, disguising it as the pure denomination of psychological, social and cultural values transformed into ideal mental states.

This power to evoke ideal mental states is important because it suggests a mode of passage – a capacity for translation and transformation – between mental and pictorial forms that *propels* images across different sites in the process of production–distribution–circulation. Photographers use concepts to create their images in ways that anticipate the interpretative strategies of stock agencies; stock agencies use concepts to categorize and promote selected images (in catalogues, for instance) in ways designed to anticipate the interpretative strategies of their clients, and these clients in turn use concepts to plan and design the image-text ensembles that they create for consumers – whose interpretative strategies they also attempt to anticipate. At each stage the notion of 'concept' articulates the meeting-point between organizationally distinct cultural and interpretative environments, meeting-points that are made manifest in communicative and interpretative encounters between media objects from one domain and audiences from another (the stock agent views photographic prints submitted by a freelance photographer, the advertising art director 'reads' or looks at a stock catalogue). And these communicative encounters are, from the point of view of those producing the object to be 'consumed', critical to their success and highly unpredictable in their outcomes. 'Concept', therefore, grants a semblance of control over an intensely risky process by appearing to *unify* these different operations and encounters by virtue of perfectly transparent communication. Its use ostensibly removes from the equation any potential 'interferences' to communication arising from diverse media properties and interpretative contexts: communication and interpretation are framed in terms of *telepathic transparency* and *equivalence* – transferable mental states for whom images are mere conduits. 'Concept' thereby helps to maintain the production–distribution–consumption process as an *intentionally coherent* and *rationalizable* system of pure communication without noise. At every stage, everyone – photographers, stock agents, advertising professionals and ordinary consumers – seems to 'speak' the same language. Or rather, 'think' it.

Of course, this conceptual coherence in visual cultural production is achieved despite the fact that 'concepts' are typically rendered through words. This point is paradoxical and yet crucial. Words are essential to the ordering and signifying capacities employed with respect to the production and circulation of pictorial images. However, the use of words must be disavowed for the discrete 'visual' power of the image, and the visual expertise of its producers, to retain its distinctive cultural status. The use of the term 'concept' not only performs this disavowal – pretending not to use words while actually using them – it also affirms the seemingly direct relationship between pictures and perceptual-cognitive processes. The cultural importance and uniqueness of visual images, and of the professions which create and manage them, are effectively valorized through the use of a term which implies that images are 'natural' (unmediated) signs – windows onto the mind as well as onto the world. I shall revisit this disavowal of words in the process of deploying them in the discussion of digital technologies in Chapter 7.

The Catalogue

Genre frees the photograph from its singular relationship with its referent, making it immediately familiar as an image type. The concept provides it with a clearly signified meaning that can be correlated with an advertised product. From the point of view of the direct client of stock photography – the cultural mediator in marketing or advertising – genre requires a form of reading based upon the equivalence of slightly differing images as representatives of the same generalized image type, while the concept requires a form of reading that is metaphorical, capable of projecting from domain to domain, and instrumental, capable of applying this projection in a specific case and to a particular end. In this sense genre is read abstractly and de-specifies while the concept is read concretely and recontextualizes. Genre works syntagmatically: the photo-graphic signifier is connected formally with other photographic signifiers that are contiguous with it. The concept works paradigmatically: the signified is replaced by another with which it is metaphorically associated. These differ-ences reflect the fact that they are both predominantly geared to different actors and moments in the cultural process: genre primarily addresses the *producer*, referring photographer and agent back to other images, and most powerfully influencing the moment of production – the question it answers is 'what should this photograph look like?'; the concept addresses the *client*, referring to the potential metaphorical projections employed by cultural intermediaries as they attempt to direct the interpretations of consumers, and is geared primarily to the moment of distribution and recontextualization in the final advertising text – the questions it answers are 'what will this image be used for?', 'what do we want it to mean?'.

This tension between abstraction into a general type and recontextualization in a particular advertisement, between generic ambiguity and metaphorical instrumentality, and most especially between producer-orientation and client-orientation, can be traced historically through the stock catalogue. Stock catalogues in general are a strange kind of object. They are simultaneously the chief functional tools of the stock industry, one of the system's key products, and productive agents in their own right: as the touchstone of 'success' and the record of generic iconographic templates, they constrain and generate certain kinds of image-production and formation, particular modes of photo-graphic performance and professional subjectivity. They are a socio-technology that orders, homogenizes and abstracts images in their process of materializa-tion – in their 'becoming' as stock photographs.

Early catalogues, produced in the 1980s, are producer-oriented, offering an interesting variation on the traditional relationship between catalogues, photo-graphy and the objects photographed. In most traditional catalogues the photographic medium remains largely transparent: in catalogues of consumer goods, for example, the image *qua image* is rarely noticed as such; its construc-tion is hidden as a concomitant of the codes of conventional realism through which the photographed commodity is presented – few viewers looking at an image of a couch in a furniture catalogue, would say 'what an expressive image! I particularly admire the lighting'. Early stock photography catalogues, however, offer a progression to another level of signification, to what we might call the 'hypercatalogue'. In terms of category organization, they reflect the domination of genre, in that they denote and emphasize the primacy of the image's visual content with such names as 'People', 'Nature', 'Science', 'Sport', 'Business'. Within this framework, the world of objects, already abstracted and transfigured in each individual photograph, is effaced entirely as the photographs achieve their presentation *as images*, in, for want of a better term, the full glory of their 'imageness'. In this respect, the stock catalogue conforms to logic of media practice that Bolter and Grusin (1999) call 'hypermediacy': the medium foregrounds its own mediating function, rather than, as in the dialectically opposed logic of 'transparent immediacy', erasing its traces in pursuit of an unmediated encounter between viewer and referent. Thus cultural intermediaries 'look at' rather than 'look through' (Lanham 1993) the images in stock catalogues: the photographs do not represent their real referents, or types of objects, so much as *their own efficacy as images*, or generic image types on whose behalf they work rhetorically (in fact, these images are doubly rhetorical: they aim to convince cultural intermediaries that they, and images like them, are useful in the task of persuading consumers).

The fact that stock images are designed for recontextualization as sources of metaphorical projections in the final advertisement has become increasingly important, however, as producer-orientation gives way to client-orientation and as the discursive centrality of advertising and marketing finally replaces any residual 'editorial' attachment to categorization by visual 'content'. This has encouraged the renaming of generic categories in categories with broad 'conceptual' terms, such as calling 'People' 'Lifestyle'.[24] The contemporary shift from the generic to the conceptual is evident in The Image Bank Catalogue 24, *Perceptions* (1999), whose category names are 'emotions', 'relationships', 'choices and changes', 'communication' and 'imagination'. Rather than a 'hypercatalogue' in which images represent whole classes of similar pictures based on the correspondence of denoted content, we encounter a metaphor-machine in which photographs are arranged according to authoritative symbolic projections. To quote from the opening text of *Perceptions*:

> A rose is a rose is a rose is love is peace is inspiration. How you see the world – whether through rose, blue, yellow or violet colored glasses – is unique to your vision. Your perceptions . . . We've organized Catalogue 24 with this in mind . . . This catalogue is a visual thesaurus of images, designed to evoke diverse emotional responses. (1999: inside cover)

The appeal to 'you' here is deliberately flattering and very accurately targeted at the professional cultural intermediary, demonstrating the thorough internalization of the advertising ethos first adopted in the 1970s. In a material and cultural economy in which marketing leads production, the meanings of stock images are presented as both unlimited in their diversity and as converging upon a single, determining point, the instrumental eye of the advertising creative. Visual meaning achieves its liberation from generic content in the self-legitimating perceptions and powers of cultural mediators.

Conclusion

In this chapter I have attempted to analyse the stock photography industry as a system of cultural production. I began with an account of other studies of photographic production. Next I examined the intersection between stock photography's cultural economy and its mode of signification, focusing on key terms and practices that are prevalent in the professional discourse – the 'doxa' of industry practitioners – but that also resonate within theoretical debates on photography and cultural production. In the process my discussion has combined, in varying measure, sociological approaches to cultural production, the close reading of specific examples of professional discourse, and more abstract semiotic and photographic theory. The next chapter shifts the conceptual focus slightly while remaining broadly concerned with the relationship between systems of cultural production and the creation of meaning. It conceives of stock photography as a dynamic archival system or 'image repertoire' that demands of images a dual rhetorical strategy which enables their survival by propelling them from sites of production into those of distribution and circulation.

Notes

1. Jensen (1984) makes the important point that 'filter-flow' and 'production of culture' perspectives – of which Rosenblum's is a good example – postulate a transmission model, in which culture is conceptualized 'as a container of messages processed along a line from sender to receiver' (108). Similar issues are elegantly addressed by Carey (1992).
2. Watney's essay was originally published in 1986. He does not specifically refer to *Photographers At Work*, but to an article by Rosenblum also published in 1978: 'Style as Social Process', *American Sociological Review*, 43.
3. The opening lines of Panofsky's famous chapter in *Meaning in the Visual Arts* (1955), 'Iconography and Iconology: An Introduction to the Study of Renaissance Art', to which – in the absence of a specific reference – I assume Rosenblum is referring, should alert us to the problems facing her. Panofsky actually equates 'subject matter' and 'meaning' in opposition to 'form' (26), unlike Rosenblum, for whom the first two terms are somehow opposed (although she never defines them). Moreover, Panofsky makes it clear that for all the distinction between the 'pre-iconographical' (formal description), the 'iconographical' (typological categorization) and the 'iconological' (symbolic/cultural interpretation), 'in actual work, the methods of approach which here appear as three unrelated operations of

research merge with each other into one organic and indivisible process' (39).

4. This influence was met with serious opposition, it should be added, from an 'interpretative' or 'ritual' view of culture as the network of symbolic forms by which people construct a meaningful and interpretable reality: Geertz's *The Interpretation of Cultures* was published in 1973, while James Carey's influential essay 'A Cultural Approach to Communication' appeared in 1975 (reprinted in Carey 1992).

5. Moreover, they do plenty of justice to the historical and discursive complexity of each stage. See for example the discussion of 'The Photographer in the Field', which addresses the socialization of the magazine's photographers, the (conflicting) versions of photojournalism prevalent at *National Geographic*, questions of objectivity and motivation, aesthetic choices and constraints (Lutz and Collins 1993: 57–70).

6. An extreme example of this is the use of stock images as 'backgrounds' for other images in the final advertisement. See for example, 'Distant Vistas, Still Lifes' in *Light Box 5*, June 1998: 13–14. Wilkinson discusses recontextualization in the context of 1930s Britain, where it was standard practice for advertisers to alter the stock images they had bought (1997: 27).

7. Unless otherwise noted, quotations from speakers at *Photo Expo East* '98 are taken from conference sessions which I attended.

8. The relationship of stock images to classificatory regimes and cultural stereotypes is discussed in detail in Chapters 4, 5 and 6.

9. Ryan's use of formatting, however, emphasizes the importance of marketing (and the identification of consumer taste) as the dominant discourse controlling cultural production. Adorno and Horkheimer stress the primacy of mass production in determining the form of cultural goods, and equate cultural standardization and pseudo-individuality with the part-interchangeability of industrial products (implicit in the 'Yale locks' simile quoted here). Gendron (1986) provides a useful critique of this equation.

10. The notion of creative transmission (and its twin, biographical criticism) is well established in both art historical and literary studies. For a famous critique of its influence in the latter, see Barthes (1977d) 'The Death of the Author'. Bal and Bryson (1991) also discuss the issue in an art historical context (and from a semiotic point of view): see especially the section on 'Senders', pp. 180–4.

11. Heron quotes Polonius' 'To thin own self be true' as an authority for this 'personal' style. As the obedient servant of authority, however, Polonius might equally be invoked to legitimate acceptance of the imposed formula.

12. Klein's brief paean to the art of photography may very well have been deliberate flattery designed to placate photographers at a time when Getty Images PLC was reducing their commissions on digital sales from 50 per cent to 40 per cent (see Chapter 5 below).

13. The 'high priest' metaphor is possibly ironic, and echoes, whether deliberately or not, Adorno and Horkheimer's use of the phrase in their critique of the culture industry.

14. The continuity between perspective and the photographic camera (facilitated in many accounts by the camera obscura) is claimed by, among others, Pierre Bourdieu (1990) and Joel Snyder (1980), and is more or less assumed by E.H. Gombrich (1980). Martin Jay (1988) follows Svetlana Alpers in connecting both 'cameras' to non-transmissive Northern representational traditions rather than to the dominant 'scopic regime' of Cartesian Perspectivalism (see also Jay 1995). The historical and discursive continuity between the camera obscura and the photographic camera is disputed altogether by Jonathan Crary (1992).

15. This viewer is also understood as immobilized by the image, in a fixity of vision that parallels the fixity of meaning and fuses significance with attention. This pinning down of the viewer occurs in both the intentional and the indexical accounts of meaning (Frosh 1998).

16. Obeying the (Derridean) double logic of the supplement, cultural codes of meaning are both surplus to pure indexicality ('a plenitude enriching another plenitude' (Derrida 1976: 144)) and take its place, signifying its radical incompleteness ('It adds only to replace. It intervenes or insinuates itself in-the-place-of' (Derrida 1976: 145)); hence the most prominent cultural connotation of the photograph is that it is purely indexical. See Derrida on the supplement (1976: 141–64) and W.J.T. Mitchell for a discussion of Barthes's notion of the 'photographic paradox' that invokes, without using the term, the logic of the supplement (Mitchell 1994: 284–5).

17. Burgin (1986: 71–82) provides a good discussion (and example) of such a 'semiotic' engagement with Barthes's work, especially with the phenomenological and ontological project of *Camera Lucida*.

18. The 'real' here is not equivalent to an objective, factual reality or even to social experience (and certainly not to the Lacanian Real): the 'real' of the generic image is created through the simultaneous presentation of possibility and actuality, the reworking of actuality (itself symbolically constructed and mediated) in the fantasy of future achievement. These complex issues – the temporality and performativity of the generic stock image – will be dealt with in detail in subsequent chapters.

19. The etymological connections between 'genre', 'generation' and 'gender' – as primary classificatory and differential modes – are extremely suggestive here. See Harraway (1991: 130).

20. Hence this 'metaphorical' meaning of the term 'concept' is different from that employed by Gombrich in *Art and Illusion*: 'He [the artist] begins not with his visual impression but with his idea or concept . . . the individual visual information, those distinctive features I have mentioned, are entered, as it were, upon a pre-existing blank or formulary' (1960: 73). Gombrich's use (he also uses the term 'schema') suggests a taxonomy of visual templates and is closer to notions of 'type' (including stereotype) and 'genre'.

21. This adoption of a philosophical term by marketing and advertising has met with (predictable) indignation by some philosophers. See for instance Deleuze and Guatarri (1994: 10): 'Finally, the most shameful moment came when computer science, marketing, design and advertising, all the disciplines of communication, seized hold of the word concept itself and said: "This is our concern, we are the creative ones, we are the idea men! We are the friend of the concept, we put it into our computers."

22. This is what makes advertising, in Barthes's terms, truly mythological: it 'is a second-order semiological system. That which is a sign (namely the associative total of a concept and an image) in the first system becomes a mere signifier in the second' (1993: 114).

23. For the purposes of the example I have replaced the word 'plenty' with 'courage' in the quotation.

24. While the shift from generic category labels that emphasize denoted content to more conceptual labels has occurred in catalogues, it has not been widely implemented in archives themselves, for reasons discussed in later chapters.

4

The Archive, the Stereotype and the Image-Repertoire: Classification and Stock Photography

'Through being photographed, something becomes part of a system of information, fitted into schemes of classification and storage . . . Reality as such is redefined – as an item for exhibition, as a record for scrutiny, as a target for surveillance.'

Susan Sontag (1977: 156)

'As for me, I'm shooting what I have always shot: the world.'

Harvey Lloyd, stock photographer, (*PDN Expo East '99 Supplement*, October 1999: 25)

Perhaps the most obvious characteristic of stock photographs is that they are intimately connected to the question of classification: operating within the distinctive ideological framework of advertising imagery, stock images participate in the selective categorization and representation of reality. In this chapter I explore a constellation of terms that will help us theorize the connection of stock photography, and the wider visual regime of consumer culture, to the issue of classification: the archive, the stereotype and the image-repertoire. Such an exploration will act as a bridge between the processes of cultural production and the professional discourses of stock photography that I have already outlined, and the analysis of the communicative modes of stock images that I perform in subsequent chapters.

The Archive in Photography Theory

The stock-photography industry as we know it emerged in the 1970s, but the connection of photography and classification is, of course, far older and far broader. Despite their claims to indexical singularity, photographs have long been objects of classification (like most other objects), categorized according to various criteria (Bourdieu, 1990 [1965]; Krauss 1984; Sekula 1989). The particular taxonomy may vary from one cultural domain to another, and may be organized according to a different rationale in each, but a principle of categorization is nevertheless usually at work. Tourist snapshots, wedding photographs and family portraits, for example, belong to the domain of ritual social representation: here the organizing principle emphasizes the context of the photographic act (although it also fixes recognizable formal and stylistic conventions). In contrast, the sphere of high culture (art photography) is replete with categories familiar from painting (landscapes, portraits, nudes), which refer primarily to content and style. Interestingly, the genre most central to the privileged truth-value claims of photography – the documentary image – refers to both context and content at the same time, turning indexical singularity (the capturing of what Cartier-Bresson calls 'the decisive moment') itself into the basis for a type. In all these classificatory systems, however, the indexical connection of the image with its referent, and the specific context of its production, are replaced by a principle of generic similarity and iconic equivalence between images. I have already discussed this substitution of the indexical with the iconic, and of the specific with the generic, in my analysis of stock photography as a system of production. Understood synchronically, however, as a *visual relationship between existing images*, it is perhaps most readily apparent in photographic archives:

> In an archive, the possibility of meaning is 'liberated' from the actual contingencies of social use. But this liberation is also a loss, an abstraction from the complexity and richness of use, a loss of context. Thus the specificity of 'original uses' and meanings can be avoided, and even made invisible, when photographs are selected from an archive . . . In this sense, archives establish a relation of abstract visual equivalence between pictures. (Sekula 1999: 183–4)

Photographs, however, are not only the *objects* of classification. In the century and a half since the invention of the daguerreotype, photographs have also become primary *agents* of classification. They have been routinely used to categorize objects and people across the globe, whether on behalf of the state (passport and identity card photographs, prison mug shots, police files, medical records), the academy (the natural sciences, anthropology), or the corporation (catalogues, advertisements, product brochures). Allan Sekula (1989), probably the principal proponent of this claim, has argued that the intersection between photography and a categorizing, disciplinary social discourse in the nineteenth century produced an *archival* paradigm of visual representation. Neither monolithic nor wholly successful in repressing photography's indexical tendency to reproduce diversity and multiplicity, this paradigm was nevertheless important in incorporating the new medium within a range of interlinked disciplinary enterprises – from police identification procedures to the rising social sciences and pseudo-sciences of the nineteenth century, among them sociology (especially social statistics), criminology, phrenology, physiognomy and eugenics. However, Sekula claims that the paradigm not only functioned *repressively*, through its imposition on the powerless ('the poor, the diseased, the insane, the criminal, the nonwhite, the female, and all other embodiments of the unworthy' (1989: 347)), but also *honorifically* in the photographic representation and categorization of the 'worthy' ('heroes, leaders, moral exemplars, celebrities'). This introduction 'of the panoptic principle into everyday life' meant that

> Every portrait implicitly took its place within a social and moral hierarchy. The private moment of sentimental individuation, the look at the frozen gaze-of-the-loved-one, was shadowed by two other more public looks: a look up, at one's 'betters', and a look down, at one's 'inferiors'. (Sekula 1989: 347)

In this way the archival paradigm found in photography a necessary (though not sufficient) tool for producing a typology of the entire social body, contributing to the maintenance of social hierarchies and influencing contemporary and subsequent photographic practice.

Similarly, Rosalind Krauss (1982) underscores the connection between the classification *of* photographs and classification *through* photography. Focusing initially on photography as an object of archival organization, she performs an 'archaeological examination' of the work of Eugène Atget – a vast collection of some 10,000 photographic plates, largely architectural in content – in order to challenge the application of traditional artistic categories and concepts to photographic production. Krauss asks how can we describe his enterprise using aesthetically derived concepts such as 'authorship', 'oeuvre', 'genre' and 'artistic statement' when the pattern of Atget's production was dictated by the card catalogues of the topographic collections and libraries to whom he sold his images? Moreover, the creation of Atget's photographs according to the specific taxonomies of actual archives also contributed to a more general categorizing imperative. In the case of Atget, this imperative did not mobilize photography to typify the social per se, but rather utilized the medium in a similar set of practices performed on the 'inanimate'. Instead of a table of social types, Atget's archives both are structured around and reproduce a taxonomy of *views*, a catalogue that tames the diversity of the architectural and scenic field.

To be sure, the archival paradigm was not simply a set of practices imposed upon photographers by employers or institutions but, rather, a broader social discourse: for other photographers operated according to an archival principle even when freed from the necessity to work on commission from organizations. August Sander is a case in point. In the original introduction to Sander's most famous work, *Face of Our Time* (1994 [1929]), Alfred Döblin compares Sander to the medieval Realists, for whom 'only generalities, universals – a biological genus, for example, or an idea, were actually real and existent' (p. 7), and claims that he has produced a scientific, *sociological* photography by revealing the truth of social types. (For a fuller examination of Sander's relationship to the archival paradigm see Sekula 1981 and Baker 1996.) Hence both within institutions, and for some photographers engaged in their own independent artistic and social projects, photography, even when also operating under the aspect of 'humanism', aided a certain kind of acquisitive, positivist knowledge operating in a 'scientific' visual mode.[1]

In short, the revolutionary ability of photographic technology to produce realistic likenesses simply, cheaply and on a mass scale – what we can call photography's mechanical iconicity – has made it a key instrument in the rise not only of the society of the spectacle (Debord 1983 [1970]) but in the regulatory and categorizing practices of Foucault's (1979) surveillance society (Crary 1992; Tagg 1988; Sekula 1989; Pinney 1992). Two related processes are at work here. On the one hand indexical singularity is repressed: the multiplicity of unique images is submitted to a categorizing imperative based on a principle of generic resemblance that is realized in photographic archives. On the other, photography is utilized as a primary instrument of that same imperative across the entire social, economic and cultural field.

It is, however, worth briefly re-examining this conflation, focusing on the term 'archive', before outlining its importance for our understanding of stock photography. In particular, it is useful to return to Foucault at this point, and to his fullest explication of the notion of the 'archive', in *The Archaeology of Knowledge* (1972):

> The archive is first the law of what can be said, the system that governs the appearance of statements as unique events. But the archive is also that which determines that all these things said do not accumulate endlessly in an amorphous mass . . . but they are grouped together in distinct figures, composed together in accordance with multiple relations, maintained or blurred in accordance with specific regulari-

ties . . . *Far from being that which unifies everything that has been said in the great confused murmur of a discourse, far from being only that which ensures that we exist in the midst of preserved discourse, it is that which differentiates discourses in their multiple existence and specifies them in their own duration.* [my italics]

Between the language (langue) that defines the system of constructing possible sentences, and the corpus that passively collects the words that are spoken, the archive defines a particular level: that of a practice that causes a multiplicity of statements to emerge as so many regular events, as so many things to be dealt with and manipulated . . . it reveals the rules of a practice that enables statements both to survive and to undergo regular modification. It is the general system of the formation and transformation of statements.' (Foucault 1972: 129–30)

This is not the appropriate context for an in-depth or extensive discussion of Foucault's 'archaeological' project. But the importance of the 'archive' (along with 'discourse' and of course the 'panopticon') to much photography theory and history make it important to engage, at least minimally, with its influence. The above quotation can show us that while the notion of the 'archive' as a general system of enunciation can be theoretically invigorating, it can also lead to problems when applied in specific historical or cultural contexts. The italicized passage, for example, disputes the idea that discourses are subject to a general principle governing their unity (a central theme of the entire book) while, in a subtle move, it asserts that a general system ('the archive') determines the very differentiation between discourses and their temporal particularity: discontinuity and specificity are adduced as evidence of a general system no less powerful, and possibly more inscrutable, than the general laws of unity, coherence or continuity postulated by traditional histories of thought (see Foucault 1972: 21–30). In the case of photography theory these problems (of which Foucault was aware, see 1972: 130) are substantially exacerbated by the dual significance of the term 'archive'. For it should be clear by now that the word combines, albeit self-consciously, two distinct referents. Sekula makes the following comment on the relationship between these two referents:

We can speak then of a generalized, inclusive archive, a shadow archive, that encompasses an entire social terrain while positioning individuals within that terrain. This archive contains subordinate, territorialized archives: archives whose semantic interdependence is normally obscured by the 'coherence' and 'mutual exclusivity' of the social groups registered within each. (1989: 347)

The notion links, therefore, the fact that as objects of classification photographs are created for and/or stored in *actually existing archives* and that as agents of classification they are produced according to the *archival paradigm* of various social institutions and discourses (the state, medicine, social science, geographical research, etc.) by which the natural and social worlds are mapped and ordered: specific photographic archives are 'contained' by the general, epochal and epistemic archive that organizes the knowledge and representational practices of 'an entire social terrain'. Note that Sekula describes the connection between the two using a deductive logic and a hermeneutic method that are mutually reinforcing. By postulating the existence of the 'generalized shadow archive' he is able to deduce the coherent, determined and meaningful ('semantic') interdependence of specific, subordinate, 'territorialized' archives (the word 'territorialized' signifying both 'bounded' and 'grounded', particular and material): nevertheless this interdependence, under the dominance of the generalized archive, is 'obscured' and shadowy – it needs to be *revealed* by penetrating demystification or archaeological discovery. Despite the sophistication and overall persuasiveness of Sekula's particular historical analysis,[2] there is something Hegelian in this argument: the universal, geist-like archival rationality achieving its particular historical realization in actual archives whose material determination by a general law, and whose 'essential unity' (347), needs to be unveiled by the vigilant (philosopher) critic. In other words there is a danger here of dehistoricizing and dematerializing the archive, insisting – with Foucault – on the internal disunity of particular discourses only to reunite them at the higher level of the episteme, turning the archive into a transcendental ideal or force above and behind history that determines its own (inscrutable) 'territorial' manifestations in the world of phenomena. Furthermore, as Sarah Kember observes, while the use of Foucault in photography theory exposes the complicity of photographic practices and Enlightenment ideologies such as positivism and humanism, and the connection between knowledge and power manifested in the archival paradigm, 'it is frequently presented as an almost unshakeable formula of perceptual mastery and control . . . What this use of Foucault fails to do for photography theory is to give an adequate picture of the instability in the terms of photographic realism and its positivist and humanist base that was always already there' (1996: 154; see also Smith 1992). This failure means that contesting practices, contrary dynamics and actual discursive disunities are rendered invisible.

Notwithstanding these important reservations, the decontextualization and generic equivalence of images that archives achieve has been widely held to indicate a historical nexus between photography, enlightenment discourse and capitalism. By participating in the disciplining and organization of the diverse and unique sights of the world as specimens in a vast catalogue, photography has provided for their general equivalence as representative forms before the 'objective' gaze of the detached observer. As Benjamin famously put it: 'To pry an object from its shell, to destroy its aura, is the mark of a perception whose "sense of the universal equality of things" has increased to such a degree that it extracts it even from a unique object by means of its reproduction. Thus is manifested in the field of perception what in the theoretical sphere is noticeable in the increasing importance of statistics' (1992: 225). This tendency to replace the singular sensuous existence of phenomena with the abstract equivalence of generic visual forms not only resonates with Adorno and Horkheimer's (1979) critique of enlightened reason, and especially the rapacious subsumption of the particular under the universal that characterizes instrumental reason, but has been (again echoing Adorno and Horkheimer) explicitly related to the progress of commodification in modern capitalist societies: the abstraction and decontextualization of the archival paradigm parallels the subordination of use-value to exchange-value in the commodity form. An oft-quoted (Ewen 1988: 24–7; Sekula 1981: 22–3; 1989: 342) early celebrator of this connection was Oliver Wendell Holmes, who in 1859 wrote of photographic and stereographic archives:

> We must have special stereographic collections, just as we have professional and other special libraries. And, as a means of facilitating the formation of public and private stereographic collections, there must be arranged a comprehensive system of exchanges, so that there may grow up something like a universal currency of these bank-notes, or promises to pay in solid substance, which the sun has engraved for the great Bank of Nature. (in Trachtenberg 1980: 81)

Sekula, unsurprisingly, emphasizes this connection: 'This *semantic availability* of pictures in archives exhibits the same abstract logic as that which characterizes goods in the marketplace' (1999: 183). Of course, some of the best-known stock agencies wear this connection on their sleeves, most notably 'The Stock *Market*' and 'The Image *Bank*'. What these stress, however – in the spirit of Holmes' declaration – is that stock images are not just like material commodities, which can be made to carry powerful semantic charges unrelated to their functional uses, but, *as they appear before cultural intermediaries*, aspire to the condition of money itself in their ability to symbolize value abstractly and to confer it upon a contiguous product. This aspiration is nothing new, according to Jonathan Crary:

> Photography and money become homologous forms of social power in the nineteenth century. They are equally totalizing systems for binding and unifying all subjects within a single global network of valuation and desire . . . Both are magical forms that establish a new set of abstract relations between individuals and things and impose those relations as the real. (Crary 1992: 13)

Stock images, however, are nevertheless only *almost* akin to money: the values they are able to represent are not entirely interchangeable and universally exchangeable. This limitation is the result of three interrelated factors. The first, dealt with in the preceding chapter, is the fact that stock images are planned and formatted: the need to predict their commercial success relies upon the production of a *parsimonious* plurality of significations. The second is the related point that the denotative content of stock photographs tends to confine and differentiate its potential metaphorical projections through its organization into generic categories. Finally – and notwithstanding Crary's insistence on the separation of photograph and referent – the repression of the indexical, what Sekula calls photography's 'messy contingency', is never wholly successful: categories cannot entirely account for 'deviance', and the singularity of the referent threatens to break through and challenge the dominance of generic encodings (1989: 353; see also McQuire 1998: 141–2).[3]

Stock Photography, Classification and Consumer Culture

Despite this historical and cultural convergence of photography, the archival paradigm, and commodity capitalism, it is important to note the complex relations of continuity and discontinuity, similarity and difference, that characterize the relationship between stock photography and the archival systems and visual regime described by Sekula and others (for example, McQuire 1998). For the latter grant primacy to the representational practices and values associated with photographic realism, as well as to the philosophical and scientific discourses of positivism and empiricism: the 'philosophical basis' of photographic archives, writes Sekula, 'lies in an aggressive empiricism, bent on achieving a universal inventory of appearance' (1999: 185; see also Sekula 1989).[4] Underlying this expansionist empiricism is the claim that 'the photograph reflects reality. The archive accurately catalogues the ensemble of reflections' (Sekula 1999: 186).

Stock photographs, and advertising images in general, do indeed share in this realist foundation in significant ways, but *only partially*. As Stuart Ewen points out in his discussion of advertising and marketing 'style',

> photography's powerful ability to mediate style is rooted in its simultaneous affinity to reality and fantasy. As Oliver Wendell Homes had observed, the power of the disembodied image is that it can free itself from the encumbrances posed by material reality and still lay claim to that reality. At the same time that the image appeals to transcendent desires, it locates those desires within a visual grammar which is palpable, which looks real, which invites identification by the spectator, and which people tend to trust. (1999: 90)[5]

This duality characterized advertising photography from its rise to prominence in the late 1920s and early 1930s. For while it possessed the advantage of realist 'sincerity' over painting and illustration, 'the very ambiguity of the relationship between things-as-they-are and things-as-we-like-to-fantasize-them was the quality that came increasingly to endear the photograph to advertising' (Marchand 1985: 152). And it is this dual relation to reality and fantasy that we noted earlier in Judith Williamson's (1978) discussion of the way in which advertising imagery projects from the 'referent system', the range of meanings associated with the 'reality' depicted in the advertising image, and the 'product system' (see also Berger 1972: 129–54; Schudson 1986; Leiss, Kline and Jhally 1997).

This means that stock images are not usually governed by a rigorous realism and empiricist code that presume and emphasize their 'truth value', their fidelity to the depicted reality: apart from anything else this 'reality' is almost always staged before the camera and usually 'enhanced' post-production, a fact that is hardly hidden from consumers. In other words, the modus operandi of stock images is overtly *symbolic* rather than documentary: their master discourse is rhetoric, not science. To go even further, this rhetorical basis actually undoes the distinctions associated with photographic realism: between objectivity and subjectivity, reflection (of an external reality) and expression (of a feeling or idea), fact (which defines an object of knowledge) and fantasy (which defines an object of desire) – all of which are imbricated within the world/mind antithesis. In their place it recovers and puts into play the manifold powers suggested by the term 'image', powers that are inextricably material *and* mental, real *and* ideal, reflective *and* expressive (Mitchell 1986: 7-46). All the symbolic potencies of the image, especially its functioning behind, across and beyond the reality/fantasy divide, are grist to its rhetorical mill, its persuasive project, which comprehends that the social reality to which it refers is always inclusive of social fantasy, that the 'imagination' or 'misrecognition' of this real is a concomitant of the gap between sign and referent: hence, for example, to depict (and designate) a 'romantic couple' is not only to represent an existing social relation, but to construct an object of envy, identification and desire.

Stock images, therefore, employ realist representational codes only insofar as they invite viewer identification and allow for the rhetorically effective projection of values and desires symbolized by the depicted 'reality'. More specifically, realist codes are utilized to create a temporal loop or oscillation that fuses the conventional reproduction of the *actual* – whose temporality is past continuous, invoked as experience, habit and memory – with the persuasive simulation of the *possible* – whose temporality is future, invoked as dream and desire. (I will develop this idea in the discussion of photographic temporality and narrativity in Chapter 6 – see pp. 158–167.) This rhetorical use of realist codes also grants the fantasy of represented social relations the apparent immunity and universality of 'normal' visual perception, such that it becomes difficult to ask precisely whose version of reality is depicted, exactly whose party this is.[6] The question it invites, instead, is (how) can I join in?

Bearing in mind this broad distinction between empiricist and rhetorical representational modes, stock photographs do nevertheless exemplify an archival principle in action. For, in the form of generic images, stock photographs are conceived, planned, and manufactured both *in order to be classified*, according to the specific archival matrices conventionally employed by stock agencies (under such categories as 'people', 'nature', 'business', 'science'), and *in order to classify*, according to the wider forms of social categorization by which advertising and marketing strive to create audiences and meanings. Categorization within stock images, archives and catalogues therefore cuts across the reality/fantasy opposition while obeying two interconnected imperatives. The first is the need for stock archives and catalogues to classify their images in a system that enables efficient image labelling and efficient image retrieval. The second is the need for each stock image to facilitate identification and projection (classification of audience identity and desire). I will briefly address each of these archival imperatives while touching upon their intricate interrelation.

Sekula describes two sorts of 'normal' orders used by photographic archives: diachronic and taxonomic. Diachronic orders follow a sequential chronology of production and/or acquisition, and retain a narrative or historical sense of the development of the archive. Taxonomic orders, on the other hand, categorize according to a synchronically applied principle: they 'might be based on sponsorship, authorship, genre, technique, iconography, subject matter, and so on, depending on the range of the archive' (1999: 185). The orders which make sense for most stock photographers and stock agencies are, according to Heron, taxonomic, based on 'subject' (referent) and 'concept' (1996: 122), with substantial cross-referencing for authorship (in the case of agencies) and iconography.[7] The logic behind the use of taxonomic rather than diachronic orders is that they are oriented toward the client rather than the producer: it may be relevant to the photographer or the archivist exactly when an image was produced or acquired, but the cultural intermediary is much more likely to ask for an image of a particular object ('subject') or about a specific theme ('concept'). As we saw in the previous chapter, however, the relationship between generic subject and concept is vexed at best, with the latter frequently requiring a specific (textual and graphic) context for metaphorical projection: the photograph of a man proposing marriage to a woman on bended knee can be made to signify 'romance', 'commitment', 'formality' or even 'courage', depending on the context. The syntagmatic solitude of concepts, their paradigmatic generality, means that the same photograph (of the proposal) can be multiply reused for different purposes, products and audiences, but it mitigates against easy and effective categorization. Bridging the gap between generic subject and conceptual application is an *interpretative* process that is difficult to systematize: this centrality of interpretation has meant that finding the 'right' image from catalogues or archives is often the work of specialist cultural intermediaries (art buyers, picture editors), frequently aided by specialist 'picture researchers' employed by stock agencies themselves ('Frequently Asked Questions about Stock Photography', *Stockphoto* Online Stock Photography Network, www.stockphoto.net, 1998). As a result, the preponderance of stock images in archives have been classified primarily by their generic subject, and only secondarily (for the purposes of promotion in catalogues, for example) – if at all – by concept.

The term 'subject' is a deceptive one, however, as is its seemingly majestic isolation from the more assertively 'conceptual' or connotative.[8] For it suggests that there are just some things – referents, denoted objects – that stock photographs naturally 'depict', and that they correspond to naturally existing entities – categories and divisions – in the real world. In fact, to say of an image of a group of four people playing on a beach – a woman, a man and two children – that its subject, or referent, is 'the family' is not simply to classify the visual content of the photograph according to a familiar category (pun intended) from our social experience, but it is also to perform two simultaneous semantic exchanges. One *anchors the image* (in Barthes' sense) by bringing to it a select cohort of the connotations of the label 'family': only those connotations, however, that match up with the image content (for example, 'quarrel' or 'feud' would be excluded, as would 'honour'). The other *naturalizes the label* by seeming to provide it with visual verification: the photograph suggests that this is what families are like (and not just what they symbolize) – heterosexuality, symmetry, leisure, play, togetherness. At a very basic level this double exchange is very similar to Max Black's 'interaction theory' of metaphor (1979), with the photograph as the 'primary subject' or 'frame' and the word 'family' as the 'secondary subject' or 'focus':

4. The maker of a metaphorical statement selects, emphasizes, suppresses, and organizes features of the primary subject by applying to it statements isomorphic with the members of the secondary subject's implicative complex . . .

5. In the context of a particular metaphorical statement, the two subjects 'interact' in the following ways: (a) the presence of the primary subject incites the hearer to select some of the secondary subject's properties; and (b) invites him [*sic*] to construct a parallel implication-complex that can fit the primary subject; and (c) reciprocally induces parallel changes in the secondary subject (Black 1979: 28–9).[9]

The use of the pictorial terms 'frame' and 'focus' makes the similarity even more interesting, for the word 'family' focuses the photograph that frames it: rather than constituting its point of internal clarity and coherence, the image's focus *comes from outside*. Of course, I have deliberately conflated Black's metaphorical use of 'focus' and the technical meaning of the term. However, the difference is not as straightforward as it seems: the technical and representational dominance of 'sharp' focus in photography is no more natural or self-evident than the metaphorical decision to focus one's interpretative capacities on a particular cultural category or object: it was achieved through experimentation and struggle, and in the face of opposition (see Smith 1992). And so, like focus, the 'subject' of the photograph comes from the outside. Just as the photographic image has no 'natural' focus, only a normative representational practice that makes claims to optical neutrality and immanent pictorial clarity, so the social centrality and obviousness of its subject (e.g. 'family') is determined discursively and externally but seems to emerge, through the image, as a prediscursive phenomenon: a perceptually 'objective' material reality.

Hence the basic classificatory possibilities that appear as subject labels in stock archives and catalogues do not spring forth magically, immanently, from the images themselves. Stock images are intended to depict according to the matrices of social categorization employed by advertising and marketing to map the world of consumers, and these matrices supply the subject labels, linking the two archival levels mentioned earlier: the classification of stock images and their work as classifiers. They do so most commonly by utilizing certain *existing* classifications within consumer society – *age, gender, sexuality, class* and *ethnicity* – for these classifications can be said to articulate, at the most fundamental levels of subjective and inter-subjective experience, matrices of identity, social positioning, knowledge and aspiration. Saying this seems self-evident and simple, but in fact it is an extremely controversial and at times fraught undertaking. To begin with, as I shall argue in my analysis of the images in Chapter 5 (see p. 117ff), classification is a constant process of reiterating normative 'regulatory ideals' (Butler 1993: 1), differential and exclusionary schema through which subjects and objects are produced. Moreover, as a reflexively undertaken project (in advertising and marketing, for example), classification is interminable *work*. For throughout the 1980s and 1990s advertisers and marketing experts systematically and repeatedly recategorized and fragmented audiences, combining, cross-tabulating and elaborating these basic variables to create multiple new permutations, in the procedure known as 'targeting'.

Joseph Turow has explored the pursuit of this project in the United States:

Marketers and their agencies piled differences in the five categories onto each other in their efforts to locate slices of America that were most useful to them. Media firms picked up on those slices and created new ones as they tried to attract advertising support through claims of efficient separation [between target audiences] and special relationship [between the media outlet and the target audience].

Curiously, advertising and media practitioners' way of complimenting a group was to further divide it. Generally, the more attractive a population segment was to marketers, the more they segmented it. An implicit theme running through the trade press was that to make best use of different segments of American consumers, marketers and media would best see them living in different worlds. (1997: 56)

Marketing and advertising (along with commercial media organizations), no less than the positivist and empiricist projects associated with the photographic archive, have traditionally concerned themselves with social distinctions and categories (Leiss, Kline and Jhally 1997: 123–58; Turow 1997: 55), as well as the constellations of cultural dispositions, values and references ('taste cultures' or 'lifestyles') with which they are associated.[10] What distinguished the concern for social categories in the late 1970s and onward from prior classificatory practices, however, 'lies mainly in the passion for detail – the desire to get more specific about consumers' activities and attitudes through a cannonade of research' (Turow 1997: 55). In the UK such passion was also associated with the rise of 'creative advertising', which not only promoted the use of new forms of consumer research (especially lifestyle research and psychographics) and the centrality of account planning, but aimed 'to construct for consumers an elaborated imaginary landscape within which the "emotional" values of the product were signified' (Nixon 1997: 195). On both sides of the Atlantic recategorization signalled a recognition – impelled by a crisis of confidence in advertising effectiveness and also by new financial constraints (Nava 1997; Turow 1997) – that the diversification of media was fragmenting TV, radio and press audiences (leading to a cycle of increasingly targeted advertising and the demand for even more precisely segmented audiences) and a shift away from demographic segmentation (based on occupation and social class) to attitudinal and motivational distinctions and categories. The concomitant of this ability to classify population segments according such to criteria as attitude, taste, aspiration and memory was the production 'of advertisements which worked directly at the level of identity and desire' (Nixon 1997: 195) and which increased 'reliance on sounds and shapes, which tapped into the feelings of consumers, rather than on logical propositions' (Mort 1996: 96).[11]

It has been the role of stock photography to provide visual images that both represent (depict) the social categories used by advertising and/or feed into their lifestyles. Such a task implies, however, a certain classificatory stability and generality, especially given the commercial bottom line of the stock image: multiple reuse. But the more precise the segmentation, the greater the difficulty in creating images which can tap most effectively into viewers' identities and desires *repeatedly for different products*. On the other hand, 'inasmuch as the new forms of advertising claimed to disavow rationality in favour of aesthetics' (Mort 1996: 100), those very changes stressed the effectiveness of visual imagery in engaging with consumers' emotions, identities and desires (as a result they also privileged art directors over copywriters within the corporate culture of advertising agencies). So by increasing the need for high-quality, advertising-oriented visual imagery *at the same time* as they destabilized and narrowed social categorization, the changes of the 1980s and 1990s presented the stock industry with a twofold challenge: greater demand, and increasingly unpredictable 'conceptual' usage. In fact, the transformation made conspicuous one of the core dynamics and problematics of advertising as a symbolic-commercial enterprise: its relationship to the social and psychic worlds it seeks to represent and mobilize. For the attempt to close the gap between (marketing) knowledge and its object, between institutional expertise and reality, between the sign-category and the consumer, almost inevitably reveals the slippage between the two: the dynamic excess of the real over the symbol-systems and archival strategies employed to pin it down.

A certain awareness of this problem can be glimpsed in the promotional text of a press release from Corbis announcing the launch of their *New Humans* Catalogue on 7 January 2002 (www.corbis.com). Headlined 'Real People Seize Spotlight From Super Models, Set the Trend in Corbis' ® New Humans Catalogue', the catalogue is designed to 'satisfy this generation's reality-hungry designers with images of real people, shot in unique ways that capture current visual trends and those destined to be hot next year'. A tension is immediately apparent between the 'real' as authentic and singular (real people, unique shooting) and the 'real' as a design compulsion and a visual trend: a stylistic category and creative option produced in opposition to the purported unreality of previous photographic styles. This tension is only further exacerbated as the text unfolds:

> Humans explodes with a diversity of photographic styles that correlate directly to emerging trends in design, style and demographics. Images include unique faces that represent today's definition of beauty, and a perspective throughout that is in tune with an international point of view . . . Both the print and online Humans catalogues feature ethnically diverse people in a wide variety of activities for broad commercial use, and is a direct response to creative professionals' need for new, innovative images of 'real people'. Because real human beings don't fit into neat, predetermined categories, Corbis has organized the photographs in Humans by personality and

lifestyle types such as 'dreamers', 'seekers', 'strivers', 'voyagers' to give creative professionals choices of images that enhance their abilities to communicate feelings and ideas.

The contradictions within this text and enterprise are barely concealed. On the one hand 'real humans' don't fit into neat categories, yet the diversity of styles with which they are photographed 'correlate directly to emerging trends in design, style and demographics', a contradiction which inventively elides the language of romantic individualism with the pseudo-scientific rhetoric and generalities of statistics. And of course, the very uniqueness of real people requires their categorization by personality and lifestyle type, which are presented as apparently non-predetermined classifications (i.e. natural, real distinctions) rendered as 'concepts'. Ultimately, of course, 'real people' (complete with quotation marks) occupies a place in its own right as the very category of human uniqueness, defined as a fashionable alternative, one assumes, to 'Fake People' (such as Super Models) – all image and no substance – who are also presumably no longer 'directly correlated' to design, fashion and demographic trends. And these 'real people' can only anchor the reality of their appearance *within* their appearance, caught in the performative paradox at the heart of advertising photography (and much else besides): the need to act genuine.

The paradoxes and tensions of stock photography's relationship to classification and representation are insoluble at an absolute (ontological) level. But they are, however, usually very manageable at a practical and professional level, as the Corbis text makes plain: 'reality' and 'uniqueness' can quite easily become generic classificatory labels without melting anyone's logic systems. What remains important, in other words, is for classificatory systems to be both relatively fixed (i.e. yield to common definition and operation) and relatively flexible, enabling sufficient sensitivity within generalizations to allow for practical application and repeated production of the new. Marketing and advertising attempted to meet this challenge through the new research methods mentioned in the above discussion, and more generally by the regular revision of their own taxonomic procedures and actual categories. The stock industry met it, at least initially, by creating the generic image as the visual correlate to cultural *stereotypes*.

The Stereotype and the Glance

'Stereotype' originates in the eighteenth century as a technical term for the casting of multiple papier-mâché copies of printing type from a single mould

(Gilman 1985: 15). By employing the 'stereotype' as the basic unit of its classificatory system, stock photography not only becomes identified, perhaps appropriately, with a process geared to the mass production of uniform graphic signs, but seems also to doom itself to recycling rigid, unvarying – and ultimately repressive – generalizations about social groups that are anything but suited to the flexibility required under the marketing dispensation. However, a number of theoretical and historical explorations of stereotypes reveal the fundamental ambivalence that underlies and accompanies the term.

Sander Gilman begins his discussion of the 'deep structure' of stereotypes by arguing that no individual, and no society, can function without them or the classificatory processes in which they participate. (A similar point has been made by many others, among them Walter Lippman (1956), Gombrich (1960) and Dyer (1993).) The creation of stereotypes is a result of the process of subjective development and individuation, the primary separation of self and world, and the secondary split between 'good' (anxiety-free) and 'bad' (anxiety-inducing) as a mechanism for coping with the loss of control over the world. At this level:

> Stereoptypes are a crude set of mental representations of the world. They are palimpsests on which the initial bipolar representations are still vaguely legible. They perpetuate a needed sense of difference between the 'self' and the 'object', which become the 'Other'. Because there is no real line between self and the Other, an imaginary line must be drawn; and so that the illusion of an absolute difference between self and Other is never troubled, this line is as dynamic in its ability to alter itself as is the self . . . Thus paradigm shifts in our mental representations of the world can and do occur. We can move from fearing to glorifying the Other. We can move from loving to hating. The most negative stereotype always has an overtly positive counterweight. As any image is shifted, all stereotypes shift. Thus stereotypes are inherently protean rather than rigid (Gilman 1985: 17–18).[12]

This protean form of differentiation guides the mental representations employed by adults in complex social contexts, representations which build upon the self/world antithesis but use 'a set vocabulary of images for this externalised Other' (ibid.: 20) that is historically and culturally produced, making up a particular society's 'tradition' of stereotyping and projecting onto difference and the Other its fear of loss of control. This 'vocabulary of images' is itself altered by the interaction of subjects with the realities which the images attempt to map, which means that

> patterns of association [between the attributes of the stereotyped other] are most commonly based, however, on a combination of real-life experience (as filtered through the models of perception) and the world of myth, and the two intertwine

to form fabulous images, neither entirely of this world nor of the realm of myth. The analogizing essential to this process functions much like the system of metaphor (ibid.: 21).

This analysis of the stereotype recapitulates several strands of our exploration of stock photographic categorization: its fusion of reality and fantasy, its reliance on and mobilization of metaphorical modes, the fixity and fluidity of its categories and its ambivalence toward its objects. In fact, we can interpret stock photographs as striking visual materializations of cultural stereotypes, the stillness of the photographic medium simultaneously coupling temporal and spatial stasis with radical narrative irresolution (see the next two chapters): here they appear – women and men, old and young, black and white – motionless in perfect colour (or arty monochrome), fixed for eternity and evanescent as the instant, staged to look real and really staged. At any particular point in time, however, the presentation of these fixed images (whether before an art director in a catalogue or before a consumer in various media) is merely a moment in a temporal dynamic characterized by the constant production of substitute images on a uniform pattern as well as more fluid, longer-term transformations in categorization, style and content. Overall we can describe this process as the 'pathological' repetition of stereotypes: it is 'pathological' in Gilman's sense that the stock industry, under the tutelage of marketing and advertising discourse, 'sees the entire world in terms of the rigid line of difference' (ibid.: 18), is perpetually anxious to maintain or create categories, and cannot perceive singularity; in this context it is worth recalling Turow's comment that 'to make best use of different segments of American consumers, marketers and media would best see them living in different worlds' (1997: 56).

Finally, the stock stereotype shares the *ambivalence* of the stereotype that Homi Bhabha describes in the context of colonial discourse. Without wishing to reduce the historical and cultural specificity of either my own or Bhaba's analysis, the stereotype in stock photography, like the stereotype in colonial discourse, 'is a form of knowledge and identification that vacillates between what is always "in place", already known, and something that must be anxiously repeated' (1992: 312). The integrity and harmonious sociability of the bourgeois nuclear family, or, in the case of the category analysed in Chapter 6, the romance and intimacy of the heterosexual and monoracial couple, display precisely this ambivalence: they restate entrenched cultural representations of selfhood and difference, mediating powerful (and in themselves protean) patriarchal, heterosexist and ethnocentric ideologies and categories. And yet they require such anxious and prolific reiteration and citation, in generic image after generic image after generic image.

This constant reiteration, this pathological repetition in a mediascape ever more crowded with similar images, emphasizes another important aspect of the stereotype: *the speed and ease with which it can be deciphered*. Writing of Walter Lippman's description of stereotypes as 'short cuts' Dyer notes 'the manner in which stereotypes are a very simple, striking, easily-grasped form of representation but are none the less capable of condensing a great deal of complex information and a host of connotations' (1993: 12). The creation of photographic correlates to cultural stereotypes harnesses this simplicity and immediacy of comprehension to the power of photographic realism's 'transparent immediacy' (Bolter and Grusin 1999: 105–12): photographic stereotypes can be read even more quickly and easily because of the photograph's apparent conformity to everyday visual codes, codes that, unlike the more abstract sign systems of spoken and written language, appear to be unmediated.

The ability of stereotypes to be easily and speedily 'grasped' or deciphered has sometimes mutated into a charge against 'industrial' photographic representation in general (see, for instance, Lyotard 1983: 333). It is probably more useful, however, to approach the speed and ease of deciphering photographic stereotypes within the context of the relationship between consumer culture, photography and the formation of observational modes in contemporary societies, as these might affect advertising viewers and especially stock-agency clients (cultural intermediaries). Tracing the prehistory of these perceptual modes, Jonathan Crary (1992, 1994) argues that a model of 'subjective vision' emerged within a broad range of disciplines between 1810 and 1840. This model understood that the 'truth' of seeing did not depend upon an ordered relation between an observer and an external world, but upon contingent psychological and physiological processes lodged within the viewer. By implication, vision could be arbitrary and unreliable. And just as significantly, this understanding was critical for the development of instrumental procedures for containing that arbitrariness, for subjecting vision to techniques of measurement, manipulation and control – a process that gathered momentum as the century progressed.

This simultaneous liberation and disciplining of vision is also linked to the unremitting creation of new forms of perceptual stimuli under modernization within 'a social, urban, psychic, industrial field increasingly saturated with sensory input' (Crary 1994: 22). Visual perception, in other words, is in a state of constant crisis, caught between the unpredictability of subjective vision in the face of perpetual stimulation, and the procedures for controlling vision arising from that very same process of subjectivization. Central among the latter is the attempt to impose 'a disciplinary regime of attentiveness' (Crary 1992: 24).

Clearly related to descriptions of sensory overload in the modern metropolis (for example, Simmel 1997: 175–85) as well as to the notion of the psychic shock of modern existence (see Buck-Morss 1992), Crary's argument focuses primarily on the nineteenth and early twentieth centuries. It nevertheless provides a framework for analysing the forces that structure the encounter with generic stock photographs and photographic stereotypes in contemporary industrialized societies. It allows us to see that they address modes of viewing which are caught within a field of arbitrariness/attentiveness in an ever more crowded visual environment. The issue of visual attention and distraction in an image-saturated culture is, of course, a primary concern of advertisers and marketers to this day.[13]

Norman Bryson (1983), in his examination of vision and painting, makes a distinction between two interconnected ways of looking at paintings that can prove useful here (perhaps because of its historical generality): the Gaze and the Glance. The Gaze is 'prolonged, contemplative, yet regarding the field of vision with a certain aloofness and disengagement, across a tranquil interval', whereas the Glance is 'a furtive or sideways look whose attention is always elsewhere, which shifts to conceal its own existence, and which is capable of carrying unofficial, *sub rosa* messages of hostility, collusion, rebellion and lust' (Bryson, 1983: 94).[14] Western art has privileged the Gaze, thanks largely to the tradition of mimesis that since the Renaissance has insisted on the elimination of the traces of temporal process and material labour in the painting, and to the corresponding construction of the viewer as a fixed abstract point removed from the dimensions of space and time: the punctual viewing subject. Within this regime, the repressed Glance – always in deferral, perpetually in motion – 'takes on the role of saboteur, trickster' (Bryson, 1983: 121).

The enforced stasis and immobility of Bryson's Gaze finds an echo in a technical precursor of the modern photographic camera: the camera obscura that Crary sees as providing the dominant model for the pre-modern discourse of visuality.[15] Such technological ancestry has led to the notion that photography largely 'inherited' the Western tradition of mimetic realism that Bryson delineates. Hence 'photography was predisposed to become the standard of 'realism' because it supplied the mechanical means for realizing the "*vision of the world*" *invented* several centuries earlier, with perspective' (Bourdieu 1990 [1965]: 191–2, emphasis in original; see also Joel Snyder 1980: 510–14). The Western perspectival pictorial tradition certainly does seem to inform popular conceptions of photographic realism as a standard, normative practice (in most news and domestic photography, for example), even if it has been significantly challenged by art photographers and increasingly by documentary, fashion and some advertising photographers.

However, we should be very careful about reading off directly from one technology (and its generalized 'mode of viewing') to another as though we were dealing with some kind of genetic transmission. 'Succession' can be a mystifying term when applied to technologies without reference to their various social applications, and the range and diversity of photographic practices – and their communicative contexts – differ greatly from those of the camera obscura.

Hence to associate photography exclusively with the Gaze and the 'punctual viewing subject' would be a mistake, notwithstanding the resilience of photographic realism. Indeed, the repression of the 'flickering, ungovernable mobility of the Glance' (Bryson 1983: 121) that such a mode of attentiveness involves is keenly felt within contemporary visual culture, almost as a kind of psychical pressure and discomfort. As Burgin suggests: 'to remain too long with a single image is to lose the imaginary command of the look, to relinquish it to that absent other to whom it belongs by right: the camera. The image no longer receives *our* look, reassuring us of our founding centrality, it rather, as it were, avoids our gaze' (Burgin 1982a: 191).

That is why, within the image-crowded field of consumer culture, most photographs are not gazed at but glanced at or *overlooked*. In fact, photographs are doubly overlooked, literally and metaphorically: they are scanned within the onward movement of the glance, but they are also taken for granted, and 'whereas paintings and films readily present themselves to critical attention as objects, photographs are received rather as an environment' (Burgin 1982b: 143). And there is almost always another photograph ready to receive and deflect our distracted look.

Ultimately it is this *environmental* dimension of photography that necessitates the incessant reproduction of stock images as visual correlates to stereotypes. The contiguity and profusion of photographs as an ordinary, enveloping visual space requires *the depletion of the individual generic image* such that it can communicate effectively and at speed without hindering the progress of the glance: hence the need for the 'short cut' to meaning that the stereotype provides. So while for Bryson the repressed yet irrepressible glance becomes a powerful critical lever against the normative representational practices of Western painting (and, more particularly, the traditional assumptions of Western art theory), it plays a different role in contemporary consumer culture. The glance can be understood as that mode of seeing which flickers arbitrarily across the surfaces of the visual field, and which tends therefore toward a certain *equivalence*: it is that visual dynamic whose momentum partakes of the levelling energy of exchange value, which denies its own duration and the singularity of its object, which requires and enacts the speedy and easy decipherment that the photographic stereotype provides. The incessantly repeated stock stereotype, therefore, proposes a solution to the routine skimming of photographs habitually employed by most viewers as an existential and perceptual imperative. Even more pressingly, perhaps, it serves and survives the page flicking and image scanning practised as a professional skill by the cultural intermediary when faced with the thousands of images presented in stock catalogues and elsewhere.

The Image Repertoire

Finally, the ambivalence of the stereotype as a basic unit of the 'archival' system of stock photography and the visual regime of consumer culture, its very fluidity within fixity, its perpetual reinscription of simplified uniformity, brings me very briefly to consider one last term within the constellation that I connected to classification: the image repertoire. For the stock industry creates and contributes to a *repertoire* of photographs and cultural stereotypes that is characterized by both reiteration and change over time. The use of the term 'repertoire' serves to distinguish the conception from what Leiss, Kline and Jhally call the 'image pool', an extensive zone of symbolic (largely iconic) reference from which advertisements 'fish out' symbolic and metaphorical associations (1997: 294). The difference between the image pool and the image repertoire is that the latter retains the sense of deliberate limitation. It is not a virtual set of potential images, but a select and changing list of actual productions: the theatrical connotations of the word 'repertoire' emphasize that images, for all their apparent stereotypical simplicity, are products that have been worked on, selected, rehearsed (in the production of similar images) and performed.

This stress on theatricality also marks out the term's usefulness in relation to the notion of the 'archive', despite their semantic proximity. For just as the production of stock photographs is not simply a drawing off from a pre-existing resource (a pool), neither is it a bureaucratic mode of filing perceptions and representations (an archive): it is, rather, a *rhetorical craft of staging*, of classification through citation and performance that refracts in complex ways the ordinary performance of selfhood and otherness in everyday life. Perhaps my ultimate preference for the term 'image repertoire' over 'archive' is my sense that they describe the classificatory and representational systems of two separate (though linked) visual regimes:[16] while the latter term is informed by the administrative rationality of the state and the institution, its purpose to survey and control, the image repertoire reaffirms the notions of *persuasion, performance, citation* and *spectacle* as enduring factors in the realm of consumer culture.

Crucially, the image repertoire (like the archive) must be understood as a dynamic, generative system: repertoires change, and not all potential images are 'auditioned' before cultural intermediaries or ultimately 'performed' before consumers. Hence for the stock image the maintenance of the image repertoire is an extremely fraught process of dialectical interchange between potentiality (the image's 'becoming') and realization (its 'being'), in which images deploy a self-promotional 'system rhetoric' designed to ensure their survival and propel them across the cultural and economic borders between sites of production (photographers), distribution (stock agencies) and circulation (ad agencies, designers, etc.), while at the same time constructing – as their 'mission' – the ordinary, everyday and unremarkable visual environment that surrounds consumers. The particularities and peculiarities of these communicative modes will emerge more clearly over the next two chapters, beginning with my reading of romantic stock images.

Notes

1. See Kember (1996) for a discussion of the connection between photography, empiricism and positivism. Berger also discusses the almost simultaneous invention of photography and the completion of Comte's *Cours de Philosophie positive* (in Berger and Mohr 1982: 99).

2. Sekula cites the prestige of phrenology and physiognomy in the mid- to late nineteenth century as the 'clearest indication of the essential unity of this archive of images of the body' (1989: 347).

3. Just as, for Barthes, the punctum pierces the studium. Crary's claim echoes Benjamin's famous discussion of the decline of the aura in the 'Artwork Essay' (1992). Benjamin's attitude to the fate of auratic singularity in the photographic age was, however, ambiguous to say the least: in his earlier essay on photography (1980 [1931]), Benjamin gives an account of early photographs which suggests that the image preserves the singularity of its referent. See Hansen (1987) for a superb analysis of this ambiguity. I have discussed it in relation to Barthes and the rhetoric of visual immobilization in photography theory (Frosh 1998).

4. One of the most famous public examples of this attempt to create a 'universal inventory of appearance' – in the spirit of a universalist humanism underpinned by empiricism – is The Family of Man exhibition, organised by Edward Steichen, which opened at The Museum of Modern Art in New York in 1955, subsequently toured much of the world, and was published as a book (which in parts resembles a documentary prototype of a stock agency catalogue). 'The exhibition . . .', Steichen wrote in his

original introduction, 'demonstrates that the art of photography is a dynamic process of giving form to ideas and of explaining man to man. It was conceived as a mirror of the universal elements and emotions in the everydayness of life – as a mirror of the essential oneness of mankind throughout the world' (1986 [1955]: 3). This proclamation of fundamental equivalence across 503 images from different cultures required a concomitant empiricist assumption about the essential facticity, neutrality and universality of photography (the photograph as mirror). Sekula claims that the exhibition, 'more than any other photographic project, was a massive and ostentatious bureaucratic attempt to universalize photographic discourse' (1981: 20). Perhaps the best-known critique of the exhibition is Barthes's essay in *Mythologies* (1993: 100–2), which similarly focuses on the exhibition's mythologizing of a 'universal human nature' through a decontextualized and dehistoricized photographic archive.

5. Whether people still do 'tend to trust' the visual grammar of photographic realism in advertising is a moot point which I will address later on. Eva Illouz, commenting on the importance of visual media and 'visualization' to the construction of 'romance' in late-capitalist societies, also notes that advertising (and cinema) gave images the 'allure of fantasy and the sharp focus of realism' (1997: 42).

6. The debate on photography's connection to 'normal' visual perception is far too extensive, and intense, to recapitulate here with any sophistication: it is the central concern of much photography theory. Umberto Eco (1982) provides one of the best known semiotic critiques of the apparent 'naturalness' of 'everyday' visual perception and its relation to the image. Tagg places such a critique within a Foucauldian insistence on discursive formations and institutional practices (1988: esp. 1–33).

7. Occasionally some of the larger agencies use the taxonomy of authorship as a promotional tool: see for example The Image Bank Catalogue 16: People which organizes its images in three primary sections, each one representing the work of a photographer or studio (Marie and Ghislain David De Lossy, John Kelly, Werner Bokelberg) and subdivided in turn by subject categories: women, men, couples and friends, families, children.

8. The problematic distinction between 'subject' and 'concept' is not a little reminiscent of the differentiation between denotation and connotation. Barthes, having utilized the distinction to great and controversial effect in his earlier writings on photography (helpfully anthologized in *Image–Music–Text* (1977)), not to mention myth, goes on to criticize it in *S/Z*, arguing that denotation is a system like any other, and there is no reason 'to arrange all the meanings of a text in a circle around the hearth of

denotation (the hearth: center, guardian, refuge, light of truth)' (1974: 7). See also my discussion in Chapter 5 at pp. 122–123.

9.   For a detailed discussion of Black's theory in the context of pictorial metaphor and advertising see Forceville (1996). Despite providing an excellent theoretical review of work on metaphor, and laudably refusing to separate absolutely the pictorial from the verbal, the book's actual analysis of pictorial metaphor in advertising suffers from an almost formalist neglect of advertising's discursive foundations and its considerable ideological force, and the centrality of metaphor to both.

10.   A well-known theoretical elaboration of lifestyle research is Mitchell (1983). Giddens discusses the concept in relation to the reflexive project of self-identity, and speculates that the term originates in the writings of Alfred Adler, or possibly even in Weber's 'style of life' (1991: 80–8). Leiss, Kline and Jhally give a useful, brief overview of the concept's use (1997: 304–7) in US advertising, while for the UK context see Mort (1996), especially 91–113. The preferred term of advertising and marketing, 'lifestyle' can easily be mapped onto a notion employed in academic sociology and anthropology: Bourdieu's (1986) 'habitus', the internalized system of socially structured gestures, tastes, aspirations, and dispositions – in which 'ideology' is located and lived. The connection between habitus and lifestyle is acutely demonstrated by Hebdige in his analysis of lifestyle packaging, or as he calls it, 'syntax selling', where an advertisement or purchase draws in its wake other products deliberately associated by marketers with the same 'cultivated habitus' (1993: 89).

11.   Overall, the changes in advertising, marketing and design in advanced industrial societies in the 1980s, especially the recategorization of social reality according to 'attitudinal' and 'motivational' parameters, constitutes an illuminating instance of what Giddens has called 'institutional reflexivity' and what others (and Giddens himself) have described as 'reflexive modernisation' (Giddens 1990 and 1991; Beck, Giddens and Lash 1994). Here institutional reflexivity involves the conscious and strategic revision of organizational forms of knowledge and practices which themselves are designed to exploit 'the susceptibility of most aspects of social activity, and material relations with nature, to chronic revision in the light of new information or knowledge' (Giddens (1991: 20)).

12.   As a result of this fluidity I find it difficult to accept as useful Dyer's (1993: 14–15) distinction (borrowed from Klapp 1962) between 'social types' – those who 'belong' in society, those who are 'in' or the same – and stereotypes – those who are socially 'out' and Other – even though it does emphasize the centrality of social power in stereotyping. Dyer himself entertains similar doubts.

13. While, for the most part, the successful elicitation of the viewer's attention is assumed in most critical analyses of advertising images: see Chapter 6, p. 145ff.

14. I have relied upon Bryson's broad bipartite distinction between two visual modes. In contrast, Martin Jay (1988) proposes three main 'scopic regimes' of modernity, the dominant Cartesian perspectivalism (roughly, the discourse of the Gaze), and two subordinate models that represent 'moments of unease' in the hegemonic regime: the art of describing (a cartographical, non-monocular, surface-oriented mode exemplified by Dutch seventeenth-century art that privileges, among other things, the discrete particularity of visual experience) and the baroque (again roughly, the realm of the Glance – a mode that accentuates a disorienting and ecstatic multiplicity of visual spaces and the opposition of surface and depth). I do not have the space to examine the advantages and problems of these distinctions. Suffice to say that both Bryson and Jay are proposing ideal-typical categories that are useful analytical tools, and that neither claims that these categories can do justice to the complexities of the modern visual field (itself an approximation).

15. Crary (1992) disputes the claim of direct continuity between perspective, the camera obscura and the photographic camera, maintaining that the classical regime of vision based on the camera obscura model had largely collapsed before the invention of the photographic camera. I will not go into the details of his historical argument here, except to echo the serious reservations expressed by David Phillips (1993) that Crary not only fails convincingly to refute the notion that the photographic camera is the 'successor' of the camera obscura, but that he is also forced at times to make confusingly similar claims himself. Phillips asserts, with some justice, that photography is the structuring absence which ultimately dominates (and undermines) Crary's thesis. See also W.J.T. Mitchell's critique of Crary's position (1994: 11–34).

16. Hence the famous opposition between Debord's 'society of the spectacle' and Foucault's 'surveillance society'. See Crary for a discussion (1992: 1–24).

5

The Image of Romance: Stock Images as Cultural Performances

Institutions authorize certain meanings and dismiss, even silence, others. Thus there is a politics of interpretation that one contends with immediately, whether one knows it or not. To interpret a photograph, or any cultural object, is to negotiate a sea of choices already made.

Richard Bolton (1989: 281)

Power in contemporary society habitually passes itself off as embodied in the normal as opposed to the superior.

Richard Dyer (1988: 45)

Textual Analysis and Cultural Materialization

What can we learn about general cultural trends from a semiotic or 'textual' interpretation of stock images as they appear in stock catalogues? Given the claims made in Chapter 1 – namely, that stock images are subject to multiple reconfigurations within and along the production chain, and that their mode of reception is contextually determined and hence not directly deducible from their form or content – such an approach would seem to be at best a rather fruitless exercise in interpretative guesswork. And at worst it could constitute an implicit endorsement of the idea that viewers are mere receptacles for meanings generated by producers and fixed irrevocably in irresistible media messages. In short, without analysing the images' actual deployment in different media texts, and their interpretation by diverse viewers in various sociocultural contexts, how can we learn anything from them about their 'meaning' and generalize from them to broader cultural dynamics?

My answer is briefly this. The appearance of stock images in stock catalogues constitutes a privileged moment of 'encoding' within the production process.

It is the moment in which their form and content are fixed as intelligible and available cultural resources, resources that cultural intermediaries will subsequently use in broader cultural practices. Operating on the boundary between stock photography as a system of manufacture-distribution, and advertising, marketing and design as modes of circulation, stock catalogues assemble and produce – in a specific textual framework – the basic archival units of the image repertoire which can be routinely understood as potentially meaningful to large consumer audiences. The catalogues therefore act as a *concentrated representational space* through which images are materialized: made to emerge as physically discrete and at least minimally communicative resources. Moreover, whatever acts of recontextualization and interpretation occur subsequent to this moment (either among intermediaries or consumers), they will be based upon *this* materialization, *these* images. Hence the catalogues provide us with a kind of palimpsest of all that is understood to be of primary symbolic usefulness within the visual environments of particular consumer cultures in a designated period, of all that it might be worth communicating to viewers in association with commodities. We cannot easily know how or whether a specific interpretation will make use of a particular materialization. But – from the overabundance of certain forms, subjects and styles, and the scarcity or non-existence of others – we can at the very least trace the significant contours of the culture within which such images are made as recognizably, ordinarily meaningful.

Procedures of Analysis

It is an occupational hazard of cultural analysis that it occasionally finds itself mimicking the very processes of production and signification that it sets out to criticize. In giving an account of the broader cultural significance of 'romantic' stock photographs, I have resorted to the necessity of further classifying the images according to particular configurations of content, style and themes. This compulsion for analytical categorization, mirroring the dynamics of rhetorical and social categorization described in the previous chapter, is I hope tempered by a modicum of reflexivity, such that the seeming self-evidence of the category and its separation from the broader flux of images will be persistently undercut.

Why, however, have I chosen to analyse images of romantic couples? First, because images of romantic couples are extremely common both in consumer advertising and marketing and in stock photography: 'relationships' and 'intimacy' are consistently named as among the most popular themes by stock photographers and agencies (see for example the contributors to 'Future Stock:

The Look of Stock in the New Millennium', *PDN* supplement to *Photo Expo East '99*, October 1999: 18–28). It is perhaps surprising, however, that while contemporary images of women and men have been extensively analysed in a variety of theoretical and material contexts, those of romantic couples have been less thoroughly investigated, at least with regard to their commercial photographic representation.[1] This is in contrast to ongoing historical and sociological concern with the construction of romantic love and intimacy as well as with the structure and function of 'pair-bonding' in advanced industrial societies (Luhmann 1986; Giddens 1991 and 1992; Hendrick and Hendrick 1992; Illouz 1997).

These images clearly raise questions regarding the visual representation of gender and sexuality which have been addressed, in other contexts, by feminist and queer theory.[2] What kinds of power relations do they represent between men and women? How are 'femininity' and 'masculinity' materialized and performed, and imbricated within particular modes of viewing? Do these images of 'couples' perpetuate patriarchal and heterosexual models of social and sexual intimacy, solidarity and reproduction? Additionally, the category reveals normative representational assumptions regarding ethnicity and class, at the very least through criteria of inclusion and exclusion. In other words, the potency of the image category lies in the way that the representation of romance *intersects with*, *structures* and *articulates* 'basic categories by which the self is defined', such as physical and social reproduction (ultimately in the face of human mortality), intimacy and self-disclosure, the importance of gender and sexuality, and the relationship of the individual to the larger social group (Gilman 1985: 23).[3] We can also understand romantic representation as providing models for the incorporation of individual self-identity, the 'reflexive project of the self' (Giddens 1991: 74–80) into a larger social unit and an assured, externally validated narrative trajectory; that is, into certain culturally sanctioned frameworks of social space and personal (non-abstract) time.

Hence these images articulate basic concerns of selfhood through the promise of romantic intimacy and, I will argue, through the ideal of non-instrumentality. However, these promises are framed within the terms of consumer culture, principally through the overall notion of 'leisure' and its practical and discursive differentiation from the world of labour and production (see Simmel 1997 [1910]: 120–9; Slater 1995a; Illouz 1997) as well as from the routine of everyday domesticity. Such a connection to consumer culture, and its complex implications for distinctions between public and private, and masculine and feminine, is ultimately related to the commodification of leisure time, and hence to stock photography's rhetorical and commercial project: for its goal, like the advertising discourse of which it is a part, is 'the selling of well-being and happiness through the selling of goods' (Leiss, Kline and Jhally 1997: 294). Indeed, among the categories of images produced by the stock industry, 'romantic' images are aimed pre-eminently and explicitly at the consumer market rather than at the corporate business-to-business market (typified, for example, by pictures of businessmen leaping hurdles or gazing resolutely at their laptops). Thus their interpretation allows for a more direct connection with broader social and ideological questions, the power relations between social groups, and their representation in contemporary consumer cultures.

Overall, then, this image category exemplifies the photographs created by the stock industry for use in consumer marketing and advertising, and (it is no mere coincidence) addresses some of the basic structures and dynamics of contemporary Western social reality. In order, therefore, to interpret the cultural significance of these photographs, to understand the ways in which they connect to these desires and structures as well as to the 'cultural economy' and 'mode of signification' of stock photography, I propose to employ four interconnected levels of analysis:

Content: This level concentrates on the main 'items' depicted in the image (people, objects, settings) and their placement within the image, tracing their principal connotative and metaphorical projections and their links to social and ideological features of contemporary consumer societies.

Style: The primary interest here is in such elements as focus, colour-tone and graininess, point of view and framing, linking them to constellations of representational practices that in turn are related to broader cultural trends.

Textual Environment: Stock photographs are designed to be inserted into an multitude of diverse texts and contexts. Nevertheless, as noted earlier, their articulation *as stock photographs* – ready-made images ripe for selection by cultural intermediaries – has traditionally occurred in one primary textual system: the catalogue. This analytical level concerns itself with the way in which the organization of the catalogues and the labels used within them interact with the images and relate to discourses and classificatory regimes prevalent in consumer culture. These issues will be dealt with as and when they arise in the discussion of the other analytical levels, rather than in a separate section.

Communicative mode: This level focuses on the communicative properties of stock photographs, notably their temporality, their narrative potentiality, their stillness, their directness of address and solicitation of a viewing gaze, and the conspicuousness of their performance or staging. Such communicative properties are closely interrelated and act as both 'bait' by which cultural intermediaries might be encouraged to select a particular image, and similarly as powers to be mobilized by cultural intermediaries in the final advertisement. In general these issues will be dealt with separately in the next chapter, where

I consider them not only with regard to romantic stock images, but more broadly in relation to the dynamics of consumption.

My reasons for stressing the linkage between these analytical levels should be obvious. The distinctions between them, especially between 'content' and 'style', are frequently nebulous. Furthermore, interpretation being ultimately an act of bringing together, of synthesis rather than of analysis (Thompson 1990: 289), my attempt to elucidate the cultural significance of these images will require their persistent interweaving. I would also suggest that these four modes highlight characteristics that are shared equally by other types of photographs and visual images, but which are put into operation in ways appropriate to stock photography as a discrete system of production. Hence these analytic levels will allow us to outline, at least in broad strokes, the distinctive representational ethos of stock photographs.

Finally, a word about the catalogues used as sources for images. These span the past decade or so, beginning in 1987 and ending in 1999, and are culled from a number of US and European agencies as follows (see the list of Primary Sources, pp. 219–20 for full details):

Tony Stone Images: UK-based (now US). Major global agency.[4]
The Image Bank: US-based. Major global agency.
FPG International: US-based. Major global agency.
A.G.E. Fotostock: Spain-based. Large European agency.
Rex Interstock: UK-based. Small European agency.
Superstock: US-based. Large independent US agency.
Index Stock. US-based. Medium-sized US agency.
The Photographer's Library: UK-based. Small European agency.
Bavaria Bildagentur: Germany-Based. Medium-sized European agency.

If, for the logistical reasons mentioned in the Introduction, this constitutes a somewhat eclectic sample – totaling some 559 photographs – it nevertheless provides a fair representation of the kinds of image produced over the last decade in mainstream stock photography, both by leading global agencies and medium-sized and small independents in the United States and Europe.

Romantic Couples

The power of advertising lies not in regimenting consciousness but rather in articulating meanings that bind consumers' desire to market forces. Romance was one of the most powerful 'channels of desire' used by advertisers to make their imagery at once lifelike and dreamlike. (Illouz 1997: 82)

In defining the contours of the category 'romantic couple' we immediately face the problem of the admixture of the denoted and the connoted, a problem that denaturalizes the term 'content' in all its crudity. For images of romantic couples are to be distinguished from photographs of couples per se by the fact that they portray couples engaged in *romantic behaviour*. Such a definition, with one important additional assumption, informs Illouz's method of selecting romantic images for her study of romance in advertising: 'I selected any image that contained a heterosexual couple apparently involved in some kind of romantic interchange' (1997: 328 and n5).[5] Aside from the questionable implication that romance occurs only among heterosexual couples, and the more interesting suggestion that it is central to the performance and representation of specifically heterosexual relationships in modern culture, the issue remains: how do we characterize a romantic interchange?[6] Illouz's solution is to select only those images in which the couple 'seemed to be involved in a flirtation (indicated by the characters looking at each other, smiling at each other, or touching each other or, sometimes, by the caption itself)' (ibid.: and n4). However, not all looking or touching among couples is romantic or, for that matter, flirtatious. Take a full-colour image of a casually dressed couple (jeans, t-shirts and trainers), the man's arm around the woman's shoulder, both facing the camera and smiling broadly not at each other but directly at the viewer as they stand in front of an open white door on the porch of a well-tended house: all of this suggests 'home-ownership' or 'domestic pride' far more than either romance or flirtation. Their actual physical proximity is far less suggestive of amorous absorption or intimacy than other images in which the couple is physically distanced but linked by a reciprocal romantic gaze. Equally, a fairly explicit photograph of a couple having sex also seems not to qualify: it connotes the fulfilment of flirtation and romance – or possibly its pornographic antithesis ('mere carnality', 'meaningless sex') – rather than their enactment.

Two points follow from this exercise in exclusion. The first is that the boundaries of the category are far from watertight: the category leaks, its meanings threaten to flow into 'neighbouring domains' such as friendship, sex, and family, which are in many cases connoted by photographs that appear on the same pages as those of romantic images. Hence we can say that categorical leakage, the slippage of meaning and its generation in the differential relationship between images, is built into the catalogue format. The second point stems from this slippage of meaning: the images do not depict or 'contain' romance as though it were a preformed material object, but are part of its ceaseless connotation, citation, reiteration and elaboration, as well as of its differentiation from other categories. That is why to classify an image according to the presence of 'romantic interchange' has such an air of tautology: for 'romantic interchange' is not found *in* these images but is precisely what their staging of reality materializes and constructs. And this staging, as discussed in Chapter 3, invites the *interpretative reproduction* of romance, both through its generic and iconic similarity to other performances of romance and through its difference from neighbouring domains.

Given the complexity of this intertextual interpretative labour, I have established my porous boundaries around the category of 'romantic couples' through a number of semantic elements or 'semes', since 'an iconic sign,' according to Umberto Eco, 'is nearly always a *seme* – i.e. something which does not correspond to a word in the verbal language but is still an utterance' (1982: 35, Eco's italics). These can signify romance both separately or in combination, but they are graded hierarchically: some are more important to the connotation of romance than others, performing the bulk of the boundary-work between romance and other interpretative possibilities.

The Romantic Look

The way in which romantic lovers look at one another is of paramount importance. The most commonplace scenario is for them to be gazing at one another, but they may be facing each other (or kissing) with their eyes closed, or gazing together into the distance. One may be looking at the other while the latter gazes wistfully away. These different manifestations of semantic 'eye-work' express, above all, the intimacy and absorbed mutuality of the romantic couple, but they also establish, as a condition of signification, one key distinction: between the large majority of romantic images which disavow the presence of the camera, and the minority for whom the camera's presence is directly acknowledged by the fact that the lovers look at the viewer rather than at one another.

This distinction is important, since the look of the romantic lovers constitutes a staging of the personal relationship within a communicative context (the relationship between viewer and viewed in commercial photography) characterized by anonymity and impersonality. Hence the intimacy of the romantic stock photograph constitutes, like sincerity, a 'performative paradox' (Scannell 1996: 58), for it cannot be genuinely intimate if it is staged primarily for an unknown outsider, the viewer. Its intimacy and absorption may be constructed, therefore, as against the larger social group. This is what the disavowal of the camera's presence involves: the lovers' gaze guarantees the seclusion of romance, and its connection to individualism and self-sufficiency, even as it performs itself in the public eye (Solomon 1981; Lystra 1989; Hendrick and Hendrick 1992; Illouz 1997). In Goffman's terms (1958: 112) the image's 'frontstage' (the models *put on an act* before the camera) masquerades as a non-performative 'backstage' (they are lovers in a moment of sincere self-disclosure).

The minority of romantic stock photographs in which both lovers *do* look at the camera, however, call to mind representational contexts and photographic practices in which photography itself has become key to the performance of (romantic) intimacy, and especially to its extension in time. They borrow and evoke the ritual photographic practices associated with amateur and domestic photography, including tourist and holiday snaps in which the photograph is designed for the future recollection of past intimacy by the *lovers themselves* (Jacobs 1986).[7] The conspicuous and self-reflexive performativity of these images makes it appropriate that they usually depict what I will call 'playful romance' (see below) while at the same time reproducing – or rather, since they are technically 'perfect' examples, idealizing – the communicative intimacy and familiarity of being photographed for oneself and one's significant others[8].

Pose

The couple's pose needs to express actual or desired *physical* intimacy as a concomitant of the mingling of selves signified by the romantic look. It needs to do this without, however, presenting an actual sexual performance that would substitute such a 'spiritual' joining of selves with the 'mere' pursuit of sexual satisfaction. The iconography of the romantic image therefore has to employ physicality in order to suggest a holistic intimacy and passion – a union of minds and of bodies in desire – while at the same time reasserting the mind/body distinction. Thus physical intimacy obeys the Derridean logic of the supplement (Derrida 1976; see also p. 88 Chapter 3, note 16): it is that addition which completes the romantic intimacy of selves, and yet it threatens to stand in for it entirely. This threat is made all the more palpable in the mute, wordless medium of photography, for physical intimacy is the very vehicle through which the coalescence of minds and selves is materialized and conveyed.

The textual arrangement of the images is extremely important in the performance and containment of this supplementarity, especially in both suggesting and delimiting the scale of connotational contrasts and differentiations along the sex-friendship axis. In one typical example, the pose of a half-naked couple in bed in an apparently 'pre-coital' image at the top left-hand corner of the catalogue page acts as both a potential narrative culmination of other, less sexually suggestive images on the page (they'll all end up in bed), and as the boundary-marker of their significatory possibilities (this is as much as we can see and still retain the sense of 'romance'). At the same time the possible

interpretation of the 'pre-coital' photograph itself as merely carnal or quasi-pornographic is largely closed off by its juxtaposition with the other, less explicitly 'physical', images of romance.

Setting

Sometimes photographs of romantic couples do not specify their social or physical setting (for example, an extreme close-up of the couple that leaves no room for visible background or other signs of setting). More often, however, they suggest a setting that nevertheless makes possible the couple's isolation. Such settings are varied, but only a small minority are connected to domestic or work environments. As noted above, categorical differentiation generates meaning, and in this instance largely backs up Illouz's findings: 'In the realm of advertising, romance is opposed to the routine of everyday life and, more specifically, to work' (1997: 88). Moreover, the settings usually – but not always – avoid the bed or bedroom, the exceptions usually serving to mark the boundaries of the image category: once again, the textual placement of images on catalogue pages is extremely important for creating differential connotations. Hence setting proves important for distinguishing between romance and its 'neighbouring domains': (1) romance is separate from the home – it is a more intense, less routine form of relationship, signifying intimacy and choice rather than familiarity and destiny; (2) it exists in the realm of leisure and consumption and is removed from the world of work and production; (3) it flourishes as a non-carnal, non-instrumental intermingling of selves that is separate from the wholly physical gratification of sexual appetites.

Conventional symbols

These include objects and actions which connote romance: flowers, especially red roses, being given by a man to a woman; lit candles on a table at a restaurant; the clinking of wine glasses in a toast; wedding or engagement rings.

These four semes serve simultaneously to demarcate the genre of romantic couples while at the same time establishing an overall framework of meaning in which more particularized versions of romance can be constructed. In order to understand these versions, it's worth working more rigorously through the types of 'content' represented in romantic stock photographs.

The Mood of Romance

Two types of romantic stock image can be distinguished according to the 'mood' conveyed by the lovers: photographs of *playful romance* and of *medita-*

tive romance. The main signifying elements of these moods are the poses, the looks and the facial expressions (smiles, pouts) of the couple. There is a large preponderance of playful images over meditative ones in every catalogue in the sample, although as the years progress the proportion of meditative images increases slightly but does not at all equal that of playful images. There is no difference with respect to location (United States or Europe) or agency.

Playful romance is signified most clearly by the broad smiles of the couple and often by the impression of their shared laughter. This laughter stands in for and demonstrates the quality of their relationship, but often it is also oriented to an external stimulus: playing with food and drink, splashing one another with water, covering each other's eyes, playing with one another's clothing, catching one another unawares. These images frequently contain 'props' (food and drink to be played with, men's hats to be taken and placed on women's heads, bicycles to be balanced on precariously) but they also rely heavily on the sense of action and movement conveyed by the pose: men lifting up their partners or swinging them around are among the most common.

The emphasis in images of playful romance is on the expression of mutuality as recreation, as doing things together in the world in a voluntary, rule-bound space of play that is nevertheless distinct and secluded from ordinary life (Huizinga 1970). It conveys not so much the profound and intense union of selves as the ritual spontaneity of bodies, the creative interaction of role-players within the structured unreality of play. Close to the 'love style' defined by Lee as 'ludus' (1988), its vignettes have a narrative suggestibility, proposing a sequence of events whose distillation of cause and effect (a man grabs a woman and she laughs, a woman puts on a man's hat and he smiles) establishes the essence of the romantic relationship *pragmatically* (romance is created in situated interaction), *dramaturgically* (romance is a performance, not a state of existence or feeling) and *morally* (romance is the freedom of two equal individuals to play).[9] Romance, according to these images, is created by how you act, not by how you are: it is a mode of *doing*, not *being*. And since you are what you do, playful romance leaves the individual lovers with *nothing in reserve*, no surplus of self or undiminished interiority that is not transformed into, and consumed by, the free and open play of mutuality.

Meditative romance, on the other hand, is signified by the seriousness or intensity expressed by one or both of the lover's faces and poses. Typically they gaze into one another's eyes, or into the distance, or their eyes are closed. Often they kiss: they do not smile or laugh. Props are rare, as is the suggestion of an action external to the physical contact between the lovers. The poses, looks and expressions of the lovers connote two seemingly contradictory meanings: self-absorption (staring into the distance conveys thoughtfulness and day-dreaming; closed eyes connote a reflexive and meditative concentration on one's own experience) and absolute absorption in the other. The images suggest stillness and repose: although they do not deny the possibility of narrative interpretation, they depict the stasis of the couple, such stasis providing the exemplary form of the romantic relationship. Romance here is closer to the 'love style' of 'Eros' (Lee 1988), presented as a combination of intense mutuality of being and of replete, self-reflexive interiority: romance is not a game, it is an experience – a way of existing and feeling. As opposed to the narrative sequence and hence limitation, or mortality, of playful romance, meditative romance transmutes the couple into the still centre of the turning world: it is the figural, photographic moment of endless love. Just as importantly, the representation of meditative romance suggests that it is free of performativity: romance just *is* – it is not created through ritual social interaction and theatrical self-presentation. The notion of authenticity is therefore central to its ideological force.

This distinction between stock photographs of playful and meditative romance parallels two historical conceptions of romantic love described by Singer (1984) and elaborated by Hendrick and Hendrick (1992): wedding and merger.

> Wedding is used metaphorically to denote a close association in which two people combine their joint fortunes, coordinate their interactions, and go forward in time together . . . For many modern couples the notion of a romantic union may be contractual only, an agreed upon association in which joint interests are pooled but separate individual identities are retained and remain well defined (Hendrick and Hendrick 1992: 30–1).

While it does not imply the emotional 'lightness', even frivolity, of playful romance, 'wedding' certainly does connect to the sense of partnership in joint activity and the narrative dimension that I discerned in these images. Additionally, in the form of contractual agreement, and in the pooling of joint interests that guarantees the difference and autonomy of individual identity, it separates external action from inner essence, the emphasis on externality presenting so stark a contrast to the images of meditative romance.

In merger, however, 'one loses one's identity as a distinct being and becomes part of that with which one merges . . . The phenomenon of falling in love is the modern archetype for the experience of mystical union . . . In a sense, falling in love is the creation of a new phenomenological reality; in sociological terms the creation of a new society of two people' (ibid.: 30). Such a concern with romantic love as an almost sacred state of psychic and spiritual union with the other, a mode of inner being and experience rather than of activity and agency in time, is clearly reminiscent of the mood of meditative love – with, however, one key difference. For while the notion of 'merger' conceptualizes or describes a state of being rather than a form of appearing and acting in the world, stock photographs of meditative romance are engaged in the paradox of signifying *essence* – this internal, phenomenological union of selves – through the externality of *appearance*. Meditative romance, to a greater degree than playful romance, is a mode of representation that disavows its own representational and performative artifice as a condition of its own existence, a condition that finds in photography its perfect medium: essence magically radiates forth from the depicted couples, just as the real is mystically, alchemically disclosed by the indexicality of the photographic image.[10]

Both wedding and merger, and the images with which I have associated them, propose differing solutions to a key problem raised by modern conditions of life. This is the need to reconcile capitalism's demand for individual mobility and self-sufficiency, promoted through a discourse of individualism, with long-term structural stability that can guarantee both social and physical reproduction (Illouz 1991, 1997). In capitalist societies:

> The mobilization and mobility of the individual as a productive unit were achieved by the dissolution of communal relationships . . . Romantic love played a very important role in providing the ideological justifications for realizing the transition from communal to individualist pair-bonding. In other words, the new organization of social relationships entailed by capitalism needed the powerful ideology of romantic love to justify a new process of pair-bonding and legitimize the fact that the community and family were not in charge of the marital selection anymore. (Illouz 1991: 239)

This ideology has a contradictory function. On the one hand, romantic love must be seen as a powerful force that individuals either find irresistible (merger) or employ as an extension of their confident individuality (wedding), potentially placing themselves in opposition to the will of the community or family in the choice of the beloved. On the other hand, love must be stable and sustainable, it must be subject to regulation and monitoring by the individual to ensure its maintenance and success in the long term: in this sense it is something to be laboured at conscientiously in the spirit of the capitalist work ethic (Ibid.: 235–8).

In this contradiction between individualism and structural stability, the construction of sexual and personal intimacy within a discourse of romantic love – in both its playful and its meditative representations – plays a crucial part. It becomes central to what Giddens calls the 'project' of the self (1991), the reflexive construction of individual identity in relation to 'ontological security' – 'the confidence that most human beings have in the continuity of their self-identity and in the constancy of the surrounding social and material environments of action' (1990: 92: see also 1991: 350–69) – in a society filled with risk.

Giddens and many others have attempted to map the consequences of modernity for subjective identity, emphasizing in particular the separation of time and space from the situatedness of place, the 'disembedding' of social institutions and social relations into abstract systems (through symbolic tokens – especially money – and systems of expertise), the transformation of daily life by globalization, and the increasing mediation of experience by symbolic media and the intrusion of distant events into everyday consciousness.[11] These consequences are of course interconnected, but one of their combined effects is to intensify the search for a core of stability within the 'maelstrom' of modernity (Berman 1982). Romantic love locates this core in the personal and sexual intimacy of the 'pure relationship' (Giddens 1991: 88–99): primary, face-to-face committed relationships of trust and self-disclosure (both of the soul and the body) that are, above all, non-instrumental – the relationship exists for its own sake, unanchored in the external conditions of social and economic life, and the other is treated as an end and not as a means. This ideal of the pure relationship can therefore serve as a counterweight to the abstraction, mediation, instrumentality and distance of most social relationships in modernity.

It is worth looking more closely at the performative or symbolic characteristics of the pure-relationship and their implications for romance as an ideology and for stock images of romance as representational practices. In Luhmann's terms, the 'semantics of intimacy' in modern experience are based on the central distinction between *impersonal* and *personal* relationships. Such a distinction has become key to the reflexive and performative tasks of self-creation in modern societies, for these are characterized by social relations in which

> the individual can – and this is new – provide cover for most of the demands made by his life only through impersonal relationships, i.e. through relationships in which he cannot communicate about himself, or, at the most, only within the narrow limits of the particular social system. This condition includes the actual creation of the self, namely one's personal development in the context of school and professional career. The experience of difference, the axis along which the self constitutes itself, is coloured in a specific manner by these socio-structural conditions. The need for another Self – and this means another Other Self and another Self of one's own – is deeply influenced by this and plays a part in constituting one's own identity'. (1986: 152)

What is interesting about Luhmann's final sentence is its stipulation that the need for 'another Other Self' (someone else) is connected to the need for 'another Self of one's own': a sequestered, private part of oneself constructed in opposition to the 'impersonal' self one performatively constructs in the majority of instrumental and functional social encounters that everyday modernity demands. Hence self-disclosure, the progressive revelation of an inner space and identity to another person, is also a construction of this identity both for and before *oneself*: reflexivity is born of interaction with another person and is a performative construction on the stage of one's own subjectivity. Developmentally, therefore, romantic 'self-disclosure' is not a progressive unveiling of a pre-existing private core of selfhood, but the creation of this core in a ritualized interaction with a reciprocating other. Ideologically, however, the performative nature of self-disclosure is itself hidden and transmuted into the positioning of romantic love as the necessary culmination of secure and fulfilled individual identity: individualism is rooted and naturalized through the mutual discovery and revelation of true, non-instrumental, inner being.

How do images of playful and meditative romance connect with these processes in their different ways? By representing distinct dimensions of romantic love – as an ideology of utopian authenticity and as a discursively acknowledged space of play – legitimating them according to the principle of *non-instrumentality*. Meditative romance deals with romantic love as an *ideology*: as I have noted, the couples embody the ideal of authentic, non-instrumental union, while the photograph denies its own artifice as a performance. In contrast, playful romance portrays romantic love as a performance by autonomous, self-disclosing individuals, but rescues it, and its representation, from the suspicion of pretence and artifice by emphasizing the non-instrumentality of promiscuous play: play as 'disinterested' and as standing 'outside the immediate satisfaction of wants and appetites' (Huizinga 1970: 28), play as the enjoyment of pure form freed from 'purposive content in the serious affairs of reality' (Simmel 1997 [1910]: 125).[12] Romance may be social ritual but neither is it inauthentic (the play does not disguise itself) nor is it malign dissembling designed to cloak the pursuit of some ulterior goal extraneous to the instance of play. Together, images of playful and meditative romance complement rather than contradict one another, suggesting a reversible and dialectical narrative interplay between surface performance and inner depth: play may be the social activity that, in its creative yet rule-bound 'free unreality' (Caillois 1962: 10), rehearses and precedes the being of merged selves: once achieved, 'merger' is externally performed and perpetuated over time through the disinterested 'wedding' of promiscuous play. Whether considered singly or in sequential conjunction, however, both image types provide the discourse of advertising, and the doubly promotional practice of stock photography, with an important means of addressing consumers: a representational mode that veils its own instrumentality by making non-instrumentality its defining motif.

Romance and Gender: The Matter of Performance

A striking initial characteristic of the two categories of playful and meditative romance is that they appear *not* to structure the representation of gender distinctions around conventional power relations between men and women. Along with Illouz – in her analysis of romantic advertisements – I failed to find any *systematic* construction of domination or subordination signified by the kinds of gender displays analysed by Goffman (1976). There are, to be sure, some images in which the man protectively embraces the woman or is active (for example, lifting her up) while she is passive. But equally there are plenty of images in which these positions and roles are reversed, and the majority of the photographs, across all the catalogues analysed, seem to emphasize the apparent equality of the romantic bond, 'the genderless face of romance' (Illouz 1997: 86).

However, while this observation leads me to confirm, at least initially, Illouz's findings concerning signs of gender, it also compels me to conclude that her analytic framework is fundamentally unsatisfactory. The failure of this search for systematic gestural signs of gender lies in its rephrasing, within the terms of iconographic interpretation, of the controversial nature/culture divide between sex and gender (Harraway 1991). It interprets gender as those cultural codes of sexual difference that are stamped upon 'sex' as a natural and neutral bodily state: the latter, by virtue of this approach, is made all the more powerful as an extra-discursive norm, as the uninterrogated blank slate upon which the signs of gender are inscribed. Aside from neglecting or denying the historical and cultural construction of 'the natural' in discourse, this has the additional effect of substantially narrowing the range of signifying elements that count as 'gendered' in romantic photographs. It searches for culturally designated markers of sexual dominance and subordination between men and women that are impressed as a signifying layer upon a naturally given, unmarked material and representational base: it reads Goffman's 'hyperritualized signs' of gender, peeling them off the surface of the image like a skin; but in so doing it creates behind them the seemingly natural, mute and insignificant 'matter' upon which these signs are written and performed – *the bodies of women and men.* In other words, Illouz's method risks reifying the 'denoted' content of the photographs she examines, turning it into a natural category that, with the matrix of sexual difference it materializes, achieves the inconspicuous power of the normative. Adding the terms of photographic theory to a well-known phrase in feminist writing, we can say that in Illouz's approach gender is to sex as culture is to nature as connotation is to denotation.

In the previous chapter I described stock photographs as 'materializations of stereotypes'. By this I meant that they 'embody' those stereotypes, or more

precisely, that they repeatedly perform social categories – and social categorization – through the visual production of bodies as 'matter': the term 'materialization' describes the incessant emergence of an object from formlessness into
physical distinctness and cultural intelligibility (and the two are inextricable).
In the case of sex this performance is part of a regulatory practice that 'produces the bodies it governs, that is, whose regulatory force is made clear as a
kind of productive power, the power to produce – demarcate, circulate, differentiate – the bodies it controls' (Butler 1993: 1). Performance, or to use Butler's
term 'performativity', 'must be understood not as a singular 'act' but, rather,
as the reiterative and citational practice by which discourse produces the effects
that it names' (ibid.: 2). Hence:

> there will be no way to understand 'gender' as a cultural construct which is imposed
> upon the surface of matter, understood either as 'the body' or its given sex. Rather,
> once 'sex' itself is understood in its normativity, the materiality of the body will not
> be thinkable apart from the materialization of that regulatory norm. 'Sex' is, thus,
> not simply what one has, or a static description of what one is: it will be one of the
> norms by which the 'one' becomes viable at all, that which qualifies a body for life
> within the domain of cultural intelligibility (ibid.).

This reiterative, citational performativity of sex connects to the 'pathological'
repetition and imitation of generic images that characterize the stock system.
Yet how can we read the 'regulatory norms' of sex through the bodies represented in romantic stock photographs? First, the men and women depicted are
overwhelmingly young,[13] well-groomed, fashionably dressed, seemingly
middle-class adults; the women healthy, slim and white-toothed, the men fit
and moderately muscular, with full heads of hair, usually hairless chests, and
clean-shaven faces. (One of the very few images in which a man has facial hair
is also one of the very few photographs in the sample that apparently depicts
a gay couple: the moustache functions as a visible marker of homosexuality.)
The lovers, in short, conform to and reproduce a conventional Western aesthetic of physical beauty that is constantly represented in advertising images.
Second, the men and women are overwhelmingly white, and even where, in
the more recent categories, images of black, Asian and Hispanic couples
appear, there are absolutely no images of 'mixed' couples in the sample. Last,
and by no means least, the couples are almost exclusively heterosexual. Hence
the regulatory norm of sex, in the case of romantic stock images, is materialized
in the heterosexual bonding of racially segregated pairs of conventionally
beautiful, middle-class, young women and men. In other words, as soon as we
interrogate not the overt signs of gender domination among photographed
romantic couples, but the conditions of their possibility and intelligibility *as*

'romantic couples', we find the intricate imbrication of differential regimes: sex, sexuality, race and class.

Such a materialization is exclusionary: it is structured against a 'constitutive outside' to the regulatory norm, possible materializations and identifications which the norm forecloses or denies. Butler, borrowing from Julia Kristeva, describes these alternatives as 'abject', culturally unthinkable and inexpressible: the abject designates 'those "unliveable" and "uninhabitable" zones of social life which are nevertheless densely populated by those who do not enjoy the status of the subject, but whose living under the sign of the "unliveable" is required to circumscribe the domain of the subject' (Butler 1993: 3). Thus such an abjected, constitutive outside to the subject is also 'after all, "inside" the subject as its own founding repudiation' (ibid.).

The abject zones of stock photography have shifted very little over time: in general they are homosexuality and lesbianism (which do, however, emerge as sanitized half-subjects in the late 1990s: the images depict – admittedly chaste – physical proximity as a sign of intimacy and affection, but almost never show kissing), the crossing of racial boundaries in sexual encounters, and class: the latter, since it is fundamental to the central marketing question of disposable income, is probably the most fully abjected of the zones mentioned, linked representationallly to the 'constitutive outside' of conventional beauty – fatness, ugliness, unhealthy teeth, lack of grooming and shabby or obviously cheap clothing. Where changes have occurred, and previously abjected groups have been materialized, it is still within a normative archival system that differentiates hierarchically between its materialized categories. This differentiation is achieved through the marking of the subordinate category in its difference from the norm. Hence, as I mentioned in Chapter 3, photographers – most of whom are white – sometimes go to great lengths to match the ethnicity of the subjects to the cultural connotations, as they understand them, of the objects which surround them (as in the placing of a Japanese screen in an image of a Korean woman), marking them as 'ethnic'. Indeed, Heron (1996: 40–1), Feingersh and others constantly stress the commercial importance of taking ethnic 'versions' of lifestyle images: once again, the assumption behind this well-intentioned, as well as lucrative, representational diversity is that it maintains each ethnic group in its deviance from the norm and in its separation from other groups. Marking can also lead to the separate categorization of images of black and other non-normative subjects in categories other than 'people' (such as 'One World'), a fact that starkly validates Richard Dyer's analysis of the representational power of whiteness:

In the realm of categories, black is always marked as a colour (as the term 'coloured' egregiously acknowledges), and is always particularizing; whereas white is not anything really, not an identity, not a particularizing quality, because it is everything – white is no colour because it is all colours . . . It is the way that black people are marked as black (are not just 'people') in representation that has made it relatively easy to analyze their representation, whereas white people – not there as a category and everywhere everything as a fact – are difficult, if not impossible, to analyze *qua* white. (Dyer 1988: 45–6)

Interestingly, the abjection of non-materialized zones and the marking of subordinate categories within these stock images can be seen as an attempt to neutralize a crisis in the ideology of romantic love and its individualist core. For according to Illouz, while romantic love addressed the need for labour mobility in capitalist societies by realizing the transition from communal to individualist pair-bonding, it threatened to privilege subjective agency over structural and class stability, to the detriment of established social hierarchies. In establishing individual choice as the criterion for pair-bonding, it under-mined one of the primary functions of marriage: 'to reproduce the social order through the organized and structured encounter of social 'likes" (Illouz 1991: 239). The materialization of exclusionary matrices of sex, sexuality, race and class diffuses the power of romantic love in this respect, containing individual agency within 'thinkable' cultural and social categories: (middle-class) black men and women are romantically intimate *only* with each other – they do not stray from the ethnic (or socio-economic) hearth. In the process these matrices also harness the 'thinkable' to the dynamic of social categorization prevalent in advertising and marketing: the inability to represent boundary crossing is a concomitant of the 'pathological' inability to comprehend social experience outside of or across sharply delineated normative categories.

Given, however, that some shifts have occurred, how robust are these natural-ized materializations of regulatory norms? Butler is at pains to distinguish her notion of performativity from a more theatrical, voluntaristic conception of performance. However, I have repeatedly argued that stock photographs *are* theatrical: both in their conspicuous foregrounding of a range of potential cultural references before the interpretative intelligence of the cultural inter-mediary, and in the more prosaic sense that they are actually and deliberately fabricated: the romantic couples we see are paid models or actors who, under the direction of a photographer, *consciously pretend* to be romantically inti-mate. To what extent such a pretence involves stepping outside of their own materialized and normative 'sex' can perhaps best be addressed through a phenomenology (and ethnography) of acting, a project which is beyond the current discussion. But the fact of conscious and conspicuous staging produces an interesting and potent paradox. The stock image is a citational materializa-tion that is continuous with the operations of 'sex' as a normative regulatory ideal in everyday experience, and yet as a *reflexive* rhetorical practice it also abstracts the regulatory ideal from the everyday, opening up a space in which the naturalization of the norm comes into view.

Butler has argued that such foregrounding, combined with incessant repetition, can destabilize regulatory norms and put them into a 'potentially productive crisis' (Butler 1993: 10). This is far from the case with stock photography, secure in its overall invisibility before consumers, which puts both the abstraction and repetition of normative ideals to good institutional use. For the potentially fatigue-inducing repetition of images within single stock catalogues (so many similar pictures), multiplied across innumerable catalogues and agencies, occurs – as I noted at the beginning of the chapter – in a concentrated representational space *that is managed by the industry itself.* The only people to encounter stock catalogues and archives, this palimpsest of social classifications and regulatory practices, are cultural intermediaries and photographers,[14] those who are professionally committed to the efficient visual materialization of normative categories. Hence this concentrated representational space enables the recuperation and refinement of exhausted normative ideals rather than any radical destabilization or productive crisis: when the images seem *too false* (abstraction) and *too tired* (repetition), they are rematerialized through altering styling, or focus, or colour – in the short term by the client (usually using digital technologies) and in the longer term by photographers creating new variants of standardized subject matter. Occasionally, when the market segment seems lucrative enough, the boundary of the regulatory norm is extended to represent a previously 'abjected' population – but within the system's own commercially-motivated exclusionary terms. Hence, according to Turow (1997: 81) advertisers and marketers in the 1990s woke up to the spending power of the 'pink dollar', beginning to target young (not old), affluent (not working-class) and usually homosexual men (rarely lesbians). It was these men who began to appear, very tentatively and almost always chastely, in the archives and brochures of mainstream stock agencies in the late 1990s.[15]

This recuperation of regulatory norms, the exploitation of their exhaustion in order to facilitate renewal within the terms of consumer culture, leads me to the issue of consumption. I have already stressed the link between romantic love, individualism and the crisis of mobility and stability in capitalism. But the connection of romantic stock photographs to advertising in particular and consumption in general still needs to be clarified. For how can these photographs 'channel' the viewer's desire from the image to the product? According to Illouz:

> The goal is to allow the viewer-consumer to penetrate the private intimacy of a romantic moment in which consumption is taken for granted as natural. In contemporary advertisements, the viewer-consumer is not targeted for a rhetoric of

persuasion – 'buy me because I will get you love' – but rather is made a voyeur to a spectacle of intimacy and *inconspicuous* consumption. (1997: 84; Illouz's italics)

What, however, is being inconspicuously consumed in these images? For the projective power of the image is not based on a direct linkage between an actual product and the actual or potential moment of its consumption, but rather on the connotation of a *general social terrain*, a field of space and time, that is devoted to the consumption of certain types of commodities: the realm of leisure. And the communication of this general field, so appropriate to the parsimonious polysemy of stock photographs and their imperative for multiple reuse, emerges mainly from the depiction of setting.

The Depleted Spaces of Romance

On reflection, perhaps one of the most predictable things about the settings of the romantic images is their generality: very few of the images specifies an identifiable location (unlike, for example, many postcards of romance which have the lovers embrace in front of national monuments).[16] Instead, the specificity of place is reduced to 'generic' scenery. Most strikingly, perhaps, the couples occupy a depopulated zone: other human figures are almost entirely absent, and where they do appear they are at best hazy, incidental background shadows (this is similar to Illouz's findings with respect to her sample of advertisements, 1997: 87). The romantic couples inhabit a topography which is not constructed by the interaction and movement of its people and objects, but by the abstract relations of geometric space. As opposed to the intricate distribution of elements and figures across the planes of the photograph's depth, these images produce a clear bipartite division: foreground and back-ground, with the lovers normally located in the former. The presence of broader social existence is eliminated. In its stead there arises an almost unvarying formal construct in a curiously impersonal fantasy, in which the setting exists for the couple alone as their idealized playground: complex socially produced place has become 'a classical space conceived as a potentially boundless field of operation of the humanist subject, constructed with all the rigor of perspect-ive' (Vidler 1993: 32). As Illouz observes:

the contemporary vision of secluded couplehood does not mean a retreat from the public sphere and an entry into the warmth of familial privacy. Rather, it signifies a complete withdrawal from the proceedings, rules, and constraints of the urban industrial world and an entry into the euphoric realm of leisure'. (1997: 87)

The space of these photographs becomes, in Illouz's terms, virtually utopian: it is no place.[17] Leisure, in other words, is an ideal space of play and pleasure that is distinguished from workplace and home in imagination and in experience: and just as the workplace is the space of production and the family home is the space of reproduction, so leisure is the ethereal, dislocated, freely-floating utopian 'space' of consumption.

Nevertheless, these depleted spaces are still identifiable in their generality, in their citation and reproduction of ideal realms. For in order to establish points of reference for the viewing subject, space cannot be abstracted to the point of being unrecognizable. The complexity of socially-produced space may be denied, but the dissipated topographies of these images are quite solidly built around three categories of location: the beach, the natural landscape and the city street.[18] Each of these ideal categories generates its own connotational field bearing directly on discourses of selfhood and social aspiration. The former two relate, in varying ways (generally mediated by the notion of 'travel'), to the connection between romance and leisure, and the establishment of leisure as a domain separated from the temporality of work and from domestic routine which is characterized by the gratification of pleasure through consumption (Illouz 1997: 81–111). For reasons of space, however, I will concentrate on the category which Illouz does not analyse: the city street.

The depletion of urban space in the 'city street' images can be understood historically as echoing the 'emptying' of European city streets after the Second World War. As McDonough notes: 'It has been argued that, with the increasingly rapid growth throughout the 1950s of mass media, the formerly contested realm of the streets was evacuated' (1994: 75). The fact that this evacuation was only partial meant that, for McDonough, the street was not exempt from the logic of the commodity-sign which had now moved into the home via television. Rather, 'it was made into the site of a mythic discourse, a discourse wholly contingent upon spectacle-culture' (ibid.: 76). Quoting Barthes' description of myth in *Mythologies*, McDonough outlines how this works with regard to the 'divided sign' of the city:

> In this operation the city as sign – which has a 'fullness, a richness, a history' of its own – is captured by myth and is turned into 'an empty, parasitical form', a floating signifier able to be appropriated for various ideological ends . . . its history is put back into play in harmless form as entertainment in, for example, tourist attractions where 'public space' is commodified for very 'private' consumption . . . The 'museumization' of Paris is one obvious example of this process. (ibid.)

The packaging of the city's public space for private consumption can be discerned in photographs that produce a despecified urban space as the vacated playground of romance. But that very mythic transformation, connected as it is to the development of media technologies and the movement of 'the spectacle' into the living-room, has also become a key motif in claims that (post)modernity is increasingly characterized by a fundamental loss of bearings and distinctions. Such claims stress the primacy of dislocation and disorientation as a social-spatial sensibility. In a characteristic description, Iain Chambers argues that metropolitan space, and more especially its images, forms and distinctive content, has undergone a disorienting expansion and mutation:

> While the earlier city was a discrete geographical, economic, political and social unit, easily identified in its clear-cut separation from rural space, the contemporary western metropolis tends towards drawing that 'elsewhere' into its own symbolic zone. The countryside and suburbia, linked up via the telephone, the TV, the video, the computer terminal, and other branches of the mass media, are increasingly the dispersed loci of a commonly shared and shaped world. Towns and cities are themselves increasingly transformed into points of intersection, stations, junctions, in an extensive metropolitan network. (1990: 53)

The upshot of this argument is that in contemporary Western culture, the proliferation of city forms and the unlimited reproduction of urban images and styles has led to a crucial loss (through multiplication) of reference points: 'the referents that once firmly separated the city from the countryside, the artificial from the 'natural', are now indiscriminately reproduced as potential signs and horizons within a common topography' (ibid.: 55). What this means is that 'precisely because of its allegorical extension, we can no longer hope to map the modern metropolis, for that implies that we know its extremes, its borders, confines, limits' (ibid.).

If we accept this broad cultural claim, we can interpret the social depletion and despecification of urban space in romantic stock images as doing more than simply reproducing the 'generic' as a type of setting: for the semantic openness of generic images in no way necessitates depopulation. Rather, we can perceive in them a particular way of handling – or countering – the disorientation that Chambers describes with regard to the city, and which Jameson has famously postulated as a general feature of late-capitalist subjectivity: the 'postmodern hyperspace' that 'has finally succeeded in transcending the capacities of the individual body to locate itself, to organize its immediate surroundings perceptually, and cognitively to map its position in a mappable external world.' (1984: 83). In effect, by producing the depleted representation of 'the street' as a stage for the performance of romance, the images serve to *re-orient* the subject within the framework of *anti-social companionship*, an intimate, self-sufficient pairing set against the wider social context. This framework replaces the 'maelstrom' of the urban industrial world that is emblematically represented by the modernist street: instead of the *flâneur*, observing the metropolitan crowd but not of it, we find the self-monitoring (for here there is no crowd to observe), self-performing, pair-demarcating companion. The dissipation of local and social space in romantic stock images does more than create a mythic cityscape: by transforming the street into the arena of anti-social companionship, it acts as a compensatory mechanism within contemporary cultural production for the very disorientation to which the latter itself contributes. And this scene of the anti-social companion, a seemingly liminal state of publicly performed intimacy that is neither in society nor outside it, is a materialization of the utopian, placeless space of consumption.

Additionally, the images' organization of space around a depleted geometric field has implications for the meaning-conferring operations of viewers. According to Vidler: 'the formulation of modern space as a field of material and externalizing activity was from the outset tied to the formulation of space as a mental category of projection' (1993: 33). Thus the abstraction of space in these images functions as a proposed projection *for* the viewer. Not only is the evacuated city street presented as the private playground of the romantic couple, but the depletion of the depicted space means that the viewer projects and expands into it, fills it up. In the case of cultural intermediaries, who scan stock images for their projective metaphorical potential, this is the moment at which the creative ego invades the image – the ego capable of filling its emptiness with meaning and giving a destiny to its trajectory as a raw cultural product. Hence the images' depicted settings intersect with the concentrated presentational space provided by the catalogue format, with the reorientation of the consumer within a utopian moment of anti-social companionship, and with the particular cultural 'moment' in which the images are viewed by their primary clients – the cultural intermediaries who will grant them their particular semantic lives.

Concluding Remarks

The trajectories of romantic images' prevalent 'content' – and its signification of mood and setting – point to the materialization of romance as a special kind of performance: one that attempts to hold together contradictions between individualism and collectivity, intimate self-disclosure and conspicuous public performance, purposive persuasive action and non-instrumentality, mythical setting and cultural disorientation. In the process they produce romance as part of the ideal space of consumption, an ideal nevertheless constrained by fairly familiar materializations of gender, sexuality, race and class.

In the next chapter I move on from a consideration of the content of stock images and its cultural implications to focus more on the images' relation to consumption. This is undertaken by way of a brief analysis of the images' stylistic features, a more extensive commentary on the 'temporality' of stock photographs, and an overall discussion of their communicative modes or 'rhetorics': the ways in which they simultaneously address cultural intermediaries and consumers.

Notes

1. Illouz (1997) is the exception with regard to images of romantic couples, analysing in depth the visual representation of romance in US culture (including advertising) and using selected romantic photographs in her interviews as triggers for discussion on romance.

2. The literature here is extensive, both for traditional artistic media (painting and sculpture) and for cinema and television. Historical and cultural analyses of the representation of gender and sexuality in photography include the following notable examples: Tucker (1973); Kelly (1979); Alloula (1987); Spence (1986); Williams (1986); Graham-Brown (1988); Spence and Holland's (1991) anthology, already mentioned, on domestic photography; Stein 1992 and Pultz 1995.

3. Gilman uses the 'crude shorthand' labels of 'illness, sexuality and race' (1985: 23).

4. At the time the catalogues were produced, the first three agencies were separately owned companies. Tony Stone was independent, The Image Bank was owned by Eastman Kodak, and FPG was part of Visual Communications Group (VCG), itself a branch of United News and Media PLC. Today all are 'brands' of Getty Images PLC.

5. My analysis of romantic stock images is, of necessity, heavily influenced by Eva Illouz's magnificent work. It complements but also significantly amplifies and extends her analysis of romantic images (which makes up only a small portion of her research), especially by outlining the 'communicative mode' of photography, and substantially differs from her interpretation on questions of gender, sexuality and ethnicity. This may be in part because, as she herself makes clear, her focus is on the intersection between romance and class (1997: 20).

6. I have not adopted Illouz's a priori exclusion of images of gay romance, though I do think her decision raises important questions about the ideological centrality of romance as a discourse that underpins and constructs heterosexuality.

7.   It was originally my intention to reproduce entire catalogue pages from the sample to enable readers to follow the analysis quite closely. Unfortunately this proved to be prohibitively expensive – the stock agencies concerned insisted on charging us for every image reproduced (between five and ten images per catalogue page) despite our appeals to their better consciences. In fact, since the sampled images were rights-restricted, using any of them in this book became impossibly costly. Instead, and with much regret, I have been forced to use only a few contemporary royalty-free images that are iconographically similar to the photographs analysed in the sample, but are not taken from the actual sample (which just goes to illustrate the arbitrariness of aesthetic distinctions between royalty-free and rights restricted images – see Chapter 7). These images come from a CD-ROM called 'Lovers' created by Digital Vision – a third-party brand sold through Getty Images – and are reproduced as an 'illustrative selection': their purpose is to illustrate the discussion undertaken in this book, especially the main arguments of this and the next chapter. For full details of the actual sample analysed see the 'Stock Catalogues' section of the list of Primary Sources, pp. 219–20.

8.   Of course, the apparent intimacy and equality of domestic photography is itself an idealization, as well as the subject of some of the most innovative research on photography as whole. See, among others, Williams (1986), Spence (1986), most of the essays collected in Spence and Holland (1991), Kenyon (1992), Kuhn (1995) and Slater (1995a).

9.   Caillois (1962) notes the ideality, and especially the artificial conditions of equality between players, that play substitutes for the constraints and inequalities of 'real life'.

10.   This elision of appearance and essence is of course fundamental to many accounts of social interaction and communication – including Garfinkle's ethnomethodology, Goffman's impression-management, and semiotic analyses – that emphasize the symbolic and performative nature of routine, everyday behaviour. See Silverstone (1999: 59-77) for a recent discussion in the context of mass media.

11.   My discussion here is heavily influenced by Giddens' attempt to bring together various approaches – sociological, social psychological and psychoanalytic – in analysing the link between subjectivity and characteristics of modernity. This combination within a single analytic account occurs over a number of works (1990, 1991 and 1992), but its most general elaboration is to be found, to my mind, in *Modernity and Self-Identity* (1991). There are, of course, many criticisms that can be made of Giddens's overall analytical framework, in particular, as Silverstone notes (1993), its under-emphasis of unconscious drives and psychic

conflict, its extremely rationalistic conception of self-identity as a reflexive project, its almost obsessive return to the existential centrality of risk as a consciously experienced factor in everyday life. That being said, however, his account does provide an extremely sophisticated model for analysing the practical and symbolic roles of modern media in general, and stock photography in particular, in the construction and representation of intimacy.

12. Simmel, writing in 1910, specifically refers to sociability here, which he describes as 'a social game' both in the sense that it occurs within society and that through it 'society' is played at (1997 [1910]: 125).

13. There are, to be sure, a small minority of photographs depicting 'mature' or elderly couples. In very few cases are these couples depicted kissing, and in general the images are mildly playful, and are almost never meditative. They suggest the kind of 'silver age' metaphorical projections described by Jon Feingersh at his session in Photo Expo East '98: images for use in life and health insurance, pension schemes, and sheltered housing projects for the elderly.

14. Apart, of course, from myself and other researchers.

15. See, for example, 'Corbis Images Appeals to Burgeoning Gay and Lesbian Market: Newest Royalty-Free CD first to offer gay and lesbian lifestyle images', Corbis Press Release, 20/9/1999, www.corbis.com.

16. Almost inevitably, perhaps, in the few cases in which recognizable national monuments are depicted, the one chosen is the Eiffel Tower.

17. Utopia literally means 'no place', and this absence supports the ironic tendency at work in even the most earnest utopian thought. Hence not only is Samuel Butler's anti-utopian satire *Erewhon* (1872) a reversal of the word 'nowhere', but William Morris called his frankly optimistic vision of the good society *News from Nowhere* (1890).

18. There are a number of subcategories of setting, such as bars, restaurants, cafés and night-clubs; spaces of transit involving props such as boats, motorbikes and cars, and occasionally more domestic settings. For reasons of space I have focused on the main categories: all of these settings, however, present socially depleted spaces in that the couple is usually pictured alone.

6

Rhetorics of the Overlooked: The Communicative Modes of Stock Images

At the beginning of this book I described the images produced by the visual-content and stock-photography industries as 'ordinary' and 'unremarkable', as the kind of images likely to be overlooked, as part of an enveloping but largely unnoticed visual environment, and as the wallpaper of consumer culture.

Cultural analysts are not, by and large, interested in the ways in which images are overlooked. They are more frequently concerned with the opposite. The photograph, says Barthes in *Camera Lucida*, 'fills the sight by force' (1984: 91): the singular image stops us in our tracks, captivates and fascinates us, assaults our vision. Or, in the void opened up by the photograph between the symbolic and the real, it pierces and penetrates us (this is the meaning of Barthes's *punctum*). Whether or not we accept Barthes's characterization of visual immobilization as (sexual) violence – and metaphors of compulsion, seizure, entrapment and arrest abound in our descriptions of the effect of images upon us – the idea of the compelling image that invites and commands engagement has underpinned many of our assumptions about visual media in general (see Frosh 1998) and advertising images in particular. This idea secures, at the very least, the sense that such images are worth analysing in the first place, and many recent advertisements have seemed to warrant both the presumption of viewer engagement and the consequent granting of critical attention. From Benetton to Calvin Klein to Absolut, whether through their spectacular subversion of social and aesthetic conventions or by virtue of their semantic complexity and intertextual playfulness, contemporary images appear to fix the gazes of viewers and critics alike, simultaneously procuring and justifying our interest.

In the study of advertising such notions have been bolstered by a number of other factors. The first is the sense among many industry practitioners, and commentators upon them, that one of the primary aims of advertising images is to attract attention. In the first chapter of his book on visual persuasion, Paul Messaris (1997) takes for granted that 'the advertiser's first task' is 'to catch the viewer's eye', and then discusses a variety of visual tools for achieving this. Similarly, Angela Goddard promotes the same idea in terms of the compelling use of verbal language in advertisements (1998: 11–27). The second factor is the prominence of 'textual' and semiotic analyses of single advertisements, which, notwithstanding their many achievements in the exploration of advertising ideology, are based on a privileging of the individual image as both unit of analysis and conveyor of meaning. As Mica Nava argues, these analyses presuppose 'that the truth not only of the ad itself but also of its history and relationships – of the cultural practices involved in its authorship and the diverse ways in which it is read and understood – can somehow be revealed by peeling back sufficient layers of visual meaning' (1997: 34).

Ultimately, however, the deciphering of ideological meanings in advertising texts requires an account of how viewers are engaged by advertisements to read them in the requisite ways, leading writers such as Judith Williamson to claim that 'the receiver is only a creator of meaning because he/she *has been called upon to be so*' (1978: 41; italics in original).[1] This brings me to the third factor underpinning the assumption of the compelling image: the deployment of (quasi-)Althusserian notions of 'hailing' and 'positioning' to describe the ways in which images arrest and engage viewing subjects. The latter term is especially troubling, for it elides two different senses: (1) the positioning of the product or brand in relation to cultural values and meanings with which advertisers hope to associate it (and in distinction from competing brands and their associated values/meanings) – this is the sense in which the term is mainly used in professional marketing and advertising discourse – and (2) a seemingly concomitant positioning of the consumer/viewer both spatially before the advertisement and ideologically in line with these values and meanings (see Bonney and Wilson 1990). In other words, 'positioning' harnesses the aesthetic assumption of spatial arrest and visual compulsion to a critical discourse of ideological domination. And this discourse, for all its deployment of complex semiotic tools, is premised upon a transmission model of communication between powerfully singular images and receptively immobilized viewers.

My interest in stock photography has led me to question these premises, specifically the centrality frequently accorded to the singular image and the notion of visual compulsion or attention that underpins many accounts of advertising and consumer culture. I don't mean to say that such singularity does not exist, but rather that it has been given, so to speak, undue prominence.

Instead, I hope to rethink and generalize the figure/ground distinction, resurrecting the significance of the ordinary, the unremarkable and the overlooked 'ground' in our understanding of the way in which many – if not most – advertising images communicate, and to replace the isolated object of the consumer-critic's interest with an unremarkable but enveloping visual environment. In effect, I wish to reinstate the second moment of the attention–distraction dialectic, recapturing the sense that Walter Benjamin had of distraction as a mode of unobtrusive collective appropriation and gradual sensory habituation (1992: 232–4).[2]

Yet this claim of distraction as a primary (though by no means exclusive) communicative mode of stock images seems to sit uneasily with the account I have given of their manufacture. For while I have described stock images as ordinary and unnoticed, I have also written that their production involves conspicuous staging and theatricality, especially before the cultural intermediaries who decide upon their 'fate' within the 'image repertoire', as they move – or fail to move – from sites of manufacture to distribution and circulation. So which is it? Are stock images 'invisible' and overlooked or attention-seeking and conspicuous?

The answer, of course, is both: though not at the same time or in the same circumstances. For as I have attempted to demonstrate, stock images are the products of exquisitely complex dynamics of manufacture and diffusion. This complexity arises, in part, from the fact that photographic images destined for advertising and marketing operate according to *two* seemingly paradoxical communicative modes or 'rhetorics', which I briefly mentioned in the Introduction and at the end of Chapter 4. These communicative modes are:

1. a 'system' rhetoric of theatrical self-promotion and persuasive efficacy which addresses the professional cultural intermediaries (art directors, designers, etc.) who put images into circulation, as well as the advertisers who ultimately pay for them. This rhetoric was most clearly in focus in my discussion of the production process in Chapters 3 and 4.

2. a 'mission' rhetoric of relentless but unobtrusive citation which is repeatedly performed before consumers. Oriented to the moment of reception, it is this rhetoric, identified with the incessant representation of particular kinds of bodies and scenes, which I chiefly analysed in the previous chapter.

In practice these two rhetorics are clearly intertwined, but by separating them out we can discern the complicated communicative strategies which are designed to *materialize* images across institutionally segregated sites of production (the photographer), distribution (photographic agencies, libraries and archives), circulation (advertising agencies, marketing departments, designers) and ultimately reception.[3]

System, mission, rhetoric, materialization: how do these terms help us to grasp how stock images communicate? Because, extending Butler's terminology to the realm of industrial cultural production, my central argument is that we cannot separate the 'being' of an image, its physical existence and cultural intelligibility as a certain kind of 'matter' at a particular time and location, from its forces of 'becoming' or materialization: those agencies that realize it as a material entity from its status as merely a *potential* image in competition with other potential images.

Stock images, as I hope should be clear by now, are precarious artefacts. What impresses about their 'biographies' (see Appadurai 1986) is how much of them can be described as a struggle for survival across cultural, organizational and economic boundaries. And even if the image does 'survive' the crossing, it may only do so in physically altered form. Hence rather than assume a ready-made, materially and symbolically stable object moving intact in a particular trajectory, I suggest we think of the image as a *possible* object, unstable, protean and dynamic, buffeted by forces of realization and decomposition which pattern the image – materialize it – across institutional-cultural zones. These forces can be separated out into distinct domains: technical (in what resolution or format does the image appear), economic (what is the commercial value/cost of the image and its use compared with other images), administrative-legal (is the image available today, what rights do I have over its reproduction and alteration) and symbolic (how does the image convey an appropriate meaning), although in practice they are usually fused together.

Why, however, should we distinguish between 'system' and 'mission' features? Because although, borrowing from others, I have argued that culture works as a circuit rather than a line, the material manufacture of stock images – their vulnerability to physical and formal alteration – *does* have a clear cut-off point: the point at which the image is put into circulation by ad agencies or designers to be encountered by viewers in moments of reception. Everything related to the (more or less) 'internal' demands, constraints and enabling techniques of the production process up until that point I characterize as 'system': this includes a preliminary moment of materialization when the image is offered to stock agencies by the photographer. The point of reception, however – the realm of the consumer – is that system's goal or 'mission', it's self-structuring, self-reproducing and self-motivating relation to an 'outside'.[4] Now, although 'system' demands are almost always intertwined with 'mission' aspirations and calculations, this division is, I argue, manifestly apparent in the communicative modes – the rhetorics – deployed in and around images as they traverse system boundaries on the way to mission fulfilment. For the organizational milieus of stock agents and their clients suggest that successful images need to be persuasive in the second degree: they need to persuade professional cultural intermediaries of their ability to persuade consumers. This second-order 'system' rhetoric is what accounts in many respects for the conspicuous theatricality of stock images. And interestingly, the proclivities of cultural intermediaries (art directors, graphic designers) as an occupational community – their high levels of cultural capital and erudition with regard to both 'elite' and 'popular' cultural forms (Bourdieu 1986: 357–60; Nixon 1997: 209–17; Mort 1996: 91–113), their possession of powerful 'creative' and 'artistic' agendas and discourses of their own – can make 'theatrical' demands of images that are not primarily connected to their mission rhetoric, to the ways in which consumers will encounter them. As Allen Russell, executive director of Photography at Index Stock, and president of PACA (Picture Agency Council of America) notes:

> Very straightforward photography is still selling very well. Photo editors at agencies love exciting new photography, art directors love to do layouts with exciting new photography, but nothing makes people more conservative than actually opening your pocketbook, and it's the client who is spending the big money on an ad campaign . . .
>
> There's a big contradiction here though because it's more important than ever to show stock agencies something that they haven't seen in order to get into the agency in the first place. So there's new pressure on photographers to shoot stock that is different for the sake of being different. But in the end, it's still probably your one cute kitten shot that sells, not the edgier stuff you shot to get the agencies to notice you . . . At Index Stock 70 per cent of our sales are of traditional photography.

(*PDN* Showguide for *Photo Expo East '99*, 28–30/10/99: 27–8).

In other words, 'edgier', less 'straightforward' photographs are frequently promotional vehicles for the photographer before two levels of cultural intermediary – stock agents and their clients. These images can be understood as 'path-breakers': they will appear in catalogues because they allow the photographer's other, more straightforward images to make the same journey from production into the catalogue, and – more often than its 'edgy' peers – all the way to mission fulfilment in encounters with consumers.

Hence 'edgy' images offer us materializations of system demands, of the photographic preferences of advertising professionals as a taste culture, that enjoy a limited autonomy from consumer orientation. Now, 'edginess' is not an easy thing to define, although it is clearly linked to notions of marked difference (from the norm), originality (something not seen before), and the avant-garde. But in the case of many genres of stock photography it emerges quite strikingly through changes in photographic style. In the brief section that follows I will look at some of these changes as they appear in romantic stock photographs, connecting them to system demands, shifts in advertising styles, and debates about representational conventions in photography theory.

The Style of Romance

What can we say about the style of romantic stock photographs, and its contribution to their cultural significance? Since 'edginess' reveals the contours of system rhetoric most clearly through innovation, I propose to concentrate on three particular elements of style where changes have been most apparent over the past ten or so years: focus, colour and the blur of movement. Other stylistic features, such as point of view and framing, have altered less dramatically, remaining largely wedded to the conventions of a common version of photographic realism, by which 'good' photographs situate their main subjects in the centre of the frame and in which subjects are seen from an angle that roughly replicates an eye-level viewpoint: all this despite certain corporate claims to the contrary and the influence of the 'avant-garde' stock agencies Photonica (see Chapter 7 at pp. 187–8) and, more recently, Getty's Stone (formerly Tony Stone). In the case of romantic photographs these largely unaltered conventions have the effect of depicting the lovers as 'whole', securely situated individuals, and as the viewer's equals.

Blur

In his analysis of the logic of the Gaze, Bryson refers to a category of utterances 'that contain information concerning the locus of utterance, to which linguistics attaches the label *deictic*' (1983: 87). Deictic forms of speech refer to their own perspective; they incorporate information about their own temporality and spatial position relative to their content. In painting, deictic references would include a display of the physical and material labour of creating the image and of its temporal process (for example, through successive versions of the work-in-progress being still visible in the final product). Yet the logic of the Gaze dictates the necessity of the image's complete self-presence, and hence it cannot refer to the process or time of its becoming: 'Western painting is predicated on *the disavowal of deictic reference*, on the disappearance of the body as site of the image' (ibid.: 89).

Surprisingly, Bryson asserts that photography, in contrast to Western painting, *is* deictic, in that it is the product of 'a chemical process occurring in *the same* spatial and temporal vicinity as the event it records' (ibid., Bryson's emphasis). I would argue, however, that only in certain cases are photographs deictic, that more often than not realist norms of focus, lighting, composition and framing mitigate against the display of information that refers to the labour and duration of their production. Indeed, this apparently natural immanence is among photography's chief ideological effects: the erasure of deixis by indexical realism. However, one technical feature of stock photographs is sometimes employed in a deictic manner – the blur of movement.

The blur of the body in motion is an important distinguishing mark of a small number of playful romantic images. These usually involve couples engaged in a mobile embrace, or track the lovers as their bodies meet. Here the blur serves as a counterpoint to the stillness of the photographic medium, a stillness which serves meditative romance so well but threatens to mortify the images of playful romance, turning the lovers into mere statues. Yet it is also deictic: as the coded sign of movement blur refers us to the image's duration, revealing the sudden, ruthless immobilization of flux that constitutes these photographs, and disclosing their nature as an artifice that depends not only on a mechanical operation but on a deliberate selection of shutter and film speeds:

> Whenever photographs incorporate the trace of visible movement, and give it a place in the image and composition, they succumb to an ambiguous force. There is, on the one hand, a raw, primal quality that brings the photographer face to face with the 'real' he or she has chosen to capture . . . But, on the other hand, nothing is less natural than these wavy lines, these thick, quivering edges that give the image a sort of second life, irreducible to the simple intent or immediacy of vision. Though it would appear to be impulse itself, blur is also one of photography's clearest techniques for pointing to itself as artifice, and (ap)pointing itself as art. (Bellour 1993: 164)

As a technique for making artifice manifest, blur makes the images of playful romance doubly flagrant in relation to notions of photographic realism. At the very moment in which blur imparts the 'life' of movement to the static couple, and duration to the still stock image, it places deixis at the service of theatrical staging, turning the photographs into conspicuous performances of conspicuous performances.

Yet the blur does not simply intervene in the relationship between photograph and event, but comes between the viewer and the viewed. It 'speaks to a kind of physical and mental agitation produced by the body as it tries to insert itself directly into the image, in defiance of all technical mediation' (Bellour 1993: 166). Since the blur of movement does not occur in everyday perception – our sight moves with our moving environment – we can treat the blur as a mark of the arrested Glance, of the temporary immobilization of vision in and by the photograph that is so important to the work of stock images before cultural intermediaries. The blur in these stock images is deictic not just with regard to representation, but in relation to the ideal perceptual conditions pertaining at a crucial systemic juncture within the image repertoire: the temporarily arrested gaze of the cultural intermediary at the moment of the image's 'audition' in catalogues, websites, or sample slides and prints. It points to the artificiality of the photograph vis-à-vis the (staged) event, and to the managed transformation of distraction into attention; to the labour of the image's initial production and to the construction of the perceptual conditions for its selection and rematerialization among its primary clients. As we shall see, such conspicuous foregrounding of the image's own processes of mediation, and of the mode of vision best suited to its reception at a given moment, is a key common feature of the other stylistic features to have undergone significant change.

Focus

In the majority of romantic stock images the couples are in sharp focus. This is, of course, unsurprising. It is likely that the overwhelming majority of amateur, commercial and news photographs taken worldwide are 'in focus', or at least are intended to be, and the standard inclusion of autofocus mechanisms on popular and many professional cameras legitimates and enforces on a technical level what has become one of the most unremarked of photography's representational norms.

Focus, however, is not as unchallenged as it appears from the images in these catalogues, and its normative status is something that has had to be worked for discursively and practically through reiteration. Moreover, as I suggested in my discussion of Max Black's theory of metaphor in Chapter 4 (see p. 101ff), focus is intimately connected to those regulatory practices by which certain categories of people and objects are naturalized as both obvious and central, while others are constructed as marginal: it establishes a commitment 'to the essentially imaginary purity of the instantaneous photograph and its sharp, too sharp lines that are all about belief in a transparent vision of life' (Bellour 1993: 164).[5] According to Lindsay Smith's analysis of the sexual politics of 'focus' in the nineteenth century, *sharp* 'focus' emerged, after a brief period of contestation (with Julia Margaret Cameron, for example), as a primary normative standard by which photographs were to be judged as both 'realistic' and 'good'. It achieved a supremacy in photographic theory and practice that was nevertheless 'made to serve existing systems of visual representation, and in particular to conspire with the dominance of geometral perspective' (Smith 1992: 243). Crucially, this normative supremacy was (and is) gendered: the 'feminine' connotations of 'soft focus' – sentimentality, dreamy romance, coy eroticism – illustrate the way in which focus can still articulate patriarchal gender distinctions.[6] Conventional sharp focus, however, like the perspectival system and objectifying gaze to which it was harnessed, was conceived as masculine. Both with respect to the photographed referent and figuratively with regard to objects of knowledge, it suggested attention, penetration and clarification of a largely docile scene by a decisive male eye and an acute muscular intelligence; and it found its most enduring expression in the symbolically centring and socially cohesive power of photographic realism (see Smith 1992; Frosh 1998).[7]

'Focus', therefore, as a technical/representational practice and as a metaphor connects the image's ordered clarity around centrally depicted objects to the analytical, classificatory consciousness of the photographer and viewer about what is *socially* 'central' as opposed to what is 'marginal' or 'other'. Hence it seems as natural for cultural intermediaries (and following them, viewers) to focus on self-evidently 'central' classificatory labels (this is not just an intergenerational group, this is 'family') as it is for the photographer to focus on and sharply delineate 'central' depicted objects. And the term 'focus' effectively cloaks this complex ideological relationship between realist depiction and gendered classificatory mastery by eliding it within a 'neutral' optical figure. Most interestingly, for our purposes, focus is a key pictorial mode of Butler's notion of materialization: it is *these* bodies that emerge, their gendered contours sharply delineated, from the miasmic formlessness of the visual field.

The suggestion that focus is a key mode of normative materialization becomes more complicated when we consider the increase in the use of 'out-of-focus' elements in more recent romantic stock images.[8] For while the majority of the photographs are fully in focus, both foreground and background, a large minority, however, have blurred backgrounds which set off the clear contours of the lovers' bodies. Allowing ourselves a little interpretative licence, we can understand these blurred backgrounds as zones of abjection, the domains of alternative, foreclosed identifications and positions, from which and against which the lovers are materialized in their subjectivity. These realms of haze, however, are also therefore realms of potentiality that in their fuzzy visibility nevertheless appear before the viewer – they are not fully realized, to be sure, but neither is their foreclosure complete. In fact, I would argue, such a realm of potentiality (whether it is a blurred street or a hazy blue sea) is perfectly appropriate to the position of leisure as the utopian space of consumption, the 'nowhere' space in which pleasures and potentialities can be explored and realized. This links the representational practice of focus to Illouz's suggestion that romance and leisure are liminal spaces, to borrow Victor Turner's term, spaces in which actual social conditions and relationships can be symbolically inverted and the individual stands aside from his or her own social conditions, as well as from the entire social system, to formulate a range of alternatives to that system (Illouz 1997: 142–5). That such liminality, also conveyed through the mood of 'playful romance', is employed to channel viewers' desires toward commodities, and attempts to mobilize a sense of subversive agency which it reduces to consumer choice, need not mean that its incorporation is complete.

And this is where we come across another paradox: the out-of-focus as the centre of attention. Following are a few quotes from a discussion of stock photography in the new millennium that appeared in *Photo District News*:

> 'For the last few years there's been a rebellion against the sharpness of objects, against perfect clarity.' Jon Feingersh, photographer.

> 'Pictures are becoming far more developed and originality is blossoming as a result. Selective focus, blurs, unconventional angles, extreme lens selections, enhanced colors and a mystical, blurry, zany innocence leads us to the dawn for the new millennium's imagery.' Roy Russmeyer, photographer.

> 'I've also been doing things like shooting with a very shallow depth of field. Focus has changed too. It used to be that you had to focus on a face, now you don't have to. A laptop in the foreground will be in focus, the business meeting behind it will be totally out of focus, but psychologically you know that it's a business meeting. Because of that I find myself focusing on things that I'd never focus on before.' Michael Keller, photographer. (*PDN* Showguide for *Photo Expo East* '99, 28–30/ 10/99: 18–28).

These same professionals will later go on to admit that *most* stock images haven't changed very much (see Chapter 8 at p. 207). Nevertheless, Feingersh's rhetoric of 'rebellion' and Keller's admission that 'now you don't have to' photograph in focus indicates resistance to and removal of a representational constraint: in the case of Keller, in fact, the lifting of this coercive convention seems almost to suggest a transformation in personal experience (thanks to the metaphorical equivalence of focus and attention) as well as professional practice.

The use of unconventional focus is perhaps most evident in the increasing number of images – still a small minority – in which the couple or one of the lovers in the foreground is out of focus. One potential effect of this is to add a conspicuous direction and duration to the viewer's gaze. Moreover, such uses of unconventional focus can serve to attract attention to focus itself as a representational practice and as a cultural code rather than as a natural attribute of perception. Hence experimentation with images depicting tradi- tionally 'central' subject categories can be simultaneously interpreted as an expression of confidence in the permanence of those categories (they no longer need the support – even partial – of photographic realism) and as a quest for new, 'hyperreal' and 'hypersignificant' visual codes at a time when the useful-ness of photographic realism to advertising's rhetorical project is felt to be exhausted. As Goldman and Papson explain:

> Hyperreal encoding points to efforts to connote a sense of unmediated reality, but always via a coding system that is mediated. Technique overwhelms substance as a semiotic system . . . Seamless technicolor realism, so popular from the 1950s through the 1970s, backgrounded technique and disguised the camera's presence. By contrast, hyperrealist encoding techniques tacitly acknowledge the insurmountable gap between photographs and that which they represent. Hyperrealism acknowledges the presence of the camera, *although once the technique gets routinized, reflexivity about the camera's presence fades* (1994: 31, emphasis added).

Experimentation with focus is one of a range of hyperreal and hypersigni-ficant techniques for decentering both the product within the image, as well the people depicted in the photograph, and is motivated primarily by the need to hold the interest of restless, over-stimulated viewers, 'to stand out and break through the advertising clutter' (ibid.: 35) for audiences suspicious and tired of traditional photographic realism. Key among these audiences are, of course, cultural intermediaries who both produce advertising clutter and need to see something different: that elusive 'original standard' image that can reduce the tension described in Chapter 3 between formulaic certainty and creative singularity. An out-of-focus rendering of a standard subject is precisely the kind of limited originality appropriate to such a compromise. Until, of course, it itself becomes routinized and formulaic.

Other hyperreal and hypersignificant techniques cited by Goldman and Papson include alterations in image-size, unusual framing and cropping that places the product or main human figure on the margins of the image, and the use of oblique and unconventional angles. Despite the claims of the photo-graphers quoted above, the majority of stock images do not employ these techniques (possibly because in terms of their mission rhetoric they are not necessarily designed to 'stand out' from the 'advertising clutter', but rather to constitute it), and my sample includes relatively few images which use them. One key hyperreal technique is, however, extremely common from the mid-1990s onward: changes in the graininess of the image and the use of colour.

Colour

Of all the hyperreal elements of these photographs, perhaps the most promi-nent is colour-tone. Increasing numbers of them are in black and white or some form of monochrome. Black and white photography presents a strange reversal. Theoretically, its relation to the colour spectrum of normal perception is one of obvious transformation and artificiality. Its iconic verisimilitude is far surpassed by full-colour photography, and indeed most personal snapshots reflect that fact. Yet faced with black and white photographs, we are more inclined to be impressed by their sense of realism than by colour photographs. This is due to the fact that black and white images, according to Dick Hebdige,

> are steeped in the ideology of the documentary photograph, the photograph as evidence, austere, cold, objective. These are real pictures of the real thing. Paradoxically, the black and white system signals that this is real. It is the system for photographers to proclaim their intention to have their work and the issues it raises taken seriously. Black and white has become the real system, the system of high contrast, the colours of confrontation (1988: 33).

The documentary realism of black and white is entirely suited to the stylized spontaneity that characterizes many of the images of playful romance, just as its photojournalistic 'seriousness' can be made to augment the existential gravity of meditative romance. And the 'seriousness' of black and white outlined by Hebdige also marks it as a sign of artistic status, a combined effect of the actual age of most canonized photographs, the classic status of many black and white documentary works among all genres of 'art' photographs, and the fact that even today a significant proportion of respected 'art' photographers – those whose work is published and displayed in the legitimate spaces of exhibition – work primarily in black and white.

This combination of documentary realism and artistic legitimacy, however, sets up a tension within most of the romantic stock images. The radical depletion of their spaces and the normative perfection of the lovers' faces and bodies contradict the realist code of black and white photography, leaving instead a strong and unbalanced sense of aspiration to aesthetic legitimacy, an *artfulness* of signification that results in the falsified effect of the 'arty'. This is magnified by the fact that a minority of the images are not actually black and white. Some are in various shades of sepia, an anachronism that only increases the impression of fabrication, while others are in muted pastel tones. Many of these black and white or monochrome images employ a graininess of texture that Goldman and Papson describe as a common form of hyperreal encoding:

> Graininess has become a primary signifier in the system of ads – the grainier the image, the more it signifies reality. Historically, the semiotics of graininess and film color derive from the time when black and white film stocks were faster than color. Until the mid-1970s color was associated with the studio, where lighting could be controlled. Thus color is identified with the musical and fantasy... Conversely, black and white was associated with documentaries because these were traditionally shot under natural light conditions. The hyperreal use of grain often exaggerates

the code of graininess until it draws attention to itself as a signifier of realism. (1994: 33)

Why, however, should the association with documentary realism be important in the codification of romantic stock images? I would suggest that the key tone set by the use of grainy black and white in these images is less one of realism than of nostalgia: a temporal projection of utopian yearning, not, in this case, focused on some consummate space of potentiality (leisure), but on an idealized moment of the lost past. Here the connotation of nostalgia works citationally through the fetishism of a 'past' technology (black and white film) which has, according to the ideology of technological progress, been technically superseded. More specifically its use evokes classic 'romantic' photographs of kissing couples from the 1940s and 1950s that were resurrected, and sold on everything from posters to jigsaw puzzles, in the 1980s – most famously, Doisneau's lovers outside the Hôtel de Ville (1950) and Eisenstadt's kissing sailor and girl in New York at the end of the Second World War (1945), which were shot in black and white. Thus while Illouz considers advertising's nostalgic aesthetic in connection with the use of natural landscapes, which invoke a *'premodern'* past – achieved, inter alia, through 'a softness in the grain of the photography stereotypically associated with the 'genteel' world of the nineteenth century' (1997: 93) – the citations I have mentioned emphatically connect to the depleted *'modern'* urban setting of the city street. Hence the use of graininess and black and white refers most powerfully to the latter part of the Second World War and the immediate post-war era. This period, the end and aftermath of the most self-destructive conflagration produced by modernity, makes a particularly apposite object of nostalgic yearning. According to Harvey Kaplan:

Nostalgia derives its meaning from the Greek word *nostos*, to return home, and *algia*, a painful condition. It was first conceptualized as a painful condition of homesickness by a Swiss physician Johannes Hofer (1678) in the late 17th century. He observed Swiss mercenaries who, in the course of fighting far from their native land, developed symptoms of melancholy, despair and hopelessness which he interpreted as a painful yearning for home and country. (1987: 466)

Nostalgia is first and foremost a soldier's complaint: the craving to leave the battlefield and return to one's home, one's family and one's beloved. It concentrates, under the extreme conditions of warfare, the experiences of mobilization, alienation, transience and spatial disorientation that were discussed earlier as characteristic of modernity. Romance addresses these experiences through the possibility of intimacy, authenticity, play and companionship.

Nostalgia adds to this the security of temporal anchorage, a feeling of reversion and familiarity in desire. And the images' main intertextual references root this position in a constructed post-war 'period feeling', created, in compliance with Fredric Jameson's notion of postmodern historicity, by approaching 'the "past" through stylistic connotation', conveying 'pastness' by the qualities of the image (1984: 67). The very 'pastness' of this position, the sense that it has happened (even if it has been lost), anchors the fraught temporality of a reflexive project of the self that necessarily unfolds in an uncertain future (Giddens 1991). In the next section I shall connect this temporality to the way in which photography in general, and the communicative modes of stock images in particular, combine repetition, narrativity and mythical monumentality.

Stock Images, Time and the Ordinariness of Consumption

The system and mission rhetorics of stock photography involve projections into the future of the image by photographers, stock agencies and cultural intermediaries. The system rhetoric imposes what we might call a 'conditional' temporality that functions sequentially: it is only through the system rhetoric (the fact of a cultural intermediary buying and using the photograph), on condition of its success, that the image's mission rhetoric can be fully consummated with actual consumers. The further back one is in the production 'chain', the more sequences or stages the image has to pass through on the road to mission fulfilment: for photographers, those stages include selection and promotion by the stock agency, selection and purchase by the cultural intermediary, and approval by the advertiser.

These sequences are, however, inseparable from the temporality of the image's mission rhetoric: its ultimate engagement with the social experience of consumers. For while stock agencies promote the images submitted to them by photographers on the basis on their sales potential to cultural intermediaries, they also know that the latter's decisions are at least partially based on the calculation and anticipation of consumer response. Hence this temporality is both 'ontological' and 'teleological': it not only defines the 'essence' of the stock image, its reason for being and its journey toward its final destination, but also provides the ultimate legitimation and authority for the sequence of 'system' decisions made along the way.

There is, however, a very strong sense in which the 'mission' rhetoric, by virtue of its legitimating power, actually becomes subservient to a system rhetoric in which the consumer is an increasingly distant and obscure terminus. For as Lury and Warde argue, 'there is very little consensus about how consumers behave and what would be appropriate ways to understand, or to predict, consumer behaviour' (1997: 87). In these circumstances, advertising 'is a function of *producer anxiety* or uncertainty' (ibid.: 89) and therefore decisions made by cultural intermediaries about the efficacy of this or that image can also be understood as legitimation strategies designed to impress anxious advertisers with the intermediaries' expert knowledge. So while, in terms of its mission rhetoric, the stock image becomes a conduit for a teleo-logical projection into its own future consumption, it is also woven into a parallel projection: the future of the image as a legitimating artefact that will promote the intermediary before his or her client, during a presentation or at other stages in the production and dissemination of the ad.

The outline I have offered so far commits the inevitable analytical sin of unravelling an elaborate braid. The prominence of mission or system rhetorics, and the specificities of their relationship at particular stages in an image's perilous journey from production to reception, is largely indeterminate. Such indeterminacy at the level of micro-decisions nevertheless results in the inces-sant manufacture and dissemination of images so similar as to invite predic-tions regarding their repeated use. Temporal projections of the future of the image are caught up in the constant citation, performance and transformation of images past, much as present narratives of the future self recall and trans-form memories. It is largely through this indeterminacy-within-recycling, which I will now frame in terms of narrativity-within-repetition, that the temporality of stock images meshes with the reality-fantasy synthesis and the potentiality-within-routine that characterizes consumption.

Photography, Narrative and Myth

Among the most obvious and oft-noted characteristics of photography is that it freezes 'reference time', the flow of events within which the referent is situated. Susan Sontag writes: 'The force of a photograph is that it keeps open to scrutiny instants which the normal flow of time immediately replaces' (1977: 11). John Berger states that 'the photograph cuts across time and discloses a cross section of the event or events which were developing in that instant', (Berger and Mohr 1982: 120) and schematizes the relationship between the photograph and the development of an event in time as a line or circle (the photograph) interrupting an arrow (time's flow). The photograph in this sense is understood as anti-narrative, as an instantaneous perpetuation of an isolated moment. This anti-narrative intervenes in reference time whether the latter includes a staged or posed event or object, or a reality apparently unstaged. As Bourdieu explains: 'An instant incision into the visible world, photography provides the means of dissolving the solid and compact reality of everyday perception into an infinity of fleeting profiles like dream images, in order to capture absolutely unique moments in the reciprocal situation of things' (1990 [1965]: 76).

Force, cut, incision, capture. We can immediately discern the violence and finality registered in the language used to describe this disruption of reference time, as though photography wrenches and captures objects and events from their natural environment, from the time of their becoming into the frozen space of the frame. The photograph, according to Christian Metz, is 'an instantaneous *abduction* of the object out of the world into another world, into another kind of time' (1985: 84, my italics). And Berger adds tellingly: 'A photograph *arrests* the flow of time in which the event photographed once existed. All photographs are of the past, yet in them an instant of the past is arrested so that, unlike a lived past, it can *never* lead to the present' (Berger and Mohr 1982: 86, Berger's italics). Here the language of violent immobilization used to describe the temporal relationship between image and referent parallels and reinforces the metaphor of violent immobilization used to describe the effect of the image upon the viewer: the image arrests time and abducts the photographed object just as it pins down the viewer and, in a phrase of Barthes that I have already quoted, 'fills the sight by force'. Both processes are crucial to the way photographic meaning is conceptualized within certain canonical texts of photography theory, especially those with a primarily ontological mission to locate photography's 'essence'.

What is at stake in this representation of reference time, as the last quote from Berger makes clear, is a specific sense of 'lived' time, the 'normal' flow of time, the *sequential* temporality associated with lived experience. This experiential temporality is closely associated with narrativity (and also with the emergence of the 'autobiographical subject' and a linear conception of historical time), the movement of events from a source in the past to an unforeseen destination in the future, in which both source and destination are constantly and reciprocally reinterpreted in the instance we call the present, the 'now'. Narrative time is premised on the openness of the trajectories available, and on the singularity of the events and the sovereign individuals from which they are formed: 'There is no repetition any longer; I am unrepeatable; there will never be another person quite like me; my story is wholly my own' (Freeman 1998: 36). Moreover, it is premised on the idea that only *duration* bestows meaning, an assumption that imposes an important condition upon the ability of the photograph, frozen and lacking in duration as it is, to escape the void of insignificance:

And in life, meaning is not instantaneous. Meaning is discovered in what connects, and cannot exist without development. Without a story, without an unfolding, there is no meaning . . . Certainty may be instantaneous; doubt requires duration; meaning is born of the two. An instant photographed can only acquire meaning insofar as the viewer can read into it a duration extending beyond itself. When we find a photograph meaningful, we are lending it a past and a future. (Berger and Mohr 1982: 89)

Berger, of course, accepts the primacy of narrativity in viewers' interpretations as a natural and experiential given. What he calls 'life' is in fact a linear, narrative temporality that, in contrast to 'mythical time' (more about which below), replaces eternal recurrence and essential sameness with change and difference, certainty with uncertainty and accident, perpetual reappearance with disappearance and death, the permanence of communal roles with the self-generating trajectory of individual identity (Freeman 1998: 33–4). Uncertainty and doubt are central to this conception of photographic narrativity, locating in the present image an intimation of a future replete with potentiality and risk, and a past that materializes and articulates the project of individual selfhood and its perilous attempts to 'colonize' the future (Giddens 1991). This notion of narrative as linear duration is certainly connected to *some* forms of meaning-making in photography, stock photography included, as I hope to show later on.

Yet only if we accept the presumption that narrative time is *existentially fundamental*, that it is the primary mode of temporal existence in human experience, can we also accept Barthes's oft-quoted comment on photographic temporality: 'What the Photograph reproduces to infinity has occurred only once: the Photograph mechanically repeats what could never be repeated existentially' (1984: 4). For, according to this view, existence is made up of singular unrepeatable instants ordered sequentially. (This is what Lloyd calls a 'cinematographic' model of time (1993: 97).) If, however, we *suspend* our acceptance of Barthes's assumption, we can see that the photograph is uncannily appropriate to an alternative temporal consciousness, what Mircea Eliade famously called the 'mythical time' of 'archaic' societies. This consciousness 'acknowledges no act which has not previously been posited and lived by someone else, some other being who was not a man. What he [archaic man] does has been done before. His life is the ceaseless repetition of gestures initiated by others . . . The gesture acquires meaning, reality, solely to the extent to which it repeats a primordial act' (1954: 5). The unique events of narrative time are, in this conception, accidents devoid of meaning and of reality, for an object or event

becomes real only insofar as it repeats an archetype. Thus, reality is acquired solely through repetition or participation; everything which lacks an exemplary model is "meaningless," i.e. it lacks reality . . . insofar as an act (or an object) acquires a certain reality through the repetition of certain paradigmatic gestures, and acquires it through that alone, there is an implicit abolition of profane time, of duration, of "history". (34–5)

Governed by the consciousness of mythical time, that only in repetition is meaningful existence bestowed, we can rephrase Barthes's statement thus: 'What the Photograph reproduces to infinity occurs more than once: the Photograph creates existentially by repeating mechanically.' Hence photography can be understood as anti-narrative not only in the sense that it interrupts the sequential flow of instances. It is anti-narrative in that it proposes and serves an alternative understanding of time. And of the various modes of photographic production (photojournalistic, artistic), stock photography, based strategically upon the interminable and overt production of imitative, generic photographs, is perhaps the most faithful to mythical temporality: it erases indexical singularity, the uniqueness of the instance, in favour of uniformity and recurrence – the systematic iconic repetition of image types.

The Stock Image, Temporal Ambiguity and Consumption

In *Society of the Spectacle* (1983 [1967]), Guy Debord characterizes contemporary 'Spectacular Time'. His description emerges from a prior distinction between 'cyclical time' and 'irreversible time' that is similar in some respects to the dichotomy between mythical and narrative temporalities that I have just outlined. Cyclical time is associated with pre-modern, largely agrarian societies, dominated by the immediate experience of nature and the rhythm of the seasons: 'Eternity is *internal* to it. It is the return of the same here on earth' (Paragraph 127, italics in original). Myth is the principal mode of thought of such societies. Irreversible time, on the other hand, is the time of historical consciousness and historical agency, and while it exists for elite groups within pre-modern cultures, it becomes a universal possibility with the victory of the bourgeoisie over feudal elites, the liberation of labour from its subservience to the cyclical patterns of nature, and ultimately with the self-conscious emergence of the proletariat as an agent of historical transformation. However:

> the bourgeoisie made known to society and imposed on it an irreversible historical time, but kept its *use* from society. "There was history, but there is no more", because the class of owners of the economy, which cannot break with *economic history*, is directly threatened by all other irreversible use of time and must repress it. The ruling class . . . must link its fate with the preservation of this reified history, with the permanence of a new immobility *within history*. (Paragraph 143, italics in original)

In consequence of this need, the pre-eminent temporal consciousness of capitalist societies establishes itself upon the model of mythic return within a repeatable history, where time is severed from development and historical agency and becomes 'pseudo-cyclical time' (Paragraph 153). Pseudo-cyclical time is the time of consumption, and also appears as the primary mode in which time is itself spent, its consumption 'exclusively dominated by leisure and vacation' (ibid.). As spectacular time it is both 'the time of the consumption of images in the narrow sense', and 'the image of the consumption of time in the broad sense' (ibid.) This social image of the consumption of time is 'explicitly presented as the moment of real life, and the point is to wait for its cyclical return' (ibid.).

What bearing does Debord's analysis have upon stock photography both as a system of image production and as an image repertoire, as the visual ground to consumer culture? Certainly the future-orientation of stock images toward system boundaries suggests a concern with (their own) irreversible development, at least at instrumental and formal levels. As does, at the level of mission rhetoric, the materialization of bodies and scenes that intersect with the self-reflexive project of selfhood among consumers. The indeterminacy and potentiality associated with narrative and agency seem to be as central to the stock project as the pseudo-cyclical consciousness that Debord describes.

Given this duality, it is tempting to conceive of stock photographic meaning 'as necessarily torn between the forces of narrativity and those of stasis' (Baker 1996: 73). And thus conceived, romantic stock images seem to energize the temporal ambiguities of photography very effectively, privileging a dialectical interplay between mutually reinforcing modes of identification among viewers.

Such strategic alternation between narrative and mythical temporalities is evident in the distinction between playful and meditative romance and in the characteristic pose of the lovers in each category. In the images of meditative romance, the static, conventional morphology of the embrace suggests neither movement nor sequence. The couples seem to have been frozen with the scene: their duration is one of petrifaction and stillness – of what we would conventionally call 'timelessness' – rather than of interaction and development.

Thanks especially to the textual presentation of the images on the catalogue page in iconographically similar generic groupings, this stillness is given the aspect of repetition so important to mythical time. Repeated in page after page, the lovers' standardized posture appears as the citation and ritual reiteration of an archetypal gesture rather than as an impulse springing from the flux of their environment and the strength of their feelings. These embraces fail to incite a highly specific interest in the history – or even the 'reality' – of the couples, in their personal narratives. In fact, these photographs re-present an intertextual iconographic code that is partially extra-photographic, and which owes much of its force to the familiar architecture of the Hollywood kiss – in its dominant form, the woman's arms around the man's neck, the man's arms around the woman's waist, the man's face tilted down. It is this pervasive extra-photographic code that supports the generalization of the specific photograph even before it has been taken, that guarantees its intelligibility to photographers, agents and viewers alike as the specific distillation of prior materializations.

The images of playful romance do function slightly differently, however. For although it too is contained by the images' repetitive textual presentation, the pose of the lovers – as I observed in my definition of the category – nevertheless conveys a narrative dimension. This dimension is both highly suggestive and productively ambiguous. We see a single moment in a scene that nevertheless suggests the scene's multiple (and potentially contradictory) developmental paths: is the man picking up the woman or putting her down?; the woman holds the man's hat above his head – has she taken it or is she returning it? In fact, the very stasis of the image distils a narrative sequence into an emblematic moment that can serve to represent several of the sequence's likely trajectories, a characteristic that well serves stock photography's polysemic imperative. Additionally, temporal duration is frequently signified here deictically, through the blur of movement, something which does not occur in meditative romantic images.

Umberto Eco, in 'The Myth of Superman', draws a distinction between the hero of classical mythology and the main character of a novel. The classical hero symbolizes the story of his or her own development: 'Even the account greatly favoured by antiquity was almost always the story of something which had already happened and of which the public was aware' (1979: 109). In contrast, the modern novel 'offers a story in which the reader's main interest is transferred to the unpredictable nature of *what will happen* and, therefore, to the plot invention which now holds our attention. The event has not happened before the story; it happens *while* it is being told' (ibid.). Thus 'the mythic character embodies a law, or a universal demand, and therefore must be in part *predictable* and cannot hold surprises for us' (ibid.).[9]

Following this, we can say that the image of playful romance is potentially novelistic: its event can seem to 'happen' while the scene unfolds. The event of the meditative images, however, is static and predictable. Through its lack of narrative particularity, its material inertia within each photograph and its incessant repetition across many of them, the conventional embrace turns the lovers into the stationary figures of myth. The couples and their poses are almost interchangeable from image to image, elements in an exchange-relation whose underlying logic is that of the commodity. That is why they cannot be singular or irreplaceable. We do not know who they are, and neither do we desire to know. They are unnamed persons, anonymous archetypes: everylovers. The irony, of course, is that unlike classical heroes, for whom external action rather than inner consciousness determined one's heroic status, these meditative lovers make *interiority* into the criterion of myth. It is the authentic, self-disclosing, sovereign individual that is placed outside of duration, beyond historical contingency, and made simultaneously the most enduring of natural conditions, the most sacred of human achievements, and the most exemplary of human aspirations.

How does this mobilization of alternative temporalities relate to stock photograph's commercial and rhetorical project? In previous chapters I mentioned that stock images combine *actuality* and *potentiality*, the past and the future: this is one of the chief effects of their temporal ambiguity. This ambiguity is a result of what we might call 'temporal collapse': the compression, into a single instant, of the period between the reference time of the photographed object and the moment of viewing. As Berger observes: 'between the moment recorded and the present moment of looking at the photograph, there is an abyss' (Berger and Mohr 1982: 87). What this represents is the insertion of a startling shortcut or corridor between two disparate zones, the shock of an instant that is not outside time, but in two times simultaneously. Barthes deals with this in his essay 'Rhetoric of the Image':

> The type of consciousness the photograph involves is indeed truly unprecedented, since it establishes not a consciousness of the *being-there* of the thing (which any copy could provoke) but an awareness of its *having-been-there*. What we have is a new space-time category: spatial immediacy and temporal anteriority, the photograph being an illogical conjunction between the *here-now* and the *there-then*. (1977b: 44, Barthes' emphasis)

This unique space-time category, according to Régis Durand, 'is not historical or narrative time. Rather, it is like an incessant back-and-forth between a before and an after, a hesitation on both sides of a threshold that would be, depending on the case, that of event, appearance or image' (1993: 124).

This hesitation on the threshold of a simultaneous past and immediate present undergoes an important shift, however. Pastness becomes actuality and the present becomes potentiality. This shift is due in part to the temporal sequentiality of system and mission rhetorics in the stock production process, both of which are *future-oriented*: the former to the barriers presented by system demands, the latter to the ultimate goal of the encounter with the consumer. It is also due to the representational conventions of advertising discourse, which typically address the present status and future behaviour of the consumer (Berger 1972, Leiss, Kline and Jhally 1997). So the temporal collapse here is one in which potentiality (the future) assumes the garb of the real, while actuality (the present) achieves the status of desire: the ideal is real and the real is ideal. Hence, in their very temporal construction, stock images straddle the reality/fantasy divide in a way that makes them perfect for 'channelling' the desires of viewers by materializing familiar aspects of social reality simultaneously as social fantasies.

This potential returns us to the necessarily dual nature of photographic meaning according to Baker: both mythical and narrative, repetitive and developmental, fixed and uncertain. Yet these are not equal forces. Romantic stock photographs, in their meditative and playful modes, do serve to mirror the pattern of consumer consumption as something based upon both *habit* (the recurrent patterning of the present by the past) and *aspiration* (narrative openness and the yearning for future transformation). However, both the fact and forms of this aspiration are themselves *habitual*: stock images present social categories as the commonly desired potential trajectories of reflexive selfhood, as 'lifeplans' carved out of fantasy and inscribed upon the future, but they achieve this through their repetitive and routinized citation, materialization and naturalization as an existing reality. Stock photographs articulate the injunction to 'become what you are' within consumer culture, proffering narrative structures of identity that operate through familiarity with a recurring and repetitive type, transforming stereotypes into archetypes. And *romantic* stock photographs do so most effectively in that they materialize normative social hierarchies of sex, sexuality, race and class, mobilizing these same hierarchies as aspirational values in the service of commodity consumption, and do so under cover of the ultimate principle of *non-instrumentality*: romance as the free play (in the case of playful images), or authentic self-disclosure (meditative images), of unfettered individuals.

So while certain (in this case, playful romantic) photographs may mobilize, *as individual images*, an interpretation that emphasizes narrative openness and potentiality, the effect is different on a macro-scale. For on this level stock images work, as I have said, as repetitive citations – including of previously established narratives patterns – but that very citational foundation establishes them as an existing and inexorable reality. Within the broad visual environment which stock images systematically produce, narrativity is contained within the overall structure of repetition. Mobilized potentiality acquires meaning and reality because *it has been cited and seen before*, and stock images engage the consumer's practical consciousness of what is ordinarily familiar and desirable by presenting potentiality as emanating from the routine reversion of actuality. The colonization of the future, the realization of agency, are achieved through the habitually repeated desire for what is already intelligible as actual and desirable. Debord's notion of pseudo-cyclical time returns with a vengeance, except that what might be described as 'pseudo' in stock photographic temporality is not its cyclical nature, but its status as irreversible, narrative time – as the time of development.

The repetitive, pseudo-cyclical temporality of stock photography intersects in one other respect with what we might generalize as the 'temporality of consumption': in the separation between the physical vehicle and specific performance of representation (a particular stock image) and the norm or stereotype it cites and materializes. For this distinction mirrors the understanding of consumption as both ephemeral and continuous (Appadurai 1986). After all, each individual stock photograph is a fleeting affair, a throwaway form, evanescent and destined to meet its end as unwanted cultural detritus. At the same time the citational basis of each image supports its generalization, allowing its 'event' already to have happened, in the controlled mutation of an exemplary pattern distilled from every other preceding image. Hence the ephemeral and the ordinary share in the monumental and intertextual timelessness of myth, ritually repeating the 'archetypal' gestures of its culture as its most powerful aspirational conditions. As Bauman has recently remarked, in a statement that could almost be a programmatic description of stock photography:

> The consumer market promises, and delivers, the reassuring certainty of the present without the frightening prospect of mortgaging the future. It supplies durability through the transience of its offerings . . . It proffers eternity in instalments, each bit coming ready for immediate use and meant to be disposed of without regret or remorse once it is used up. (2001: 24)

Conclusion: The Roar on the Other Side of Silence

Finally, how does this complex temporality intersect with the inconspicuousness of most stock images before the consumer, the glanced-at, wallpaper-like quality with which I began both this chapter and this book? By making the depleted spaces and materialized stereotypes depicted in stock images like the glance that encounters them: without duration or power of compulsion as events and experiences that are marked and remarked upon. By rendering aspiration as habitual, routine and ordinary, and by communicating primarily through incessant repetition rather than through the manifest interval of narrativity or the arrested gaze. As Paddy Scannell says:

> Now the 'awesome fact' is that ordinary life and ordinary experience have no storyable features. There is, literally, nothing to say about it. 'What did you do at work/ home/ school/ the office today?' 'Nothing.' It is not, of course, that in some cosmic sense *nothing* happened, but that what happened was in every way usual, routine and ordinary. (1996: 94)

Scannell then goes on to quote from *Middlemarch*, where George Eliot suggestively represents the sight of ordinariness in aural terms: 'If we had a keen vision of all ordinary life it would be like hearing the grass grow and the squirrel's heartbeat, and we should die of that roar which lies on the other side of silence' (quoted in Scannell 1996: 94). Stock photography, in this sense, emits the 'background noise' of consumer cultures: vast numbers of similar images which are repeatedly produced and performed as ordinarily familiar and ordinarily desirable.[10] Such production is 'ordinary' in that it is partly constitutive of viewers' 'practical consciousness', their non-discursive emotional and cognitive orientations to the stability of social reality (Giddens 1991: 35–6): this is why these images are largely *unremarkable* – they do not engage viewers as distinct experiences upon which they are likely to comment – there is, *pace* Scannell, nothing to say about them. And it is images such as these that help create, in their multitude, the visual ground of cultural intelligibility in consumer societies, the overlooked environment within which selected acts of attentiveness and specific encounters with singular figures become possible. But they are also deliberately organized noise, and the environment they make is neither neutral nor blank. It is the result of an intensive, unremitting and systematically ordered labour of production and dissemination. And it enables the constant and 'invisible' performance of the ordinary as simultaneously the most reassuring of enduring conditions and the most desirable of human goals.

Notes

1. See John Sinclair's critique of Williamson, and her reliance upon the advertisement's 'appellation' of the consumer (1987: 49–52).
2. I hope also that my understanding of distraction will avoid what Meaghan Morris calls the construction of the distracted masses as dopes or bimbos (1992: 24).
3. This notion of 'mission' and 'system' rhetorics is an application, in a specific case, of Wernick's (1991) more general description of 'promotion' as a widely diffused rhetorical form characterizing contemporary culture. Advertising photographs, designed to promote lifestyles and products, necessarily promote themselves as effective promoters.
4. These 'system' and 'mission' relations can be understood in Luhmann's terms as the 'self-reference' and 'other-reference' observations of a media system. See Luhmann (2000) on the mass media and (1990) on self-reference, the 'autopoesis' of social systems and the question of meaning.
5. Focus has been the subject of a well-known debate within film history and theory, particularly around the question of 'deep focus' and depth of field.

See especially Bazin's famous and controversial opposition of 'the shot in depth' to the use of montage (1992 [1955]: 155–67), and Bordwell's (1998) discussion of the issue in the context of film history and production processes.

6. See Craik (1994) on the use of soft focus in fashion photography.

7. It is also worth noticing that the metaphor of focus, like those of illumination, revelation and visual clarity in general, has become an almost unavoidable trope within critical writing, invoking, regardless of the best intentions of writers, its discourse of perceptual and conceptual mastery.

8. I use the cumbersome phrase 'out-of-focus' in preference to 'soft focus' in order to avoid the 'feminine' connotations of the latter mentioned above, since the use of out-of-focus elements is different from the conventional deployment of soft focus: in fact, conventional soft focus (where the couple is shrouded by a hazy blur) is rare in romantic stock images.

9. Bakhtin (1981) makes a similar distinction between the epic and the novel.

10. For reasons of space I won't connect the aural metaphor used here to the concept of 'noise' in communication theory, but the resonance is very suggestive.

7

And God Created Photoshop: Digital Technologies, Creative Mastery and Aesthetic Angst

'On average, an image is downloaded from the www.tonystone.com website every 12 seconds of every day.'
'Getty Images' Tony Stone Images Announces Success of First Online Catalog Preview', Getty Images PLC Press Release, www.gettyimages.com, 27 July 1999.

To analyse the impact of digital technologies on the stock-photography industry is to risk immediate obsolescence. As I write, a range of converging technologies, as well as the technical, cultural, and commercial discourses and practices which frame them, are transforming the stock business in radical and unanticipated ways. Accompanying this rapid, fundamental change is the sense that 'stock photography', as an internally coherent phenomenon with a unified structure, purpose and identity, no longer exists. It has been engulfed, it seems, by something new: a global, technology-driven 'visual content industry', dominated by transnational corporations, that is erasing the discursive and institutional boundaries between advertising, documentary, historical and fine-art photographs, and between moments of production, distribution and consumption.[1] Thus the impact of digital technology on stock photography might be described first and foremost by the word *extinction*.

Having said this, the present juncture can also be narrated as stock photography's ultimate triumph, its evolution into another, 'higher' stage, consummated by the very forces held responsible for its sudden demise. In this interpretation, the stock industry's commercial, aesthetic and archival logics find their perfect incarnation in the potentialities of an ensemble of digital technologies – fast, effective and increasingly unconstrained image-manipulation, maximally efficient data storage and management, unlimited duplication with no loss of quality, and almost instantaneous on-line delivery worldwide. And this immaculate self-transcendence is made manifest, by the global visual content industry, in a far broader range of products and markets than ever before.

In this version of events one must resist conceiving of technology in terms of its 'impact', as though technology were a hurtling meteorite and stock photography a fragile and unheeding planet. Rather more prosaically, technology 'emerges from complex processes of design and development that themselves are embedded in the activities of institutions and individuals constrained and enabled by society and history' (Silverstone 1999: 20). Any technology takes its form within pre-existing and often dynamic systems of power, practice, knowledge and representation, and can be shaped by these systems as it affects them in turn. Stock photography, conceived as a cultural industry and as a mode of visual representation, is such a system. Moreover, the upheaval it is both promoting and undergoing is not the result of technology alone: it is connected to at least two additional agents of change; cultural and organizational-financial. Finally, to complicate matters even more, the transformations themselves are intricately tied to significant counter-pressures – continuity with the past and resistance to change – that further muddy any simple picture of a technologically-determined breach with a prior regime.

By insisting on the articulation of digital technologies within existing discourses, and their complex interaction with older systems and practices, I am in sympathy with the arguments of theorists and critics such as Martha Rossler (1991), Kevin Robins (1996), Sarah Kember (1995, 1996), Martin Lister (1995) and Don Slater (1995a), who have provided a valuable alternative to the occasionally sophisticated but often millenarian mainstream discourse (academic and journalistic) on digital and 'virtual' technologies. In its dominant celebratory mode this discourse ascribes utopian possibilities to the mere use of new visual technologies, and in its distopian antithesis laments their emergence as inevitably signalling the end of authenticity, certainty and innocence.[2] In contrast, the writers I have mentioned broadly subscribe to the statement that the question of technology 'is not at all a technological issue' (Robins 1996) but a social, cultural, and political one, examining the ways in which technology can act as a conservative as well as a transformative force – and as an agent of subordination as well as subversion – in specific historical and cultural circumstances.

In this chapter I hope to explore some of these complex interactions, connecting them to the central cultural, commercial and technological dynamics of the digitized stock-photography industry, focusing on the expectations and anxieties underlying professional discourses and practices and their relevance to broader questions of value, power and ethics in contemporary visual culture. Hence this chapter connects in very obvious ways to the historical mapping of the core values of stock photography – the institutional priority of advertising clients, the emphasis on production quality, the adoption of professional marketing techniques, and orientation to global operations – that took shape in the industry's 'classic' period, as well as to the analysis of its cultural economy and mode of signification in Chapters 2 and 3. Less obviously, perhaps, it will also tie in to discussions of the archive in an age of digital image replication and simulation (sometimes construed as an archive, or museum, 'without walls', or in Hal Foster's phrase, an 'archive without museums' (1996)), that return us to themes at the heart of Chapter 4. Finally, while it will be less occupied with the analysis of photographs and communicative modes (as opposed to professional discourses about them) than the previous two chapters, it will briefly touch upon one of the central issues of this research throughout its various sections: the question of *image diversity*, in this case as it is framed within stock photography's contemporary, or 'postmodern', regime of signification.

Moments in the Life of the Digital Stock Image

The best way to approach the dynamic interactions of cultural, commercial and technological forces in contemporary stock photography is through the specific applications of digital technologies at key moments in the life of the image: production, storage and distribution.

Production

Up until the turn of the millennium it was still relatively rare for advertising or stock photographers to take pictures using digital equipment: according to the *1999 APA (Advertising Photographers of America) National Photographer's Survey*, only 1.8 per cent of jobs were shot in digital format during 1998.[3] This reluctance to embrace digital equipment is partly the result of a widespread feeling among professional stock photographers that digital cameras and film do not yet provide the level of accuracy or resolution achieved by their conventional analogue 'ancestors': hence its increased adoption in the future is largely a matter of technical capacity (more memory and processing power, greater picture resolution), cost and time. Accompanying this justification, however, is the attachment to non-digital equipment and processes resulting from routine daily familiarity and years of financial and emotional investment, plus the lingering affection of some for the 'alchemy' of the old chemical technology and the 'artisanal skills' associated with it (Brian Seed, *Photo Expo East '98*, 30/10/98).

Hence the primary use of digital technologies to date mainly occurs after the photograph has been taken and converted into digital form. In this phase software programs such as Adobe PhotoShop are employed to 'retouch' or 'enhance' the image, and it is the apparent threat that such 'manipulation' poses to the credibility of the photograph (and the credulity of the spectator) that has made it one of the most common preoccupations of philosophical and theoretical writing on digital imaging technologies:

> As still photography leaves its optical-chemical past and enters the optical-electronic-computer future, new possibilities and challenges emerge for the news media. Long held notions of what constitutes credibility of source, credibility of information, and philosophical concepts of truth are rapidly becoming outmoded (Bossen 1985: 27).

I will not dwell here on the assumptions regarding the non-digital photograph underlying such preoccupations, assumptions about the photograph's 'analogical perfection' in relation to the real (Barthes 1977a: 17), the claim that it does not 'translate' real appearances through a code but 'quotes' them directly (Berger and Mohr 1982: 96), the sense that photographs 'really are experience captured' (Sontag 1977: 3).[4] Neither will I rehearse the arguments of those who celebrate the effect of digital technologies as a liberation from the prison-house of this (mythically objective) referentiality (see Mitchell 1992; Tomas 1996) or, conversely, of those who mourn it as the withering of photography's essence, the defining necessity – 'the fatality', as Barthes calls it (1984: 6) – of the photograph's indexical relationship to its referent and its status as a form of evidence (for example, Ritchin 1990), although I will return later on to a possible ethical consequence of this 'loss'. Suffice to say that both rejoicers and lamenters are both marking a type of ontological fracture, a crisis in the very being of photography:

> The substance of an image, the matter of its identity, is no longer to do with paper or particles of silver or pictorial appearance or place of origin; it instead comprises a pliable sequence of digital codes and electrical impulses. It is their configuration that will decide an image's look and significance, even the possibility of its continued existence'. (Batchen 1998: 22)[5]

Several commentators have already noted a key difficulty with this sense of a decisive break with a pre-digital mode of photographic signification, since photographic 'truth' has been widely questioned for several decades at the very least (Bossen 1985; Kember 1996). This suggests that the departure from a previous formation may be less connected to ontology and technology than to differences in the material and discursive contexts in which photography and image manipulation occur. It also highlights the shortcomings of designating 'photography', whether analogue or digital, in the *singular*, as a unity that spans, accommodates and integrates photojournalism, fine-art photography, domestic photography, advertising photography and other practices (see Lister 1995: 14). What is perceived as causing an ethical crisis for photojournalism, for example, may be seen in an entirely different light by commercial and advertising photographers.

Nevertheless, the shift in the 'identity' of the photographic image caused by digital 'enhancement' technologies *has* impacted upon the discourse of stock photographers. Rather than producing an ethical or ontological crisis, it appears as an epistemological and practical transformation, a fundamental change in what it is possible to *know about* and *do to* a photographic image. We can call this transformation the 'disenchantment' of photography. By this I mean that digital technology removes photography from the sphere of alchemy and magic by allowing for the image's conversion into numerical sequences, for the decomposition of its continuous textures and forms and for their arbitrary reconfiguration. This is perhaps a strange claim to make, given photography's historical and discursive connection to positivism and science, and its seeming primacy, therefore, 'within the most thoroughgoing appropriation of the world as pure object, and thus within a project of total disenchantment' (Slater 1995b: 223). How, if photography is itself an agent of disenchantment (of the visible world), can it be amenable to disenchantment by digital technology?

The answer lies in a paradox of modernity described by Don Slater, in which the visibility so central to scientific validation and technical demonstration is also necessarily one that inspires belief. Hence scientific demonstrations, for example, do not simply furnish visible experimental 'evidence' but

> take the form of social events shaped into complex cultural forms, with highly dramatic and spectacular qualities. The problem is that as cultural forms these spectacles move in the opposite direction from the disenchanting mission of modernity: in the very process of making public the disenchanted facts of the world, they can be re-enchanted through visual spectacle. (1995b: 223)

The spectacular quality of science involves creating 'an audience *for modernity*, (for the consumption of modernity as a spectacle)' (ibid.: 226), before whom scientific technologies both make nature wonderful and, in their mastery of nature's laws, become wonders in their own right. These technologies are for

Slater a form of 'natural magic', since 'the power of science and technique at the height of their rationality appear to us (who do not understand them) as a new form of magic' (ibid.: 227). Photography, understood as a revelation of optical and chemical laws that, in the terms of both Daguerre and Fox Talbot, allows nature to represent itself, and also conceived as a performance of the technical ability to command nature and replicate its appearance on demand, seems clearly 'magical' in this sense. Moreover, the magic of photography is inseparable from its indexicality (or in Slater's phrase, its 'ontological realism' (ibid.: 222)), which seems to make the image uniquely co-substantial with its referent, an emanation or shadow of the real: this much has been noted by some of the foremost commentators on the medium (Benjamin 1980 [1931]: 202; Bazin 1980 [1967]: 242; Sontag 1977: 155; Barthes 1984: 88). In the experience of ordinary amateur photographers, such enchantment is perhaps most keenly felt in the appeal of the Polaroid: it is not just the instantaneous emergence of the indexical image from its paper-chemical womb, but its performance of the darkroom development process as a private spectacle for a broad market of non-specialist consumers, the birth of the photograph before one's very eyes and in a way that nevertheless remains inexplicable. And similarly it is the staging of that chemical process, and the fetishization of the laboratory environment, that allows a few older stock photographers to regret the loss of the 'alchemy' of pre-digital technology.[6]

As I have said, new digital technologies, by dematerializing and reconfiguring the photograph before our eyes, by allowing for our absolute mastery over its every particle, disenchant photography just as photography disenchanted the visible world. In the process, as Kevin Robins contends (1996), they extend the project of rational control to the very core of the image-making process, massively empowering their users. But at the same time the new technologies themselves become magical, staging themselves as wondrous spectacles of replication and simulation.

Hence stock photographers and agencies are almost completely unperturbed by ethical considerations that might arise from *their own* use of digital image-manipulation technologies (as we shall see, they are less sanguine about the use others might make of them), and they are almost overwhelmingly over-awed and enchanted by the power of these technologies. This combination of mastery and miracle is nicely encapsulated by Patrick Donahue, former Director of Photography at Tony Stone Images, who noted that in the late 1990s 80–90 per cent of the photographs they promoted had been digitally manipulated. 'Adobe didn't create PhotoShop,' he said. 'God did' (*Photo Expo East '98*, 31/10/98). Most stock photographers have responded to digital imaging technologies with similar enthusiasm:

With the advent of digital, if we choose, we now have more control, in every way, than we ever did before (John Lund, digital photographer, quoted in Kristina Feliciano, *PDN Photo Expo East '98 Showguide*, 10/98: .22)[7]

> Retouching is a major use of digital imaging for stock. It's easy to remove a blemish that makes stock less saleable . . . Another common use of digital retouching is to add background to enhance the shape of a photo . . . But the most exciting aspect of imaging is the ability to create new, unimagined photos. Merge several photos, distort them, alter color, change perspective. Make a real-looking scene more perfect than you could shoot it. Or create an impossible universe from your imagination (Heron 1996: 176).

Digital manipulation is welcomed as an empowering and providential extension of the photographer's rhetorical craft, a craft that includes the miraculous perfection of the real through its fabrication. It has become an integral part of all image production in the stock business. And a concomitant of this unambiguous passion for image manipulation is the utter irrelevance of evidentiary truth value or 'ontological realism' to the work of stock photographers, the purposes of their images, or the perceived expectations of their ultimate viewers. Like advertising images in general, and due partly to the framing of advertising photography within a prior tradition of advertising illustration (Wilkinson 1997: 27), stock photography is not concerned with the unmediated and ideally objective reproduction of the material world in a neutral photographic 'document'. Rather, and as I have outlined at length in previous chapters, the purpose of the stock photograph is to convey a 'concept' (Heron 1996: 26), a metaphorical or narrative structure only selectively and tangentially representative of social experience that when associated with a product will work rhetorically to sell it. Thus the only questions asked about an instance of digital image manipulation – say, the addition of a patch of sky to a landscape photograph because its target audience (Americans, in this case) 'tend to like to see the horizon' (Tracy Richards, Director of Photography, Panoramic Images, *Photo Expo East '98*, 30/10/98) – concern its compositional feasibility and, above all, its rhetorical efficacy: indexical fidelity to an external reality is beside the point. And stock photographers and their clients in design firms and advertising agencies assume that consumers, long accustomed to the formal conventions and promotional goals of advertising images, do not expect such fidelity from their photographs.

However, the legitimacy of image manipulation is not only conferred upon photographers themselves. Traditional, rights-protected stock photographs are primarily sold to professional cultural intermediaries – art directors and art buyers, picture editors, graphic designers – in advertising agencies, design studios and marketing departments for use in promotional material. Such usage involves, as we already know from the analysis of stock photography's cultural economy, the recontextualization of the image, its combination with other graphic and textual elements (including other photographs), at which point the photograph can be substantially altered. For some, however, digital technologies make possible recontextualizations that are so radical, so disfiguring to the initial image, that they pose a new type of threat:

> Interactive multimedia technology enables users to manipulate data, alter images, turn still paintings into animated sequences, and combine music and art in idiosyncratic ways. While this may be exciting and innovative to the user, in the eyes of the creator such manipulation may compromise the value of the original artwork. (Karen A. Akiyama, Manager of Business and Legal Affairs, *Rights and Responsibilities in the Digital Age*, www.corbis.com, 9/98)[8]

However, while such transformative power is new in degree, it is not new in principle: Helen Wilkinson's research on the UK stock agency Photographic Advertising in the 1930s shows that almost all its images were altered by the client, even to the extent of being made to look like drawings (1997: 26). Thus stock photography has always had to deal with potentially a far more explosive issue than the simple theft of images: the 'completeness' or 'unity' of the photographs it promotes, and, given their availability for alteration by legitimate, fee-paying customers, the definition of their 'value'. The industry has typically contained possible clashes over the unity of images by permitting clients to make specifically sanctioned types of alteration. The transfer of artistic and cultural authority – the power to pronounce a work open or closed, complete or incomplete, more than or equal to the sum of its parts, and to change it and reproduce it in multiple, unanticipated contexts – is regulated through a precise legal and financial mechanism: the negotiation of reproduction rights and fees that lies at the heart of the traditional stock-licensing system. On their own, therefore, digital image-manipulation technologies have not radically challenged this system: they have been incorporated into a framework which already, from its inception, was designed to profit from the short-term resolution of what we can call the 'existential angst' of the photographic image, although the increase in the range of alterations that these technologies make available to powerful clients and willing agencies has caused some disquiet among photographers. The real trouble begins, however, when the power of digital manipulation bolts through the open door of digital distribution. But before we cross that threshold, let us turn briefly to another moment in the life of the digital stock image: storage.

Storage

According to what rules of classification can digital photographic images be held in an archive? 'Computers are wonderful for organising and storing information, but how do you find something once it's stored in invisible digital form?' (Frequently Asked Questions About Stock Photography, www.stock photo.net). The simple answer is that the taxonomy should provide an efficient means of retrieving the image for clients: this entails the use of verbal labels or descriptions that mirror the thought processes of clients rather than of image producers. In the debate over 'subject' and 'concept', the latter has become gradually more prominent in printed catalogues (in which, unlike computer databases, the images are materially visible and easily glanced over). However, 'concept' has not replaced 'subject' as a basic organizing principle in non-digital archives: as spelled out in Chapter 4 (see p. 100), moving from the denoted 'subject' to the connoted 'concept' is a context-dependent labour of interpretation that is extremely difficult to systematize. In this respect at least, computer databases (and websites) still resemble actual archives far more than printed catalogues: images are not present for viewing, they need to be 'retrieved' from their location in the database. And the subject labels they often employ (people, nature, business, science, etc.) are just as familiar.

At one stage, however, it appeared that computers themselves could take on the interpretative work of fitting images to concepts. Through the power of 'keyword' searches, they could 'process' different verbal descriptions and match them with images searched from vast databases far faster and more efficiently than people. Yet although it is now absolutely crucial to the archival systems of most agencies and many photographers, and ubiquitous on websites, keywording has proved to be deeply problematic. It is intensely complex, time-consuming and expensive, with an average cost of $10 per image in costs and labour (multiply that for a small archive of 1,000 images and the scale of the expense is immediately apparent), and with most descriptions of images totalling over a hundred words each. It has proved exceptionally difficult to systematize even the most basic descriptions of 'subject', not to mention 'concept', since people use different words in their descriptions and computers are unable to simulate the interpretative linguistic and visual processes that human photo researchers have traditionally used to compensate for such differences (Frequently Asked Questions About Stock Photography, www. stockphoto.net). As a result, some photographers have even decided against having any search engines on their websites, instead encouraging clients to e-mail, fax or phone requests so that researchers can offer a selection on-line a few minutes later ('Selling Stock Direct on the Web: Three Case Studies', *PDN* 1/2000, www.pdn-pix.com).

These difficulties have led Comstock, employing a bombastic tone not uncharacteristic of the agency, to denounce all keyword searches in an attempt to place 'visual thinking' at the centre of its archival system:

> You are no more likely to find a great **photograph** with a 'keyword' search than you would be to find a great piece of **music**. **You didn't become an artist to do crossword puzzles.** You became an artist because you understand that the **power of the visual** is *unique*. You have that rare ability to **think visually** and **communicate visually.** And that's why it is a supreme irony that the best way photo agencies have figured out – so far – to help you 'connect' with the imagery that works for you, is by using **words** ('Why Keyword Searches Don't Work', Comstock, 3/3/00, www.comstock.com; emphasis in original).

Comstock's alternative, aimed at matching images to the client's 'concept', is a facility called 'Dynamic Visual Linking'. The user enters a keyword, the computer responds by proposing a verbal list of image categories related to the keyword, the user selects one of these categories, the computer retrieves a selection of miniature 'thumbnail' images for the selected image category from which the user then chooses the image closest to his or her 'concept', at which point the computer presents a further verbal list of image categories suggested by that choice. The process continues, presumably, until the ideal image is found or someone gives up.

Apart from speaking directly to the self-esteem of designers as 'visual artists', and to their business interests (keyword searches are presented as a waste of money and time: they don't deliver the best image for the purpose required), both Comstock's rhetoric and its solution suggest a fundamental ambivalence regarding the relationship between images and words in the world of digital visual culture. For its bombastic and moralistic insistence on the rights of the visual over the verbal, and on their incommensurability, expresses what W.J.T. Mitchell calls 'ekphrastic fear' (1994: 151–81). This is to be distinguished from 'ekphrastic indifference', which expresses a simple common-sense acknowledgement of the difference between words and pictures. It is also opposed to 'ekphrastic hope' – the moment in which the image/text distinction 'is overcome in imagination or metaphor, when we discover a "sense" in which language can do what so many writers have wanted it to do: "o make us see"' (ibid.: 152) – this being different in degree, but not in kind, from the goal of conventional keyword searches. In contrast 'ekphrastic fear', which Mitchell links to the fear of otherness, is alarmed by the possibility of ekphrasis, resists the equivalence of image and word. It insists on their distinction as an aesthetic and moral imperative, an imperative partially incarnated in the institutional separation between visual and verbal expertise in many media and 'creative' professions.[9]

Notwithstanding the anti-verbal tone of Comstock's text, however, the search engine it has designed works by moving constantly *between* images and verbal categories, playing one off the other in a sequential process of elimination. In fact, despite Comstock's claims and intentions, 'Dynamic Visual Linking' is not terribly different from the conventional keyword searches in use elsewhere. What this contradiction between rhetoric and reality seems to indicate is a fissure between aesthetic discourses and commercial practices with regard to digital technologies. For even were ekphrastic hope a (fearful) possibility in the pre-digital era, today it appears as the commonplace technical achievement of a digital code which converts both images and words into patterns of numbers, breaching the wall between them by equalizing them as data: 'Might visual culture', as Hal Foster asks, 'rely on techniques of *information* to transform a wide range of *mediums* into a system of *image-text* – a database of digital terms, an archive without museums?' (1996: 97; italics in original). It is important to note that the 'image-text' emerges here not in its own self-created ekphrastic glory, but as a subspecies of the binary system, while each medium – visual and verbal – purportedly loses its own material specificity in the ether of universal numerical exchange.

Hence Comstock's attack on the verbal realm displays an anxiety to maintain the singularity and difference of words and images in the face of media (such as the computer) and representational practices (such as stock photography itself) which aspire to their coterminous abstraction and equivalence. While Comstock's search engine necessarily goes with the digital flow, the ekphrastic fear of its rhetoric reasserts the importance of symbolic and professional distinctiveness, and especially of visual 'purity', against a dynamic that appears to level all other representational forms. Paradoxically it is this same dynamic of equivalence that – in the shape of recyclable similarity and its shadow of commodification – is at the heart of 'industrial' mass cultural production, digital or otherwise. In effect, digital technologies have come to embody the system-stabilizing desire for visual–verbal transparency and interchangeability so (imperfectly) performed though the use of such terms as 'the concept', while at the same time awakening fears that a technologically perfected equivalence will engulf whatever uniqueness the cultural product can claim. Such a fissure in stock photography's professional discourse has been seen before, in the antithesis and fraught cohabitation of corporate and artisanal notions of 'success', and will reappear below in concerns around the 'integrity' of the photographic image. Ultimately, of course, such ekphrastic fears are unfounded. Whatever their capacities regarding image manipulation, storage, distribution and reproduction, digital technologies make pictures and texts equivalent only for computers, or for those working instrumentally with computer code. As the imperfections of keyword searches make amply clear, human beings are still stuck with the frustrating and highly productive slip-pages between two of their primary 'interfaces': images and words.

The problems of keywording point to two other developments impacting on the nature of the digital archive: the sheer quantity of images made available from diverse sources, and the way in which digital technologies have made them accessible to large markets of non-professional consumers who, unlike the traditional clientele of cultural intermediaries, are left to navigate the archive (on CD-ROM or website) without the intervention of human experts who can interpret their needs. The first development, to be dealt with later, bears on the voracious ingathering of 'visual content' that characterizes the stock industry today. The second development leads me to consider the next moment in the life of the digital image: distribution.

Distribution

The two main technologies behind digital image-distribution systems are CD-ROMs and on-line (usually web-site) delivery.[10] Just as digital production has not yet become the dominant technology for taking photographs, so digital delivery systems still only account for a minority of images distributed, although this is changing fast: in some companies, such as Getty Images, online or 'e-commerce' sales account for a majority of overall sales – 61 per cent in the last quarter of 2001, 48 per cent in the third quarter of the same year ('Getty Images Reports Financial Results for The Fourth Quarter and 2001', Press Release 6/2/2002).[11] Of the two technologies, on-line distribution is probably the more radical, since it erases time as a factor in delivery. It fulfils a similar function to that once performed by the telegraph in relation to news reporting, severing 'content' (the image) from its fixed attachment to a material 'vehicle' (the photographic print or slide) and allowing for its instantaneous transmission across the world at massively reduced cost, independent of postal or courier schedules and charges.

But perhaps the most significant transformation engendered by both CD-ROM and on-line delivery technologies is the prospect of inexpensive, faultless duplication, providing the stock industry with a low-cost solution to one of its biggest technical and financial challenges: the expense of analogue duplication and the constant struggle to keep costs down by ensuring that clients return the slides or prints of the images licensed to them (loss of these usually incurs a hefty fine, and in the case of lost or damaged original slides currently approaches around $1500 per image ('Licensing Still Images', Index Stock 4/6/2000, www.indexstock.com/publications.htm)). The efficient distribution of perfect duplicates has revolutionized stock photography by making the delivery of images to a *mass market* (rather than a restricted market of professional cultural mediators) a practical, cost-effective possibility, as well as a major source of anxiety. Karen A. Akiyama describes this as the 'paradox of mass distribution', whereby 'artists fear that their works will be distributed without adequate protection or compensation to millions of on-line consumers with the click of a mouse. Yet, the very possibility of such fast and far-reaching distribution is exactly what makes digital communications so appealing in the first place' (*Rights and Responsibilities in the Digital Age*, www.corbis.com, 9/98).

It is this radical potential for broadening the market that has led to the rise of a new 'royalty-free' (RF) sector operating alongside stock photography in the 1990s. Royalty-free photographs are sold on a single-fee, multiple-use, mass-distribution principle, which means that, in contrast to rights-protected stock photography, purchase of the image includes purchase of a very broad, non-exclusive licence to use the image as, when and however often the purchaser sees fit.[12] Generally sold on CD-ROM for anything between $100 and $500 for several hundred (and sometimes several thousand) photographs, royalty-free images are also available individually via the internet.[13]

The initial response of established stock agencies to the emergence of royalty-free was anything but positive, even though at first the two systems did not officially compete for the same markets: RF was aimed at small business users and general consumers who could not afford the prices of rights-protected stock. Nevertheless, RF producers were frequently condemned as pirates flooding the market with 'low-end' (i.e. low-quality and low-cost) content that threatened both traditional stock and assignment photography (the same argument was made against stock by assignment photographers in the 1970s and 80s) ('Future Stock: Comstock Goes Clip, Henry Scanlon Explains Why', *PDN* 9/97: 66). RF producers countered that these claims were commercial self-interest dressed up as high moral and aesthetic principle. Competition between these image producers soon intensified, however, as royalty-free images began to enjoy increasing popularity among graphic designers and corporate marketing departments: in 1997 royalty-free accounted for 46 per cent of image usage in 'creative' (i.e. professional advertising, marketing and design) markets, as opposed to rights-protected stock which had dropped from 38 per cent in 1996 to 24 per cent (*Communication Arts*, 8/98: 209), with 63 per cent of respondents to a US graphic design trade journal's survey reporting that they used royalty-free images (stock agencies were used by 87 per cent of respondents) (*Graphic Design USA*, Stock Survey, 8/98: 78). This has led to growing product differentiation and market segmentation within the royalty-free sector, with industry giants such as PhotoDisc focusing on the 'high-end' creative professional market, and encroaching on 'rights-protected' stock's traditional clientele (*PDN* 8/1995: 71).

In the past few years the relationship between traditional stock and RF has shifted from hostility to accommodation and collaboration. RF is now applauded for pioneering new, non-professional, markets as well as for driving up the prices of traditional stock – because (so goes the claim) rights-protected stock can guarantee the quality and exclusivity that top clients will willingly pay more for (*PDN* 9/97: 64–6; Jonathan Klein, CEO of Getty Images PLC, 'Content in the 21st Century' (Keynote Speech), *Photo Expo East '98*, 31/10/ 98). This accommodation to RF has been sealed with the acquisition of RF companies or the establishment of RF divisions by the big stock agencies: Getty Images PLC, now the largest 'visual content' agency, was formed through a merger between the owners of leading traditional stock agency Tony Stone Images and RF pioneer PhotoDisc (Getty Images Press Release 16/9/97); Corbis bought RF producer Digital Stock in February 1998 (*PDN* 9/97: 22; *Photo Source News* 'Corbis Buys Digital Stock': 3/98, www.photosource.com); The Image Bank (prior to its acquisition by Getty) bought Artville in November 1998 (*Photo Source News*, 'Photos for Sale', 12/98, www.photosource.com; 'TIB Enters R-F Business', *PDN* 12/98, www.pdn-online.com), and Visual Communications Group (again, prior to its purchase by Getty) opened an RF division at FPG International in late 1999 (FPG Press Release, 'Visual Communications Group (VCG) Launches Interactive Website for its FPG Stock Photography Brand – Includes New Royalty-Free Line', 11/99, www.fpg.com) and at around the same time acquired Definitive Stock, an on-line provider of royalty-free imagery.

This convergence of royalty-free and rights-protected systems has been marked by attempts to redraw the boundaries between them. The danger of competition between RF and stock agencies owned by the same conglomerates, and the need for super-agencies to offer product diversity, has led to the alignment of distribution and licensing systems with particular instrumental advantages; namely, the exclusivity of expensive rights-protected stock as opposed to the low-price and ease-of-use of RF. However, these systems have also been attributed with specific *aesthetic* characteristics. The most prominent claim, frequently made by the senior management and marketing departments of the super-agencies themselves, is that much of the 'low-end', 'generic' and clichéd content produced by traditional stock agencies has moved over to RF, with traditional agencies emphasizing 'quality', 'creativity' 'uniqueness' and 'individual vision' in the images they promote (*Communication Arts*, 'Stock Photography', 1–2/93: 108; *Graphic Design USA*, 8/98: 81–2).

The extent to which traditional stock has indeed undergone a 'quality' revolution in the last decade is subject to some dispute (see *Creative Review*, 'Best Sellers', 8/99: 36–7, as well as the brief discussion below), as are the causes of such a transformation, which are lodged as much in cultural and organizational-financial trends toward market differentiation and less homogenous advertising design as they are in technological forces (see Chapters 3 and 4). But the claim intersects with questions of digital manipulation and recontextualization in very illuminating ways, since it amounts to a discursive and practical strategy for containing anxieties about the unity of stock images.

Comstock (which opened its RF division in June 1997), for example, is among the claim's most vocal proponents. Not only does its CEO, Henry Scanlon, distinguish between 'the hardy few' 'visionary' photographers creating quality work for stock and the mass of 'technicians' manufacturing derivative RF images ('Future Stock', *PDN* 9/97: 64), but the company's promotional material, in particular its website, draws a distinction between its rights-protected and royalty-free 'brands', adding an explicitly aesthetic dimension which other agencies tend to leave unstated.[14] In *'Rights Protected' vs. 'Royalty Free' – Which is for you? An Insider's Essential Guide to Making the Right Choice*, (Comstock 1998, www.comstock.com), the company gives the following advice to its clients:

> Rights Protected stock photos are intended to be used intact, shot to communicate a powerful message. Sure, good stock photos are always composed to give you flexibility for type, cropping and re-sizing. But, in general, they represent a 'complete' composition with all elements of that composition designed to support a central theme or idea – a 'story' (12).

Characterized at the level of form by compositional unity, and at the level of meaning or effect by narrative potency and communicative clarity, the distinction of these images is further bulwarked by their pedigree and the status of their source: they 'represent the best creative work of some of the world's foremost professional photographers working at the top of their form' (ibid.). All three dimensions – form, meaning, origin – can be subsumed in the term 'integrity': the image is valued for its integrity as the perfectly composed and powerfully communicative work of an exceptional individual. Conversely:

> a great royalty-free image is an image you look at and can't wait to change. You want to get it into your computer and begin to work with it. You want to take a part of it and flip it or manipulate it or put it with another picture and another and begin to create a unique, personal composition. Arguably, good royalty-free imagery is a direct result of the way computerized graphic design has vastly expanded – in essence *liberated* – graphic design from traditional structures. The increasing reservoir of royalty-free imagery is making this kind of multi-image composition (where, indeed, the image is often used not so much for its 'story-telling', but, simply, for its graphic substance), both possible – and affordable (ibid.: 13).

This manifesto for cultural differentiation that valorizes, on the one hand, elitist image conservation, and on the other, massive and radical image manipulation, represents probably the most sophisticated and explicit strategy for the incorporation and containment of digital technology's challenge to image integrity. The dichotomous conceptions of value it formalizes, 'integrity' and 'graphic substance', specify precisely which photographs acquire purpose as the authorized and unchangeable works of sanctified artists, and which are the raw visual material – a colour here, a texture there – gathered up by merely competent technicians.[15] Of course, the 'graphic substance' of many a uniquely powerful stock photograph, not to mention of a royalty-free image, may itself originate, at least in part, in graphic substances provided by other digital images, themselves the products of prior acts of materialization.

This 'liberation' of graphic substance from the (always fragile) unity of the photographic image is actually a radical extension – or implosion – of the archival paradigm at work in pre-digital stock photography. For the liberation of the graphic substance of the royalty-free image takes the archival principle one crucial step further: *into* the very material constitution of the photograph. Rather than treating images as the basic units of the archival system, to be stored, retrieved and valued intact, it sees each image itself as a repository of exchangeable components, as a further 'anthology of images' (Sontag 1977: 3): it creates a new foundational unit for the digital archive – the 'info-pixel' (Foster 1996). To borrow Heidegger's term (without necessarily endorsing the premises of his whole analysis of modern technology), the photograph loses its object status and becomes a 'standing-reserve', valued solely as an arrangement of constituent elements for the purpose of a further deployment in a potentially endless succession of recontextualizations: 'Everywhere everything is ordered to stand by, to be immediately on hand, indeed to stand there just so that it may be on call for a further ordering.' (1993: 320). This drive to excavate the very graphic substance of the photograph not only manifests an archival logic but also a commercial one. It makes possible a significant expansion in the range of chargeable exchanges immanent to each image: a photograph may be multiply resold for use intact, and once it loses its integrity as a traditionally licensed image (say, for reasons of fashion) it can be recycled as a royalty-free image to be mined for its retrievable parts.

Yet the centrality of the info-pixel as the archival unit of the digital visual database necessitates the vigorous reanimation of (never dormant) artistic discourses and commercial practices on behalf of image integrity. And the insistence on the integrity of the rights-protected stock image is also continuous with the commercial and aesthetic logic of pre-digital stock. Like the dynamic of the standing-reserve to which it is opposed, it builds on the tension mentioned in previous chapters between generic recyclability and the need for stock images to compete with the singular, personally attributable images of top assignment photographers. That is why mainstream super-agencies continue to promote their mass of generic content along with the selected work of 'brand' photographers who have reputations outside the stock business (see, for example, the stress on 'world renowned photographers' in 'Launch of New Tony Stone Images Catalogue', Getty Images Press Release, 18/7/99). In fact, the renewed emphasis on formal singularity and the centrality of the individual photographer has itself taken the shape of a stock agency: Photonica (www. photonica.com). Founded in Tokyo in 1987, Photonica began its international expansion with the opening of an office in New York in 1990. According to Miller, the agency represents the stock industry's 'avant-garde' wing: 'The imagery is highly specific rather than generic, and the style foregrounds the signature style of individual photographers' (Miller 1999: 129). Promoting abstract forms, highly specific content, unusual cropping and camera angles, non-conventional use of focus and colour, and above all emphasizing the individual 'signature' styles of selected photographers (its website is organized around the work of individual photographers rather than by 'subject' or 'concept'), it has created a market for photographs that are definitively opposed to the aesthetic of the generic image.[16] Its success has led to the increasing production of 'photonica-like' images by the large mainstream agencies (Miller 1999: 129; BAPLA Directory 1998/9: 105).

In one sense, Photonica represents an oppositional tendency at the heart of stock photography, or embodies – ironically in corporate form – the values and interests of the artisanal culture of production described in Chapter 3. These values resist the dominance of corporate formula through a discourse of photographic creativity that privileges personal artistic autonomy and authenticity. Moreover, Photonica opposes generic images with photographs that fail the 'concept' test proposed by photographer David Arky: they are 'unsuccessful stock images', in that they 'do not have a clear metaphorical application . . . they are more complex and challenging' (*Photo Expo East '98*: 30/10/98). Interpreted more cynically, however, Photonica's strategy is simply exemplary brand positioning: working out what the stock industry lacks and represses, and then creating a stock agency to supply it: on-demand, unconventional, elusive and mystifying, individual and always 'artistic' images. Such a strategy is particularly effective when one considers that the primary clients of stock agencies are sophisticated cultural specialists with their own powerful 'creative' and 'artistic' agendas and identities. Specifically, Photonica's 'artistic' pretensions serve these clients' aspirations to cultural legitimacy while its oppositional stance toward mainstream stock photography matches their cultivated rhetoric of subversion and difference (Lash 1990).

The emphasis on image integrity and artistic vision, and its opposition to graphic substance and merely technical competence, also serves an important function within the system of labour relations that characterizes the contemporary stock industry. It suggests the emergence of a two-tier hierarchy among photographers: a small group of relatively well-treated 'stars' who can be marketed, along with their photographs, to high-fee-paying cultural intermediaries in advertising and graphic design, and a far larger number of anonymous photographers serving the RF sector and their broader, low-fee-paying, markets. As I mentioned earlier, photographers working as freelancers in traditional stock contractually receive around 50 per cent of the income from non-digital domestic sales of their images. In contrast, RF photographers are entitled to about 10 per cent of sales revenue: the actual amounts received allow them to make a living, according to industry management, because of the sheer volume of sales in a mass market. These percentages are set and precariously maintained within a context of increasing professional uncertainty regarding future industry trends that will directly affect livelihoods, and especially against a background of strained relations between photographers and many agencies, particularly the powerful corporate giants of the visual content industry.

Anxious for the rights of 'average' photographers (Scanlon's 'technicians'), the ASMP (American Society of Media Photographers), which represents most US stock photographers, involved itself in a very public conflict with PACA (Picture Agency Council of America), the US stock industry's principal trade association, over PACA's alleged encouragement of business practices and contractual agreements that are unfair to photographers ('An Open Letter to PACA', ASMP Press Release, 29/4/99, www.asmp.org).[17] Confirming some of the ASMP's worst fears, the largest super-agencies have begun to challenge the 50 per cent figure for traditional stock, strategically using the question of technology in order to reallocate revenue. Arguing that photographers benefit from the new markets opened up by digital technologies while the agencies bear the financial burden of capital investment in those same technologies, Getty's Tony Stone Images reduced commissions for domestic digital sales from 50 per cent to 40 per cent in September 1998 (*PDN*, 10/98: 23–5).[18] This reduction is all the more severe when we consider that it refers to the commissions actually specified in photographers' contracts: according to the ASMP, as much as 23 per cent of sales revenue can still be deducted to cover marketing and other costs, leaving the photographer with relatively little ('ASMP's Stock Survey Results – May 1999', ASMP Press Release, www.asmp.org). Hence through their position as the gateway to new markets and also as a major corporate expense, digital technologies have become sources of friction as well as tactical weapons in the power relations between photographers and agencies, affecting the industry and its products not only as a direct result of their particular capacities regarding the photographic image, but also through the financial and organizational structures to which they are tied. It is these structures that are at the centre of attention in my final chapter.

Notes

1. The term 'visual content industry' is increasingly in use among stock photography professionals, especially those associated with super-agencies such as Corbis and Getty.
2. William Mitchell (1991) exemplifies the sophisticated end of the utopian spectrum, arguing, for instance, that digital technologies are ideal critical devices for deconstructing the assumptions behind photographic objectivity. Among his chief problems, outlined by Robins (1996) and Lister (1997), is that his characterization of pre-digital photography is based on a very selective view of the medium which assumes that it is primarily defined by the values of documentary realism. This problem is echoed in my claim that stock photography (and advertising photography in general) are rhetorical and performative practices which have always been at some remove from the discourse of photographic objectivity. See Chapter 4 and below.
3. Available at www.apa.org, the survey is by no means conclusive. It is based on 164 returned surveys, representing roughly 25 per cent of APA members. Additionally, not all APA members shoot stock images (according to the survey 9 per cent of average income comes from stock-usage fees, as opposed to 81 per cent from assignments), and there are plenty of US-based stock photographers who are not APA members. However, in the absence of more concrete and comprehensive data, it does offer some useful indications about professional trends in US advertising photography as a whole.
4. I have dealt with some of these claims in previous chapters.
5. In all fairness to Batchen, he himself neither rejoices nor laments, since he does not argue that digital technologies are causing a fundamental alteration in photography's identity. Rather, he stresses that the representation/reality dichotomy is a central problem and anxiety at work in photography from (and before) its inception. See Batchen 1998: 22–4; 1997.
6. For a broader discussion of media technologies and enchantment, see Silverstone (1999: 21–2).
7. John Lund, however, was at the centre of a row that showed just how much – or little – control photographers actually have, providing an

illuminating example of the trauma caused by digital image-manipulation technologies to traditional conceptions of authorship and image
integrity. One of Lund's photographs was licensed for use to Fat Cat
Digital, a digital retouching company run by two photographers. The
company, according to Lund's agent Richard Steedman at The Stock
Market, then 'tampered with the image. It's been digitally altered in a
sloppy or haphazard way. How a couple of professional photographers
would allow this to happen to someone's work is so indecent, so unfeel-
ing . . . You can't take an artist's work and denigrate it' (PDNewswire,
PDN 7/12/2000).

8.   This article was unfortunately removed from the Corbis website in late
     1999, and I have been unable to find an alternative source for it. Karen
     Akiyama does not appear on the current list of senior Corbis employees.

9.   The example of advertising provides us with a clue to the difficulties of
     making any absolute separation between visual and verbal spheres. The
     development of professional careers and expertise based on an institu-
     tional separation of the visual and verbal is evident in the creation of
     two distinct functions, copywriters (verbal specialists) and art directors
     (visual specialists), which at critical periods in advertising's history have
     apparently been in competition for status and power (see Marchand
     (1985: 149–56) on the impact of photography on the 'decisive triumph
     of art over copy' (153) in 1930s US advertising; Mort (1996) and Nixon
     (1997) on the struggles within British advertising in the 1980s). However,
     since the 1960s the key creative unit in the advertising firm has been the
     creative pair: a copywriter and art director working together. Hence the
     'fusion of verbal and visual expertise in equal work partnerships stands
     at the core of work with symbols in advertising' (Hirota 1995: 329).
     Within these partnerships the tradition of bouncing ideas around in a
     kind of purposeful free association often leads to the dissolution of the
     very visual-verbal distinction upon which such partnerships are ostens-
     ibly based: 'the established roles of art director and writer collapse, with
     the art director freely suggesting copy and the writer imagining sets,
     props, and other visual details' (Ibid.: 334). What emerges from this
     collapse – the resulting 'product' – is the 'concept': the central symbolic
     theme linking the product to its target audience.

10. These are also the two pillars of the digital promotion of images. How-
     ever, most stock agencies and clients still rely heavily on conventional
     printed catalogues (*Graphic Design USA*, 9/98: 79–80). I would specu-
     late that this has something to do with the different purposes for which
     habitual modes of seeing are deployed, as well as the specific advantages
     (portability, tactility, breadth of access) still retained by print. One

technologically oriented designer I spoke to, for example, emphasized that he uses the promotional CD-ROMs issued by agencies when he knows exactly what kind of image he is looking for, but still prefers to flick through the printed catalogue in order to get a general overview of what's on offer (interview with Ilan Peeri, Peeri Communications, Tel Aviv, 10/12/98).

11. E-commerce does not include digital delivery on CD, so the total figure for digital distribution for Getty is actually higher. The large growth in Getty's e-commerce sales between the last two quarters of 2001 is explained in the press release by the launching of a new website in October of that year.

12. In other words, royalty-free embodies a pay-per-image principle, in contrast to rights-protected stock which embodies a pay-per-use principle. However, 'royalty-free' isn't necessarily royalty-free: almost all royalty-free producers place restrictions on the rights of users. In particular, the fine print of royalty-free 'terms and conditions' clauses usually prohibits 'items for resale', which means that while the images can be used to promote products they cannot always be incorporated into products (including other images) which are then sold, because this effectively involves the resale of the images. See '"Rights-Protected" vs. "Royalty Free" – Which is for you? An Insider's Essential Guide to Making the Right Choice', Comstock 1998, www.comstock.com; *Photo Source News*, Front Page News, 'Will It Survive? Commercial Stock Photography', 1/98, www.photosource.com).

13. Variations in price are primarily determined by the number of images on a disc and by their resolution, measured in pixels per inch and file-size (mega-bytes). High-resolution-image collections are usually aimed at professional designers rather that at the broad consumer market. Similarly, the price of individual RF images bought from websites also increases with resolution and file-size: small, low-resolution images are often available free to registered website users for use in 'comps', mock-ups and draft versions.

14. The cultural distinction is detectable in the names given to the brands: Comstock's rights-protected division was initially called *Comstock Classic*, while its royalty-free division was for a time named *Comstock Klips*, the use of the letter 'K' being not a little reminiscent (perhaps deliberately so) of other brand names in related fields – 'Kall Kwick' copying, for instance.

15. Comstock, unlike most of the other large agencies, can perhaps afford to be so forthright in its characterization of the majority of photographers, its own included, as mere 'technicians'. Rather than promoting

images supplied by copyright-holding freelancers (who frequently need to be cultivated and humoured, despite their overall dependence), it mainly relies on images shot by in-house staff photographers who are paid a wage. Comstock owns the copyright to these photographs.

16.   Many industry observers would argue that from the very late 1990s onward Tony Stone Images, rebranded as 'Stone' within the Getty group of companies, has also pioneered innovative imagery and pursued new directions in catalogue design.

17.   Just to indicate the general drift of photographer–agency relations, the ASMP's 1999 survey of stock photographers shows that while 61 per cent of photographers report no change over the past five years in their share of sales, 25 per cent report a decrease (14 per cent report an increase). Furthermore, 25 per cent report an increase in deductions from payments to photographers that were made to cover agency costs, with less than 1 per cent reporting a decrease (74 per cent reported no change). See 'ASMP's Stock Survey Results – May 1999', ASMP Press Release, www.asmp.org.

18.   This *Photo District News* article included an interview with Getty CEO Jonathan Klein on the question of photographers' income. Klein's remarks received a scathing response from the executive director of the ASMP ('ASMP Executive Director's Letter to PDN on TSI and Erosion of Photographer's Revenues', ASMP Press Release, 3/12/98, www.asmp.org).

The Realm of the Info-Pixel: From Stock Photography to the Visual Content Industry

Industry and Empire

Why has 'the visual content industry' been so named, and what is its central ethos and governing tendency? We can begin to answer these questions by focusing on the stock photography super-agencies which lead it. Among these, Corbis is probably the best known outside the industry, doubtless because of its association with Microsoft's Bill Gates. In addition to its stock photography and royalty-free brands it owns the reproduction rights to the Bettmann archive, which includes the United Press International (UPI) photo library and extensive material from Reuters and Agence France Press, as well as the digital reproduction rights to much of the world's fine art ('Company Overview', Corbis, 9/98, www.corbis.com; see also Batchen 1998).

However, it is Getty Images PLC that probably provides the best example of how marketing-led industry consolidation interacts with digital technologies. Prior to September 1999, Getty Images had employed an aggressive acquisition and technological development strategy to become the largest of the super-agencies. It owned one of the biggest stock-photography agencies (Tony Stone Images), one of the leading 'high-end' royalty-free brands (Photo-Disc), EyeWire (royalty-free audio and graphics for designers), Energy Film Library (stock film footage), Art.com, which sells art ('Monet, van Gogh, Picasso, Herb Ritts and Robert Mapplethorpe') and 'art-related products' on the internet,[1] leading agencies specializing in sports (Allsport), news and reportage (Liaison), and celebrity photography (Online USA), and the Hulton Deutsch Collection – bought in 1996 and subsequently renamed the Hulton Getty Picture Collection – which comprises 15 million images from the major

British newspaper and press archives of the nineteenth and twentieth centuries ('Company Overview', www.gettyimages.com). Getty's principal aims are to digitize saleable content and as many of its transactions as possible (emphasizing especially on-line promotion and sales, or 'e-commerce'), to target existing markets with specific 'brands' while allowing for the profitable integration of content from diverse archives and agencies, and to open up new (especially internet-based) markets, frequently through joint ventures (e.g. 'Getty Images' PhotoDisc Inks Deal with Amazon.com', Getty Press Release 27/4/99; 'Getty Images' Art.com Partners with Key Women's Web Sites', Getty Images Press Release, 3/6/99). Digitization provides the opportunity for multiple promotion of the same content to several ostensibly distinct markets: in particular, the vast reserves of the Hulton Getty Picture Collection can be mobilized to serve traditional editorial sectors, nostalgic marketing and advertising campaigns, and on-line art consumers (see, for example, 'Getty Images Broadens Access to Hulton Getty Collection Through Art.com', Getty Images Press Release, 25/5/99).

In September 1999, Getty stunned the industry by announcing that it was acquiring The Image Bank, one of its most venerable competitors and arguably the stock industry's most famous 'brand', for $183 million, adding huge global contemporary stock photography and stock footage agencies, a leading royalty-free company, a fine-art photography agency, a film-footage archive, and the largest North American historical archive of still images to its already immense resources ('Getty Images to Acquire The Image Bank: Acquisition to Bring New Opportunities for Online Distribution and Brand Leverage', Getty Images Press Release, 21.9.99). Responses in the industry were mixed, with some emphasizing the extent of Getty's debt as a result of the acquisition and its pressing need to please shareholders by showing immediate profits, further increasing the downward pressure on photographers' percentages of sales. Others praised its scope and vision: 'This creates a monster with global reach' commented David Moffly, former president of stock agency FPG International. 'It creates huge synergies and economies of scale' ('Getty to Buy the Image Bank', PDN 10/99, www.pdn-online.com). Digital technologies, and predictions regarding their most lucrative future developments, were crucial to Getty's strategy: 'The Image Bank's footage business is particularly strong because that agency has invested heavily in film storage, retrieval and distribution technology. And footage is expected to become a major growth area in the stock business as Internet bandwidth improves' ('Getty to Buy the Image Bank', PDN 10/99).

This was, however, only the beginning, for in February 2000 Getty announced that it was acquiring its largest competitor, Visual Communications Group (VCG), for $220 million. This act of consolidation, if not of industry domination, exemplified the way in which such developments in the stock industry were only a part of broader consolidating tendencies across media firms. For the announcement of VCG's sale coincided with the (unsuccessful) attempt by its owner, United News and Media PLC, to merge with Carlton Communications – momentarily threatening to form one of the largest UK media conglomerates – and reflected a new focus on 'core' mass-media businesses (especially television). VCG had been performing poorly in recent years, largely as a consequence, according to industry observers, of underinvestment in new digital and web-based technologies ('United News and Media to Unload VCG', *PDN* 2/2000, www.pdn-pix.com; 'Getty Images Acquires Visual Communications Group', Getty Images PLC Press Release, 28/2/2000, www.gettyimages. com), but the acquisition turned Getty into a behemoth, providing it with an additional four major US and European stock agencies – FPG International (USA), Telegraph Colour Library (UK), Bavaria Bildagentur (Germany) and Pix (France) – several speciality image collections (fine art, celebrity images, space, natural history) and a royalty-free company. Ironically, in the light of this sudden and overpowering incorporation of two of the four 'super-agencies' by a third, the hope of resistance to prospective domination by Getty was now lodged in Corbis, itself no mean consolidator. As Richard Steedman, the president of The Stock Market (a large commercial US stock agency), explained upon its acquisition by Corbis in May 2000: 'It's nice to have that support [of Corbis] to fight against the Getty organization' ('Corbis to Acquire the Stock Market', *PDN* 5/2000, www.pdn-pix.com).

Content as Information

In this context the introduction of the phrase 'visual content industry', for which Getty is chiefly responsible, can be seen to express three of the industry's main structural tendencies. First, that although it makes extensive use of digital visual technologies it is to be distinguished from those sectors that specialize in the production of such technologies. In other words, it is a *culture industry*, and ultimately defines its own identity and tasks in cultural and commercial terms: the creation and circulation of valuable and relevant symbolic goods. The visual content industry is not therefore chiefly concerned with technological 'hardware', except instrumentally, as a means to the production and sale of images, and as a catalyst for increased demand. As Getty Images CEO Jonathan Klein explains: in the future 'demand for visual content of all kinds will increase, for two reasons: we are all becoming more visually literate; technology is creating distribution mechanisms that demand more images – which in turn are making people more visually literate' ('Content in the 21st

Century', *Photo Expo East '98*, 31/10/98). Klein's second point – the demand for still images created by new technologies – is amply illustrated in the case of multimedia products: 'a typical "electronic book" could use 1,000 stills along with video and sound clips. Video games need still-image backgrounds, educational software uses still examples of situations or locations, and training products use stills for both' ('Licensing Still Images: Basic Information for Multimedia Producers', Index Stock, 4/6/2000, www.indexstock.com/about/publications.htm).

The second tendency of the visual content industry is its centrifugal, 'imperialistic' trajectory: its dispersal of increasing numbers of products to more and more consumers across the world, to larger and more lucrative markets. Klein's projection starkly reveals the multiple roles of digital technologies in this dynamic: delivery tool, source of demand for images, and socializing agent of viewers.

Yet the third tendency made manifest by Klein's analysis is probably the most significant: the dismantling of the technical boundaries between previously distinct media (photography, painting and drawing, film, video) and their convergence and mutual convertability. This centripetal dynamic, this adamant ingathering of 'all kinds of visual content', is of course intimately related to the militant universality of digital code which transforms the Babel of incommensurate symbolic forms into a miraculous numerical equivalence (Binkley 1993: 92–121; Lister 1997: 254–5). But such an ingathering is not merely a technical feat – it is also, and perhaps primarily, an institutional and discursive transformation. This is because of a radical disjunction between the moments of image production and later moments of distribution and reproduction, brought about by what can be described as the 'corporatization' of almost all photographic archives. In the past it was relatively safe to assume that the photographers and news agencies who produced news and documentary images maintained ownership and control over their reproduction, and that there was a direct organizational and professional connection between production and distribution. This link was in fact based on a separation, both discursive and institutional, between historical and photojournalistic photographers and archives, fine-art photographers and archives, and those working in advertising and marketing. The distinction ensured a certain continuity of communicative milieu between production and subsequent reproduction – a photojournalistic image may have been reproduced in a history book, for example, but very rarely in an advert – that guaranteed the validity and constancy of contextual assumptions upon which the interpretation of photographs conventionally depended.

It comes as no surprise that these boundaries have disintegrated. Or rather, that the domains of historical and photojournalistic photography, and also of fine-art photography, have been enfolded within the tender embrace of the master discourses of marketing and advertising under the aegis of the visual content industry. Admittedly, the connection between the production and distribution of photographs has been increasingly tenuous since the emergence of photography as a media profession, but these latest trends, with the acquisition of historical archives and exclusive reproduction rights by transnational corporations that specialize in 'visual content', signifies the absolute decontextualization and abstraction of images. Thus not only are the distinctions between media erased, so are the differences in the values and purposes associated with different types of photographs. The visual content industry converts the complex material and symbolic specificity of images into an abstract universal, '*content*', severing each image from the context of its initial production, circulation and consumption and reinscribing it within the overarching system of commercial exchange. Such a reinscription parallels, on the discursive and institutional plane, the abstraction and equivalence of forms achieved by digitization on the technical plane. And it makes it almost impossible for viewers to trace the relations of power back through to the initial context of production, to determine who is exercising the authority to represent the world in this particular way.

This deployment of the word 'content' parallels in important ways the prevalence of the term 'information' in all manner of contemporary discourses: academic and scientific, industrial and commercial, governmental, legal, administrative and journalistic – even artistic. In fact, I would argue that 'information' is the paradigmatic term here, setting the semantic and conceptual framework within which new meanings for other words such as 'content' and 'knowledge' come to be activated – new meanings which both enable and limit certain understandings of cultural activity, and the practices to which these understandings are tied.

So what can we glean from the use of 'information' as a pre-eminent characterization of 'knowledge' in a specific milieu, and how can it help us to grasp the cultural shifts that the term 'visual content' portends? Geoffrey Nunberg, in an important essay on the subject, argues that the generally abstract meaning which 'information' carries in such phrases as 'the information age' is a relatively new sense of the term, which refers 'not to "knowledge . . . concerning some particular fact, subject or event", but rather to a kind of intentional substance that is present in the world, a sense that is no longer closely connected to the use of the verb "inform", anchored in particular speech acts' (1996: 110). This intentional substance has a number of important qualities: it is indifferent to the medium in which it resides and to the kind of representation it embodies; it is quantified and atomized, allowing for discrete, measurable pieces to be broken off and transported while preserving their (numerically calculated) value. Information therefore *appears* as an abstract universal, without history or geography, that is separable both from the material practices and media of its production and from the communities of 'receivers' (one can no longer specify 'readers', 'viewers' or 'listeners') for whom it may have been intended. It subsumes all particularities and maintains autonomy from their specific contexts, ensuring its eminent and uninhibited transferability between temporally and spatially connected points. Thus depicted, information – as a conceptual reification of the media in which it is inscribed – is not simply the technical product of computer technologies and digital code, but is an institutional and discursive accomplishment of the highest order. And its characteristics, as Dan Schiller (1994) describes in great detail, are eminently adapted to the needs of commodification.[2] Indeed, in its symbolic autonomy, universal transferability and context-free value, 'information' aspires to the ideal condition of money itself.

'Knowledge', in contrast, is frequently interpreted more holistically as inherently connected to particular realms of inquiry (such as 'scientific knowledge') and as still connoting, in some measure, such unquantifiable and non-transferable notions as 'understanding': it is not free-floating but connected to the qualities of the one who knows (thus 'human knowledge' defines a field in relation to both a subject and an object). Yet even here the term is undergoing the same kind of reifying processes manifested in what we might call 'the informational model': the information society is also a 'knowledge economy'; those skilled in tasks associated with mental rather than manual capacities are 'knowledge workers', and the British Film Institute, I was amazed to discover, currently employs a senior executive with the title 'Head of Knowledge'. With information as the guiding model, similar decontextualizations are befalling other terms: Andrew Saunders, Vice-President of Getty Images PLC, is also 'Director of Imagery'.

As I have suggested, 'content', in its deployment in the phrase 'visual content industry', seems to share in these characteristics of information, qualities of transferability, atomization and manipulability that are based on a new unit of storage and representation, the 'info-pixel'. What does the emphasis on 'content', abstracted, flattened and universalized, leave unstated? First, material form: the structural intertwining of a cultural product's physical properties and representational proclivities, enabling its emergence and circulation as a physical object and its intelligibility and resonance as a symbolic one. The informational model of 'content' conceals the fact that cultural products are always forms *in process*, not just symbolically but materially. The nature of that process, the fluidity or viscosity of its flow, so to speak, depends upon the second factor 'left unstated' in the discourse on content: the networks of cultural, technical and institutional power which make materialization possible. These networks – of media organizations, technologies, professional groups, key individuals, legal and financial structures – manifest, among other things, the power to make a product open or closed, to mine it for its retrievable parts or declare it inviolate, to treat it as recyclable, transferable, detachable 'content' (or even 'information') or as a singular 'composition' or 'work', to deem an image worthy of digitization or not, and above all to fix the technical, legal, commercial and aesthetic practices which generate images. Just as abstract 'content' conceals the potential fluidity of a cultural product's 'becoming', so it also hides the web of complex determinations that always governs the productive process and stabilizes it sufficiently to create a coherent yet transferable 'being'. For if the abstract universal 'content' – the informational product of visual digital technologies – is subject to virtually infinite mutability and transportability, how can it be stabilized sufficiently in order to be owned? If digital media separate symbolic forms from any necessary connection to a material or physical 'vehicle' (except, of course, the computer), if they are designed to make such a separation or 'dematerialization' an easily performed actuality for all who possess them, how can they support concentrations of property and power? In other words, digital technologies and the practices in which they are embedded appear to destabilize not just traditional media technologies, but the power which their control can grant.

It has become almost a cliché to claim that information 'wants' to be free. In reply to this I would say simply that information 'asks' to be chained. It has to be controlled institutionally and ideologically if it is to grant control.[3] The more that photographs, films, illustrations and painting become easily interchangeable and alterable content – by virtue of technical capacity and cultural convention – so the need to control exactly *who* can transfer and alter *what* becomes ever more crucial to those seeking to profit from content's sale. Hence the recourse to traditional discourses of cultural authority, especially of romantic authorship, and hence the enormous concern over unauthorized image usage, on-line security, copyright and reproduction rights that is bound up with a broader expansion in intellectual property law to cover areas previously outside the property system (Boyle 2002).

The informational model of visual 'content' elides the differences between media, contexts of production and material forms in the name of (technical and commercial) transferability and mutability while at the same time reanimating the need for stabilizing practices. The precarious organizational achievement of this delicate equilibrium between culturally productive instability and commercially secure stability can be detected in the corporate structures and acquisition policies of companies like Getty and Corbis. These clearly show that the main players in the visual content industry are attempting to encompass and integrate types of 'content' that are associated with distinct media, such as photography, graphics and illustration, fine art, animation, film and video, understanding them all as technically and commercially equivalent communicative tools. This does not mean to say that distinctions no longer exist within these organizations, but rather that they are increasingly designed around perceived differences in client needs rather than differences between media or contexts of production.

For example, Getty's operations, as they are presented to potential clients on their website, are currently divided into 'Getty Images Creative', aimed at 'creative professionals' in advertising, marketing, design and new media, and Gettyworks.com, which provides communication materials (photographic images, illustrations, music, sound effects, movie clips, fonts) to small and medium-sized businesses. The relationship of these client gateways to the various archives and organizations now owned by Getty, in which the featured products are actually manufactured, is one of partial subsumption. On the one hand these sites of storage and manufacture are defined as brands whose products cut across the two client gateways, and can appear in both: hence they are characterized by transferability and mutability. On the other hand the residual requirements of branding do gesture toward the contextual specificity of production: the 'original contemporary photography' of 'Stone', art directed and devised with 'creative intelligence' is positioned as slightly more upmarket and avant-garde than that of The Image Bank, which is described as a 'global leader in mainstream contemporary stock photography' (note the absence of the term 'stock photography' in the description of Stone) ('Getty Images Corporate Profile: About Us. Imagery', 2002, www.gettyimages.com). Discourses of artistic distinction are associated with specific brands insofar as they are likely to stabilize and promote the value of the 'content' purveyed, a distinction which simultaneously goes against the grain of the equivalence and abstraction characteristic of 'information' and at the same time signals the ingathering of all content and its instant availability according to the primary criterion of distinction: the client's present needs.

This orientation toward a primary distinction tells us one more thing about 'content'. It is that, however abstract and autonomous it appears, *content is never just content*; it possesses intentionality and directionality: it is always 'content *for*'. This means that at a fundamental level 'content', to be recognizable and conceivable as such within the digitized visual content industry, must be distinguishable from 'non-content', and it is precisely the absence or nonvalidity of a potential client which designates the latter category.[4]

There is, finally, another key limitation on content and its informational abstraction, transferability and mutability, which is performed by the term 'visual'. This term provides a way of enclosing and stabilizing the potential universality of content without having to specify media or contexts of production: it qualifies one abstraction with another. 'Visual' is a slippery word when combined with 'content' (and for that matter with 'culture', 'communication' and 'media'). It is both explicitly expansive and furtively exclusive: it embraces all the products of 'visual' media (photographs, film, video, illustrations, paintings) with one major exception – written or printed text. In other words, 'visual content' really means primarily 'pictorial content', only it can't say so, because that would be tantamount to anchoring the abstraction of 'content' in a particular symbolic form, hence endangering its informational qualities. In order to avert the threat of restricting informational 'content' to the content *of* pictures (inviting questions about where it comes from, how it was made), content is anchored *perceptually*. Such a stabilization grants content the ideological benefits which have accrued to the sense of sight in modernity: the sense of naturally given plenitude, unmediated directness and imaginative command which 'vision' enjoys.

Why should the visual content industry be so wary of texts? Because of the dialectic of information mutability and control that I mentioned before. Content may be abstracted and generalized, but its control requires some basic industrial operations, notably the specification of fundamental units that compose the product's material structure (the info-pixel), the delineation of units of 'intelligibility' which allow professionals and clients to recognize what the product *is* at given moments in its development (the image), and direction-ality (who is this content *for*). Texts fall outside the definition because to include them would expand the category of 'content' to such an extent as to render it meaningless. (The same thing might be said to have happened to 'culture'.) Texts are therefore at best supplementary tools for organizing, retrieving and promoting visual content, and at worst (as in the strictures of Comstock) a barrier, an impediment to the direct encounter with the universal language of images.

I have already shown how this attempt to exclude words is bound to fail, and how central certain kinds of image–word relationship are to the *production* of stock images (and not just to their subsequent organization and distribu-tion) – both within pre-digital stock and in the contemporary visual content industry (Chapters 3 and 7 respectively). Texts and photographs work together in the image repertoire as part of a generative and self-monitoring process of image creation, auditioning and performance – a process whose coherence and integrity is in constant need of stabilization. If, then, the image-repertoire is increasingly guided by an informational model of content, however radically incomplete and fissured it may be, what might be the repercussions of such a model for social power and cultural experience? Of course, it is impossible to predict all of the potential implications of these cultural, structural-financial and technological interactions. However, a number of interlinked dynamics do seem to be emerging. I will first consider these dynamics as they relate to questions of social and cultural power, before concluding with an attempt to outline their representational and ethical dimensions.

Questions of Power

Centralisation of distribution

'There is a detectable tendency for the new media to create a society with an excluded middle, in which . . . the mediating centre, the mid-sized firm and indeed the nation state are being squeezed out of contention by the forces of the large and the small, the global and the local' (Silverstone 1999: 26). Validating Silverstone's claim, medium-sized stock agencies are finding it hard to compete with the delivery systems, costs (thanks to economies of scale) and marketing power of the super-agencies on the one hand, and the prices of royalty-free companies and specialist capacities of niche agencies on the other. As Superstock president Gary Elsner recently admitted: 'Any midsized company in this industry is in a pickle now because of competition from royalty-free providers and mega-agencies' (Superstock Cuts Prices', *PDN*, 3/2000, www.pdn-pix.com). Niches can include not just subjects such as 'golf' or 'medical', but also 'group' niches, such as women's agencies and lesbian and gay stock libraries. However, some also doubt the ability of even specialist agencies to distribute their images to a large market without the aid of the super-agencies, especially because of the high costs of digitization (scanning, storage and data management, key-wording, website creation and maintenance, security, etc.): Getty Images invested $13 million in digitization in 1998 out of a total capital expenditure of almost $28 million (*PDN* 10/98: 23). This in turn threatens to restrict the choices realistically available to clients as well as to photographers looking for representation.

Control over history

Digitization has its benefits, but it also has its burdens. 'Embracing its role as a cultural steward', Corbis announced, in April 2001, that it was planning to build an underground 'state-of-the-art, sub-zero film preservation facility in western Pennsylvannia' to house the 17 million-image Bettmann Archive, and the archives of United Press International (UPI), International News Photos and Acme (Corbis Press Release, 16 April 2001). According to the press release the decision was motivated entirely by the need to conserve a national historical treasure: the images are deteriorating, and their digitization, while proceeding apace, would take time to complete. In the interim period it was essential to preserve the remaining images.

Others in the industry (and elsewhere) have been a little more cynical about Corbis's motives. When the announcement was made around 225,000 images from the Bettmann archive had already been digitized. This constituted less than 2 per cent of the total that was to be consigned to subterranean cold storage. True, this is partly a matter of time: high-standard digitization performed with due care for the original image can be a lengthy operation. But it is also very much a matter of money:

> Most estimates suggest that it costs around $10 to digitize a single image, and as much again to retouch, resample and catalogue the file. If those numbers are right, then Corbis has spent around $4.5 million digitizing just a small fraction of the Bettmann Archive, and would probably face a total bill comfortably in excess of $250 million.
>
> (Jon Tarrant, 'Stand By Your Scan', *PIX* 7(3) in
> *PDN* XX1(6), June/July 2001: 25)

Of course, corporations are generally inclined to spend this amount of money only if it seems likely that they will profit in the long run. But, according to others involved in the commercial digitization of photographic archives, only a small proportion of images generate the majority of sales: 'I would be very selective about what I digitized: you're probably going to make 80–85 percent of your sales on fewer than 10,000 images – maximum 20,000 images' (Russell Glenister, President of Image 100, quoted in Tarrant, 'Stand By Your Scan'). So it is manifestly in the interests of Corbis and other corporations in a similar position (most obviously Getty) *not* to digitize the historical archives they have purchased, but rather to make available only a selection of the most apparently 'saleable' photographs.

Other commercial constraints and imperatives also impact upon the question of access to non-digitized archives. An overall downturn in the general economic environment, coupled with policies that prioritize investment in digitization over continued analogue operations, have led to staff cuts at Corbis that affect print and transparency distribution, with customers being directed as much as possible to use images from the digital archive ('Layoffs at Corbis', *PDN* XX1(3) March 2001: 16–17). So although questions of conservation versus public access have longed plagued archivists, the labour intensity of preserving, accessing and distributing analog images compared with that of digitized images (which can be searched for and distributed on-line) means that even when non-digital archives *are* preserved (as in Corbis's new facility), customers may be enthusiastically *dis*couraged from using them.

What kind of impact will such 'cultural stewardship' have on our visual culture and our historical memory? Writing about the relationship between film and history, Anton Kaes has argued that:

the sheer mass of historical images transmitted by today's media weakens the link between public memory and personal experience. The past is in danger of becoming a rapidly expanding collection of images, easily retrievable but isolated in time and space, available in an eternal present by pushing a button on the remote control. (1990: 120)

This is persuasive up to a point, although the problem it outlines is really a state of luxury which we have not yet achieved. For the argument – about the separation of an image-based public memory from personal experience – automatically assumes the *rapid expansion* of easily available historical images.[5] Whereas what actually seems to be happening, if the example of Corbis is any guide, is a significant *contraction* in the availability of these images.

PDN's Jon Tarrant makes the stakes fairly clear: 'the danger must be that only the most commercial images will be deemed worthy of electronic preservation. Thanks to digitisation, the age of the photograph as a pure commercial commodity is now here in a final and incontrovertible way' (Tarrant, Stand By Your Scan: 26). If, in the past, the logic of the commodity was manifested in external competition between different institutional and discursive forms of cultural authority, lodged *separately* in archives of images that were deemed to be of commercial value and archives deemed to be of historical or artistic value, that separation has disappeared. Or, more accurately, the distinction commercial/non-commercial has become thoroughly internalized – it has become the distinction between *content* and *non-content*. It has entered the historical archive, leading irrevocably to the conclusion that our image of history – the collective visual memory of the past that depends upon access to its images and their public dissemination – will be increasingly determined and constrained by the rhetorical needs of consumer advertising and marketing.

The Decreasing Power of Photographers vis-à-vis Agency Management

The financial and marketing clout of the super-agencies makes photographers extremely dependent upon them for exposure and sales. The new 'democracy' of the web doesn't appear to benefit photographers here, unless, again, they cater to specialist niches.[6] They can set up their own websites in competition with the big agencies, but without large marketing budgets and campaigns most potential customers won't know that they exist. This seems to be true of many industries on the web: 'without promotion, you're just a lemonade stand on the highway' says the head of one media conglomerate (Herman and McChesney 1997: 124). Searching the web using key words such as 'stock photography' calls up thousands of web-pages, so marketing becomes the key to attracting customers. As Jonathan Klein puts it 'the web is chaotic – therefore it is a natural place for aggregators' ('Content in the 21st Century', *Photo*

Expo East '98, 31/10/98; see also Jenn Shreve, 'Time to Take Stock, *PIX* 7(3) in *PDN* XX1(6), June/July 2001: 25). This means that while photographers are officially encouraged to be 'creative' and pursue their 'unique vision', they may have to conform more and more to a few house-styles, including, ironically, one that promotes a 'Photonica' look.

This closer adhesion to house-style is actually becoming increasingly institutionalized among higher-end agencies such as Getty's 'Stone' (formerly, Tony Stone) through the establishment of new working relationships between photographers and agencies. Rather than photographers submitting images for selection and inclusion in catalogues, catalogues are now being approached as coherent artistic projects with a unifying theme and style. For example, Stone's Catalogue *Meet Me* is described thus: 'The body: receptacle of mental, physical and emotional stimuli. Meet Me explores the effects of other people on our bodies'. Or *Organoteque*, which urges us to 'reconsider the play between flesh and technology. 1,800 new images render the ever more intimate twining of technology and human nature'. The making of these catalogues has involved the effective distribution of assignments by Stone to selected photographers, the selection of subject matter and concept by Stone creative personnel, the presence and active intervention of Stone stylists at the shoot itself.

This relatively new and still limited practice signals two important changes. First, it establishes the *direct* intervention of agencies in the primary materialization of the image, whereas in the past this would have been the prerogative of the photographer (albeit heavily influenced by previous catalogue images and the corporate discourse of 'success'). Stone tells photographers what to photograph and is involved in decisions on location or in the studio. Second, the source of 'creativity', the locus of cultural authority, is transferred in the very first instance from the photographer to the agency: the original creative concept, and much of the technical execution, is initiated and undertaken by Stone, with the 'high-end' photographer transformed into a well-paid, but manifestly commissioned and directed, technician.

Some of these changes represent a transition, at the most prestigious end of the stock system, to photographer–agency relationships that resemble the model used in commercial assignment photography rather than in traditional stock. It also fulfils the logic of 'branding' and industrialization already at work within the stock system since the rise of The Image Bank, extending it into the very depths of the image-production process: a Stone image is no longer one merely selected and marketed by Stone, but one recognizably made by Stone (and not by anyone else). Creativity passes from the personal identity and capacities (however constrained) of an individual to the identity and 'vision' of a corporation. It is still too early to say what effects this still nascent practice will have on artisanal and corporate discourses, and on representational practices and image diversity. However, coupled with the trend toward centralization and the sheer size and power of the super-agencies within the industry, it threatens a potential narrowing of subjects and stylistic options. Interestingly, one of the most promising areas of resistance to this potential narrowing can be found in the creative departments of companies like Stone itself, where discourses of experimentation and innovation are essential to the continual performance and reproduction of brand identity (Interview with Andrew Saunders, VP of Getty Images and Director of Imagery at Gettyone, 18/1/2001). How such a commitment to diversity and difference will fare in the long term, at the heart of a mainly conservative commercial industry, remains to be seen.

Globalization

The global reach and instantaneous distribution offered by on-line delivery systems threatens to alter the power relations between corporate headquarters (based in the United States or Europe) and representatives in non-Western cultures who distribute on their behalf. It means that – at least in theory – stock agencies can retain a global clientele without the expense of maintaining local offices or franchisees across several continents. Indeed, one of the chief fears of many local franchisees is that in an age of e-commerce, websites and instantaneous transactions they are an expensive irrelevance to global corporate strategy. While many industry insiders argue that there is no substitute for the culture-specific promotional and 'policing' (tracking unauthorized uses) tasks local offices undertake, on-line digital delivery increases concern about the relationship between globalization and the dominance of Western cultural perspectives and commercial interests.[7] And, with the possible exception of landscapes, digital 'enhancement' technologies may even aid the fabrication of 'non-Western' photographic images at (or near) corporate headquarters, should this prove cost-effective.

The limitations of image-diversity

As I mentioned earlier, stock's generally acknowledged rededication to 'quality' is due at least as much to cultural and commercial forces as to technological factors. In line with general corporate and cultural trends toward market differentiation and more complex and reflexive advertising imagery, the large stock agencies have diversified somewhat from the generic stereotypes of the 1970s and 1980s both to more abstract 'fine art' and conceptual images and to images that address ethnic minorities and other previously unrepresented groups (see Chapters 3 and 4).[8] Interestingly, digital technologies have the potential to augment and advance this limited diversification of content. The flexibility, accessibility and relative efficiency of digital delivery means that it has become easier and cheaper to distribute a diversity of images to a far greater range of users than previously. However, while 'such attempts *have* broadened the repertoire of stock imagery' (Miller 1999: 128, Miller's emphasis), they occur within a context whereby most of the photographers and management are still white heterosexual males who are frequently blind to the cultural distinctions and interpretations that their audiences take for granted.[9] Moreover, given the overall framework of advertising practices, almost all stock photographs need to address the tastes and enthusiasms of the relatively small percentage of the population with large disposable incomes (see Chapter 3). The upshot of this is that while images that use unconventional focus, cropping and lighting are now far more common than previously, the bulk of stock imagery has not changed very much at all. This was a recurring theme in a *Photo District News* survey of stock professionals who were asked to comment on 'The Look of Stock in the New Millennium' (*PDN* Showguide for *Photo Expo East '99*, 28–30/10/99: 18–28):

> In terms of content, what was good in 1900, good in 1930, good in 1999, is still going to be good in the year 2000, 2010, 2020. Relationships between people do not change . . . I put my hand on the shoulders of my sons in the same way my father did, and his father did.
>
> Jon Feingersh, stock photographer.

> In terms of content, we're rushing into the next century with images of people with cellulars and pagers, true. But images of Americana – the front porch, the tire swing – are ever more with us . . . The biggest change in stock today is not in content- which doesn't change much at all.
>
> Richard Steedman, president, The Stock Market.

> Best-selling images are those that very quickly convey a message. It's safe to say that the same concepts are always going to be popular: love, family, strength, success . . . Unfortunately, there are a finite amount of options.
>
> Paul Henning, consultant.

> 'It's fun to take chances, and I am getting great response from my newer stuff. But I think a smart photographer would still do some of the old tried-and-true shots. There's still a big market for straight and almost corny shots. Those are still my bread and butter.
>
> Michael Keller, photographer.

So, largely irrespective of the digital transformation, the forces for image uniformity – the relations of structural and financial dependence between photographers, agencies and clients, and the discursive and institutional priority of marketing and advertising – are as powerful today as they were in stock photography's 'classic' period. Digital technologies have shattered the ceiling on the *number* of images that the industry can produce and deliver, and have met cultural and aesthetic shifts with a limited diversification in the content, and more especially the style, of stock photographs. The increase in the quantity of images means that inevitably – and thankfully – some are new. But it also means much, much more of the same.

Questions of Ethics

What might be the ethical consequences of these dynamics? I would briefly suggest the following interconnected themes.

Exclusionary representational power

Like any archival system, including pre-digital stock photography, the visual content industry operates on an exclusionary basis. Its repertoire of images is selected, ordered and performed in accordance with the classificatory regimes employed by advertising and marketing discourse to specify meanings and target audiences (most fundamentally: class, gender, sexuality, ethnicity and age), and with these industries' almost pathological inability to comprehend social experience outside of or across sharply delineated normative categories (Turow 1997 and Chapter 4 above). As we have seen, such classificatory regimes function, like Sekula's 'shadow archive' both *honorifically* and *repressively* (Sekula 1989: 347): they define their 'inside', their archival integrity, in opposition to a constitutive 'outside' of possible materializations and identifications which are abjected – foreclosed or denied.[10]

The ethical question raised here is clearly connected to representational power: the inability of certain groups to control representations of themselves, or even to be represented at all. Such a concern is raised by any archival system: so what makes the visual content industry different? Indeed, the concentration of extensive and diverse archival material within a handful of transnational conglomerates, combined with their global reach and the universality of digital code, suggests that the age-old dream of a universal library, a uniquely non-exclusionary archive, is about to become a reality. However, this invocation of digital technology and the powers it seemingly bestows is at the heart of the problem: for the fabled technical universality of digital systems actually disguises the functioning of power in an industry structured and driven by commodity exchange, an industry that selects and orders images in terms of their saleability. The word 'content', so neutral and inclusive, is a key indicator of this concealment of exclusionary representational power through the magic of the binary code. And it is the claim of universality that is truly mystificatory here: for the visual content industry *is* universal, but mainly in the sense that money is: and money is one of the most potent excluders of all.

Loss of autonomy

Even as the visual content industry is fissured by – and profits from – discourses of artistic vision and originality that intersect with the 'artisanal' notion of creativity discussed in Chapter 3, its dynamics of power strongly suggest that it threatens the autonomy of individual photographers. To say that this is an ethical issue, one concerning the constitution of individuals as creative, reflexive subjects in relationships of mutual responsibility with others, is not to pretend that 'autonomy' is either a universal, trans-historical possibility, or that it has only recently come under threat. It is, however, to second Hal Foster's argument: 'For many of us autonomy is a bad word, a ruse in aesthetic discourse, a deception in ego psychology, and so on. We forget that autonomy is a diacritical term like any other, defined in relation to its opposite, that is, *subjection*' (1996: 117, my italics).

Representational Mastery and Experiential Depletion[11]

The visual content industry does, in several respects, empower viewers. It makes a vast number of images available to average income-earners, and gives them the technical and legal opportunity to alter those images and use them in works of personal creative expression. Such a form of empowerment, and particularly its unambiguous celebration, does come with a price however, and that price – at the risk of sounding like an utter technophobe – is a depletion in our ability to experience otherness through representation, and to feel responsible to the represented. Pre-digital photographic technology entails a 'referential excess' (Baker 1996), the indexical tendency of the photograph to reproduce aspects of the rendered reality irrespective of the photographer's intention or the viewer's expectations: it makes encounters with the radically unknown and unanticipated at least possible (as in Barthes' *punctum* (1984)), if not probable, and in encouraging a sense of the (ontological) reality of the depicted, it engages, at least minimally, with questions of responsibility toward them. Even when the photograph, like most stock images, is thoroughly staged, or altered during and after development, these repressions of referentiality require hard, skilled work, a kind of laborious paying of dues as the price for gaining representational mastery.[12]

In contrast, the visual content industry is premised on the absolute eradication of photographic referentiality and on the provision of representational mastery to all – viewers no less than photographers. The bottom line of this mastery is that the image becomes an extension of the ego, its tailor-made world: the other evaporates, along with any sense of duty toward it, into so many alterable info-pixels that stand at the service of the photographer and the viewer. And since the visual content industry appears to gather in all the images of the world, the ego becomes coextensive with the total phantasmagoria of the digital archive: otherness is no longer a radically unknown ontological reality, but that which is easily fabricated and speedily acquired in a global system of infinite image transformability. Such a dynamic makes the accidental encounter with the other, the shock of the unmasterable, *otherness as an experience of the self's limitation*, a structural and discursive improbability: it threatens to give photographers and viewers alike a sense of power without responsibility.

Institutional Invisibility

Finally, the visual-content industry, like the pre-digital stock photography business, is largely hidden from the public which consumes its images: most people have never heard of it or the companies that dominate it. The industry is concealed from its viewers by its clients, the cultural intermediaries in advertising agencies, marketing departments, graphic-design studios and elsewhere who directly employ the images in their material while making no overt reference to their source. And it is cloaked by the corporate acquisition of historical and artistic archives and the collapse of discursive and institutional boundaries between types of photograph, a collapse which destroys the continuity between production and consumption and the interpretative assumptions such continuity traditionally underpinned. Together these factors make it almost impossible, as I have already said, for viewers to follow the traces of power back through the images to the context of their manufacture, and to glimpse exactly who is exercising the authority to create these representations of the world.

The key ethical concern is, once again, power without responsibility. Only this time it is not just the power of producers and consumers to manipulate images on a computer, but veiled, hegemonic power over a vast empire of image creation. And it is a central irony of this concealment that the invisibility of the visual content industry lies *behind* its perpetual production of the visible – its trajectories and limitations – as though its very products shielded it from view. All this in a globalizing and digitized culture of consumption ever more dependent upon the images it makes.

In Conclusion

At present the trends that I have discussed in the last two chapters are in their nascent stage, although the pace of change could lead to their rapid maturation. Together they paint a complex, obscure but nevertheless unsettling picture: the fusion of miraculously transformative technologies, the collapse of discursive and institutional barriers between image types, the colonization of new markets and the containment of the process of image diversification, the use of technology as a weapon in the struggle to subordinate photographers, all carried out within the globalizing and commodifying logic that drove the pre-digital stock industry itself. This development is not without its moments and dynamics of resistance and empowerment – the increased diversity of images, previously unrepresented groups coming into visibility, 'viewers' enabled by digital technologies to take part in (and to take apart) the image-producing process – moments that the visual content industry seeks to neutralize or exploit. But perhaps most troubling of all is the last point in the section on ethics above: the concentration of power through which digital visual technologies themselves are being directed and shaped in the very instance of being deployed, and the invisibility of the institutions which possess this power to most of the consumers of their products.

Notes

1. Art.com is Getty's gateway to the vast 'global consumer art market', which is estimated to be worth $9 billion, making it a much bigger fish than the traditional stock photography market. See 'Getty Images Acquires Leading Online Consumer Art Brand, Art.com: Acquisition marks leading visual content provider's expansion into online consumer marketplace', Getty Images Press Release, 5/5/99).

2. Schiller's article thoughtfully delineates the intellectual context in which this abstraction of 'information' was able to occur, notably the rise of information theory and cybernetics and the later discourse on post-industrial and information society. This discourse, exemplified by the work of Daniel Bell (1976), is marked by what Schiller calls 'information exceptionalism', an insistence on the essential difference between theoretical knowledge based on science and technology (information), which

possesses intrinsically transcendent universal properties, and all other modes of activity, including labour. Needless to say Schiller characterizes this claim as an ideological 'sleight of hand' (1994: 95).

3. See Robins and Webster (1999) on the connection between information and control in modernity.

4. My analysis here of 'content/non-content' is indebted to Luhmann's description of the information/non-information code that underpins the system of the mass media (Luhmann 2000: 15–23).

5. Kaes's argument, while heavily indebted to Baudrillard's notions of simulation and the hyperreal, is effectively an indictment of contemporary visual culture *per se* in contrast to the authenticity of personal experience, memory and imagination, as well as text-based history. In this respect it corresponds to a long tradition of iconoclastic or anti-pictorial writing.

6. There are, however, photographers who have successfully used the web and argue that the fact that they cater to specialist niches is incidental to their success. See 'Selling Stock Direct on the Web: Three Case Studies' (*PDN* 1/2000, www.pdn-pix.com).

7. This is, of course, an extremely tricky question, and most of the literature on globalization stresses its dialectical relationship with forces of localization, or at least that globalization is 'the condition whereby localising strategies become systematically connected to global concerns' (Poppi 1997: 285; see also Appadurai 1990, Friedman 1990, Morley and Robins 1995; Tomlinson 1999; among many others). Globalization of distribution systems need not necessarily mean centralization of image production in the United States and Western Europe, though the two have tended to coincide. Israel, for example, has three 'general' stock agencies: The Image Bank, Visual Communications (which primarily represents large foreign agencies), and ASAP – a home-grown library that focuses specifically on 'Israeli' imagery but also represents some US and European agencies. Overall the preponderance of stock photographs available, not to mention royalty-free images distributed on CD-ROM, is American or Western European in origin.

8. Such as lesbian and gay consumers: see 'Corbis Images Appeals to Burgeoning Gay and Lesbian Market: Newest Royalty-Free CD first to offer gay and lesbian lifestyle images', Corbis Press Release, 20/9/1999, www.corbis.com.

9. According to the APA National Photographers Survey 1999, only 14.5 per cent of advertising photographers are women, representing a decline in the number of women since the last survey, in 1992. No figures were available for photographers from ethnic minorities.

10. I am grateful to Sarah Kember for suggesting the ethical dimension of Sekula's argument.
11. The following point is heavily indebted to the work of Kevin Robins (1996).
12. The price of representational mastery over staged photographs is in part a monetary one: models used are required to sign 'model release forms' which state that they have been remunerated for the use of their 'image' in the initial work contract and have no claim on the photograph's subsequent earnings. Similar contracts are employed with the owners of properties that appear in stock images. Most agencies will not accept images provided by a photographer unless model release forms have been signed by all those who appear in them.

9

Epilogue

My dialogue with stock photography began many years ago, while I was working as the senior copywriter of a very small advertising agency and publishing house based in Tel Aviv. Then, as now, I was fascinated by its contradictions, by the way it seemed, in its very formulaic repetitiveness and monumental redundancy, simultaneously to embody the most debased, manipulative and uninteresting of cultural artefacts and yet still to convey, in its very pathology, both a desperate yearning for authenticity and an almost utopian innocence – for how else could anyone treat seriously the incessant and deliberate production of such apparent uniformity. In the years since that first encounter I have learned much more about how that contradiction inhabits, and inhibits, stock photography, finding along the way that its products are both slightly less uniform, and often much less innocent, that I had initially supposed.

Those years have also allowed me to formulate the 'big question' with which I opened this book and that has animated my concerns throughout: how do media help create the 'background' of our lives, the largely unnoticed, routinely encountered framework of knowledge, trust and expectation which allows us to orient ourselves within extremely complex societies. My basic assumption in answering this question has been that creating such a background, and making it generally unobtrusive to most media 'users', involves highly skilled, deliberately organized and unremitting labour by media organizations and the professionals they employ. This is not to insist that media organizations and cultural professionals always conceive of their work in these terms. As we have seen from the example of stock photography and the visual content industry, much of their activity is ostensibly more selectively focused on the fulfilment of specific 'system' demands, and even the stock industry's 'mission' orientation – to persuade consumers – is normally measured by practitioners in narrowly commercial terms: hence the dominant monetary definition of a 'successful' image.

So this 'big question' has led me to analyse the connections between the formal properties of media 'texts' (in this case, commercial photographic images), the institutional and cultural contexts in which they are produced and distributed, and the representational conditions which would allow them to become routinely 'intelligible' – amenable to everyday recognition and interpretation. I have also been concerned with the kinds of social identities and values facilitated by such 'intelligibility', and the power relationships between different social groups that it implies. In pursuing these interests, as my research has progressed, my attention has increasingly fallen on the ways in which media and cultural products, whose success is frequently based upon their openness to multiple recontextualizations and radical alteration, nevertheless appear as stable and internally coherent entities with clear meanings. How do these entities-in-process become solidified into achieved products, objects whose contingent materialization seems as naturally recognizable as the focal point of an image, and therefore endowed with apparent necessity and inevitability? How is the self-evident 'being' of images – among other cultural artefacts – produced by dynamics of 'becoming' that are systematically, *generatively*, volatile? And how does this constant solidification and foreclosure of potentiality intersect with the stabilization of power relations between social groups – pre-eminently those represented (or neglected) by these images, those addressed by them, and those responsible for them?

The dialectic of instability and stability has always been particularly apparent in the stock photography industry. As the last chapters made plain, however, the advent of new digital technologies has brought that dialectic more plainly into view by facilitating enhanced powers of image dematerialization and distribution, thereby challenging – and in some cases reanimating – cultural practices and discourses (such as the romantic notion of artistic vision) aimed at particular types of stabilization. Digital technologies, while certainly not the sole cause of changes in the stock business, have intersected with a range of other cultural and organizational forces to produce new understandings – *embedded in altered practices* – of what a visual image is and how it might be determined and controlled. One result is that the stock photograph, always premised on multiple reuse and radical recontextualization, has been transformed into *the* paradigmatic form of 'visual content'. Extending the logic of their pre-digital dynamics, the rootless mobility and material precariousness of stock images is now shared by a variety of other, seemingly more noble forms: documentary and art photographs, illustrations, film footage, video clips and sanctified artworks themselves.

Finally, in addition to my interest in this 'big question', and my desire to shed some light on stock photography and the visual content industry for its own sake, I have written this book as part of a contribution to the analysis of industrialized or mass culture. Now 'mass culture' has long been used as a term of derision: semantically it hovers on the brink of self-contradiction. For some commentators it is among the most devastating of oxymorons, the brute connotational force of 'mass', with its associations of 'mob' and 'multitude', crushing the elitist sensibility of 'culture'. For others it signifies the incursion of industrial methods and values into the realm of art – mass culture as *mass production* – thereby effecting an irreversible fall from grace into economic instrumentality. What I hope I have shown in the preceding chapters is that mass cultural production is much more than a purely industrial process (whatever that might be). It is – like all economic activity – also a cultural one. For too long cultural production has been treated as monolithic and unconflicted, both by those who unconditionally endorse the charges of 'mass-culture' theory and by those who locate the site of interest for media and cultural studies almost exclusively in the realm of consumption and its putative modes of 'resistance' to the production system. What this book promotes, I hope, is not the view that production is the determining moment in the cultural process, and that therefore its products cannot be recontextualized by consumers: if anything, I hope that my interpretation of production and distribution has stressed their *systematic openness* to recontextualization. Rather, this book is written as a testimony to the privileged complexity of cultural production, 'mass' or otherwise, a complexity no less significant than that of consumption for our understanding of how culture works.

Sources and Bibliography

Primary Sources

Stock Catalogues

Tony Stone Images: UK-based (now US). Major global agency.
1987 'Edition 7': Romantic images appear in category – *People; People on Holiday.*
  N (no. of romantic images in sample) = 11.
1989 'Edition 8': Category – *Singles & Couples; Vacations.* N = 12.

The Image Bank: US-based. Major global agency.
1993 'Catalogue 13: European Focus': Category – *People.* N = 47.
1994 'Catalogue 14: Bokelberg Edition 3': No category title. N = 11. This is a small
  catalogue, devoted entirely to images of people, which was the result of a joint
  venture with the German publishing house Gruner and Jahr. All of the photographs
  are by Werner Bokelberg, whose name figures prominently on every page of the
  catalogue.
1995 'Catalogue 15': Category – *People.* N = 43.
1995 'Catalogue 16: People': Category – by photographer's name. N = 98.
1995 'Catalogue 17: Ideas': Category – *Relationships.* N = 11.
1996 'Catalogue 18: Annual': Category – *People.* N = 27.
1998 'Catalogue 24: Perceptions': Category – *Relationships.* N = 22.

FPG International: US-based. Major global agency.
1993 'Selects Volume 5': Category – *Couples.* N = 39.
1995 'Selects Volume 6': Category – *Couples.* N = 32.
1997 'Selects Volume 7': Category – *Early Adulthood.* N = 30.

A.G.E. Fotostock: Spain-based. Large European agency.
1995 'Fotostock Volume 3': Category – *People* (lifestyles/ couples/ relationships/
  tenderness/ special moments/ intimacy/ love/ timeout/ leisure/ vacations). N = 34.
1996 'Fotostock Volume 4': Category – *The Art of Living* (couples/ friends/ tenderness/
  intimacy/ love/ characters/ leisure/ vacations); *Family Life* (first love); *Holidays.* N
  = 39.

Rex Interstock: UK-based. Small European agency.
1997 'Rex Interstock': Category – ***People***. N = 11.
1998 'Rex Interstock Two': Category – ***People***. N = 4.

Superstock: US-based. Medium-sized US agency.
1995 'Portfolio 5': Category – ***Lifestyle***; ***People***. N = 30.

Index Stock. US-based. Medium-sized US agency.
1995 '13': Category – ***Lifestyle***. N=14.

The Photographer's Library: UK-based. Small European agency.
1990 No Title: Category – ***People***. N = 6.

Bavaria Bildagentur: Germany-based. Medium-sized European agency.
1995 'The Creative Stockbook 21': Category – ***Beach***; ***People***. N = 38.

Trade Publications

BAPLA Directory 1998/9 – Listing of members of the British Association of Picture Libraries and Agencies, the stock industry's trade association in the UK.
CEPIC Directory 1998/9 - Listing of members of the Coordination of European Picture Agencies Press and Stock, the stock industry's official European Economic Interest Group (EEIG) in the European Union.
Communication Arts – Prestigious US professional design and photography magazine.
Creative Review – Monthly UK commercial design magazine.
Graphic Design USA – Small monthly professional graphic-design journal.
Light Box - The quarterly magazine of BAPLA (British Association of Picture Libraries and Archives), the British stock industry's trade association.
PACA Directory 1998/9 - Listing of members of the Picture Agency Council of America, the stock industry's main trade association in the United States.
PDN (Photo District News) – Leading monthly US commercial photography trade journal with extensive online version.
PhotoStockNOTES – The monthly newsletter of PhotoSource International, a marketing-service company serving stock photographers and photography buyers.
Stock Photo Report – A small publication devoted to stock photography published by long-serving industry observer Brian Seed.
Zoom – Bi-monthly international professional photography magazine.

Stock Photography Websites

Agencies
Comstock – www.comstock.com
Corbis – www.corbis.com
Gaze – www.gaze.co.uk

Getty – www.gettyimages.com
FPG International – www.fpg.com
Index Stock – www.indexstock.com
The Image Bank – www.imagebank.com
Tony Stone – www.stone.com
Visual Communications Group (no longer active) – www.vcg.com

Organizations, On-line Journals and Professional Sites
The American Society of Media Photographers – www.asmp.org
Advertising Photographers of America – www.apa.org
BAPLA – www.bapla.org.uk
PACA – www.paca.org
Stockphoto Online Stock Photography Network – www.stockphoto.net
PDN Online – www.pdn-pix.com or www.pdnonline.com

Bibliography

Adorno, T. and Horkheimer, M. (1979) *Dialectic of Enlightenment*. London: Verso.
Alloula, M. (1987) *The Colonial Harem*. Manchester: Manchester University Press.
Anderson, B. (1983) *Imagined Communities*. London: Verso.
Angus, I. (1998) 'Constitutive Paradox: The Subject in Cultural Criticism', *Continuum* 12(2): 147–56.
Appadurai, A. (1990) 'Disjuncture and Difference in the Global Cultural Economy', in M. Featherstone (ed.) *Global Culture: Nationalism, Globalization and Modernity*, London: Sage.
Baker, G. (1996) 'Photography between Narrativity and Stasis: August Sander, Degeneration and Decay of the Portrait', *October* 76: 73–113.
Bakhtin, M. (1981) 'Epic and Novel: Toward a Methodology for the Study of the Novel', in C. Emerson and M. Holquist (eds) *The Dialogic Imagination*. Dallas: University of Texas Press.
Bal, M. (1996) *Double Exposures: The Subject of Cultural Analysis*. London: Routledge.
Bal, M. and Bryson, N. (1991) 'Semiotics and Art History', *The Art Bulletin* LXXIII (2): 174–208.
Balio, T. (ed.) (1985) *The American Film Industry*. Madison: University of Wisconsin Press.
Barthes, R. (1974) *S/Z*. New York: Hill and Wang.
Barthes, R. (1977a) 'The Photographic Message', in *Image – Music – Text*, ed. and trans. Stephen Heath. London: Fontana.
Barthes, R. (1977b) 'Rhetoric of the Image' in *Image – Music – Text*, ed. and trans. Stephen Heath. London: Fontana.
Barthes, R. (1977c) 'The Third Meaning: Research Notes on some Eisenstein Stills', in *Image – Music – Text*, ed. and trans. Stephen Heath, London: Fontana.

Barthes, R. (1977d) 'The Death of the Author', in *Image – Music – Text*, ed. and trans. Stephen Heath, London: Fontana.

Barthes, R. (1984) *Camera Lucida: Reflections on Photography*. London: Fontana.

Barthes, R. (1993) *Mythologies*. London: Fontana.

Batchen, G. (1997) *Burning with Desire: The Conception of Photography*. Cambridge, MA: MIT Press.

Batchen, G. (1998) 'Photogenics', *History of Photography* 22(1): 18–26.

Baudrillard, J. (1981) 'Toward a Critique of the Political Economy of the Sign', in *For a Critique of the Political Economy of the Sign*. St. Louis: Telos.

Baudrillard, J. (1988a) 'Consumer Society', in M. Poster (ed.) *Selected Writings*. Cambridge: Polity.

Baudrillard, J. (1988b) 'Simulacra and Simulations', in M. Poster (ed.) *Selected Writings*. Cambridge: Polity.

Bauman, Z. (2001) 'Consuming Life', *Journal of Consumer Culture* 1(1): 9–29.

Bazin, A. (1980 [1967]) 'The Ontology of the Photographic Image', in Alan Trachtenberg (ed.) *Classic Essays on Photography*. New Haven: Leete's Island Books.

Bazin, A. (1992 [1955]) 'The Evolution of the Language of Cinema', in G. Mast, M. Cohen and L. Baudry *Film Theory and Criticism*. Oxford: Oxford University Press.

Beck, U., Giddens, A. and Lash, S. (1994) *Reflexive Modernization: Politics, Tradition and Aesthetics in the Modern Social Order*. Cambridge: Polity.

Becker, H. (1976) 'Art Worlds and Social Types', in R. Peterson (ed.) *The Production of Culture*. London: Sage.

Bell, D. (1976) *The Coming of Post-industrial Society: A Venture in Social Forecasting*. New York: Basic.

Bellour, R. (1993) 'The Phantom's Due', *Discourse* 16(2).

Benjamin, W. (1980 [1931]) 'A Short History of Photography', in Alan Trachtenberg (ed.) *Classic Essays on Photography*. New Haven: Leete's Island Books.

Benjamin, W. (1992) 'The Work of Art in the Age of Mechanical Reproduction', in *Illuminations*. London: Fontana.

Berger, J. (1972) *Ways of Seeing*. London: Penguin.

Berger, J. and Mohr, J. (1982) *Another Way of Telling*. New York: Pantheon.

Berman, M. (1982) *All That Is Solid Melts Into Air: The Experience of Modernity*. London: Verso.

Bhabha, H. (1992) 'The Other Question: the Stereotype and Colonial Discourse', in Screen Editorial Collective (eds) *The Sexual Subject: A Screen Reader in Sexuality*. London: Routledge.

Billig, M. (1997) 'From Codes to Utterances: Cultural Studies, Discourse and Psychology', in M. Ferguson and P. Golding (eds) *Cultural Studies in Question*. London: Sage.

Binkley, T. (1993) 'Refiguring Culture', in Phillip Hayward and Tania Wollen (eds), *Future Visions: Introduction and Development of New Screen Technologies*. London: BFI.

Black, M. (1979) 'More About Metaphor', in A. Ortony (ed.) *Metaphor and Thought*. Cambridge: Cambridge University Press.

Bolter, J.D. (1996). 'Ekphrasis, Virtual Reality and the Future of Writing', in G. Nunberg (ed.) *The Future of the Book*. Berkeley: University of California Press.

Bolter, J. and Grusin, R. (1999) *Remediation: Understanding New Media*. Cambridge, MA: MIT Press.

Bolton, R. (1989) 'In the American East: Richard Avedon Incorporated', in R. Bolton (ed.). *The Contest of Meaning: Critical Histories of Photography*. Cambridge, MA: MIT Press.

Bonney, B. and Wilson, H. (1990) 'Advertising and the Manufacture of Difference', in M. Alvarado and J.O. Thompson (eds) *The Media Reader*. London: BFI, 181–98.

Bordwell, D. (1998) *On the History of Film Style*, Cambridge, MA: Harvard University Press.

Bordwell, D., Thompson, K. and Staiger, J. (1985) *The Classical Hollywood Cinema: Film Style and Mode of Production to 1960*. New York: Columbia University Press.

Bossen, H. (1985) 'Zone V: Photojournalism, Ethics and the Electronic Age', *Studies in Visual Communication* 11(3): 22–32.

Bourdieu, P. (1986) *Distinction: A Social Critique of the Judgement of Taste*. London: Routledge.

Bourdieu, P. (1990 [1965]) *Photography: A Middle-Brow Art*, trans. Shaun Whiteside. Cambridge: Polity. Originally published in French.

Bourdieu, P. (1993) *The Field of Cultural Production*, trans. Randal Johnson. Cambridge: Polity.

Boyle, J. (2002) 'The Second Enclosure Movement and the Construction of the Public Domain'. Preliminary Discussion Paper for Conference on the Public Domain at Duke Law School.

Brookes, R. (1992) 'Fashion Photography. The Double-Page Spread: Helmut Newton, Guy Bourdin and Deborah Turbeville', in J. Ash and E. Wilson (eds) *Chic Thrills: A Fashion Reader*. London: Pandora.

Bryson N. (1981) *Word and Image: French Painting of the Ancien Regime*. Cambridge: Cambridge University Press.

Bryson N. (1983) *Vision and Painting: The Logic of the Gaze*. New Haven: Yale University Press.

Buck-Morss S. (1992) 'Aesthetics and Anaesthetics: Walter Benjamin's Artwork Essay Reconsidered', *October* 62.

Burgin, V. (1982a) 'Looking at Photographs', in V. Burgin (ed.) *Thinking Photography*. London: Macmillan Education.

Burgin V. (1982b) 'Photography, Phantasy, Function', in V. Burgin (ed.) *Thinking Photography*. London: Macmillan Education.

Burgin V. (1986) *The End of Art Theory: Criticism and Postmodernity*. London: Macmillan Education.

Butler, J. (1993) *Bodies That Matter: On the Discursive Limits of 'Sex'*. London: Routledge.

Caillois, R. (1962) *Man, Play and Games*. Glencoe, IL.: Free Press.

Carey, J. (1992) *Communication as Culture: Essays on Media and Society*. London: Routledge.

Chambers, I. (1990) *Border Dialogues: Journeys in Postmodernity*. London: Routledge.

Chase, M. and Shaw, C. (1989) 'The Dimensions of Nostalgia', in M. Chase and C. Shaw (eds) *The Imagined Past: History and Nostalgia*, Manchester: Manchester University Press.

Chia, R. (1996) 'The Problem of Reflexivity in Organizational Research: Towards a Postmodern Science of Organization', *Organization* 3(1): 31–59.

Craik, J. (1994) 'Soft Focus: Techniques of Fashion Photography', in *The Face of Fashion*. London: Routledge.

Crane, D. (1987) *The Transformation of the Avant-Garde: The New York Art World 1940–1985*. Chicago: Chicago University Press.

Crary, J. (1992) *Techniques of the Observer: On Vision and Modernity in the Nineteenth Century*, Cambridge MA: MIT Press.

Crary, J. (1994) 'Unbinding Vision', *October* 68.

Culler, J. (1981) 'Apostrophe', in *The Pursuit of Signs*. Ithaca: Cornell University Press.

Debord, G. (1983 [1967]), *Society of the Spectacle*. Detroit: Black & Red.

Deleuze, G. and Guattari, F. (1994) *What is Philosophy?*. London: Verso.

Derrida, J. (1976) *Of Grammatology*. Baltimore: Johns Hopkins University Press.

DiMaggio, P. and Hirsch, P. (1976) 'Production Organizations in the Arts' in R. Peterson (ed.) *The Production of Culture*. London: Sage.

Döblin, A. (1994 [1929]) 'Faces, Images and Their Truth', trans. Michael Robertson, Introduction to Sander, A. *Face of Our Time*. Munich: Schirmer/Mosel.

Du Gay, P. and Pryke, M. (eds) (2002) *Cultural Economy*. London: Sage.

Du Gay, P., Hall, S., James, L., Mackay, H. and Negus, K. (1997) *Doing Cultural Studies: The Story of the Sony Walkman*. London: Sage/Open University.

Durand, R. (1993) 'Event, Trace, Intensity', in *Discourse* 16(2).

Dyer, R. (1988) 'White', *Screen* 29(4): 44–64.

Dyer, R. (1993) *The Matter of Images: Essays on Representations*. London: Routledge.

Eco, U. (1975) *A Theory of Semiotics*. Bloomington: Indiana University Press.

Eco, U. (1979) 'The Myth of Superman', in *The Role of the Reader*. Bloomington: Indiana University Press.

Eco, U. (1982) 'Critique of the Image', in V. Burgin (ed.) *Thinking Photography*. London: Macmillan Education.

Eco, U. (1989) *The Open Work*. Cambridge, MA: Harvard University Press.

Eliade, M. (1954) *The Myth of the Eternal Return: Or, Cosmos and History*. Princeton: Princeton University Press.

Elkins, J. (1995) 'Marks, Traces, *Traits*, Contours, *Orli*, and *Slendores*: Nonsemiotic Elements in Pictures', *Critical Inquiry* 21 (4): 822–60.

Ewen, S. (1988) *All Consuming Images: The Politics of Style in Contemporary Culture*. New York: Basic.

Feldman, A. (1997) 'Violence and Vision: The Prosthetics and Aesthetics of Terror', *Public Culture* 10(1): 24–60.

Ferguson, M. and Golding, P. (eds) (1997) *Cultural Studies in Question*. London: Sage.

Forceville, C. (1996) *Pictorial Metaphor in Advertising*. London: Routledge.

Foster, H. (1996) 'The Archive without Museums', *October* 77: 97–119.

Foucault, M. (1972) *The Archaeology of Knowledge and the Discourse on Language*. New York: Pantheon.

Foucault, M. (1979) *Discipline and Punish: The Birth of the Prison*, trans. Alan Sheridan, New York: Pantheon.

Freeman, M. (1998) 'Mythical Time, Historical Time, and the Narrative Fabric of the Self', *Narrative Inquiry* 8 (1): 27–50.

Freund, G. (1980) *Photography and Society*. London: Gordon Fraser.

Friedman, J. (1990) 'Being in the World: Globalization and Localization', in Mike Featherstone (ed.) *Global Culture: Nationalism, Globalization and Modernity*. London: Sage.

Frosh, P. (1998) 'Filling the Sight by Force: *Smoke*, Photography and the Rhetoric of Immobilization', *Textual Practice* 12(2): 323–40.

Frow, J. (1991) 'Tourism and the Semiotics of Nostalgia', *October* 57.

Garnham, N. (1986), 'Contribution to a Political Economy of Mass-Communication', in R. Collins, J. Curran, N. Garnham, P. Scannell, P. Schlesinger and C. Sparks (eds.) *Media, Culture and Society: A Critical Reader*. London: Sage.

Geertz, C. (1973) *The Interpretation of Cultures*. New York: Basic.

Gendron, B. (1986) 'Theodor Adorno Meets the Cadillacs', in T. Modelski (ed.) *Studies in Entertainment*. Bloomington: Indiana University Press.

Giddens, A. (1990) *The Consequences of Modernity*. Oxford: Polity.

Giddens, A. (1991) *Modernity and Self-Identity: Self and Society in the Late Modern Age*. Cambridge: Polity.

Giddens, A. (1992) *The Transformation of Intimacy*. Stanford: Stanford University Press.

Gilman, S. (1985) *Difference and Pathology: Stereotypes of Sexuality, Race and Madness*. Ithaca: Cornell University Press.

Goddard, A. (1998) *The Language of Advertising: Written Texts*. London: Routledge.

Goffman, E. (1958) *The Presentation of Self in Everyday Life*. Edinburgh: University of Edinburgh Social Sciences Research Centre.

Goffman, E. (1976) *Gender Advertisements*. New York: Harper and Row.

Goldman, R. and Papson, S. (1994) 'Advertising in the Age of Hypersignification', *Theory, Culture and Society* 11: 23–53.

Gombrich, E.H. (1960) *Art and Illusion: A Study in the Psychology of Pictorial Representation*. Princeton: Princeton University Press.

Gombrich, E.H. (1980) 'Standards of Truth: The Arrested Image and the Moving Eye', *Critical Inquiry* 7(2): 237–73.

Graham-Brown, S. (1988) *Images of Women: The Portrayal of Women in Photography of the Middle East 1860–1950*. London: Quartet.

Gregory, K. (1983) 'Native-view Paradigms: Multiple Cultures and Culture Conflicts in Organizations', *Administrative Science Quarterly* 28(3): 359–76.

Hall, S. (1972) 'The Determinations of News Photographs', in *Working Papers in Cultural Studies*, Birmingham, England.

Hall, S. (1980) 'Encoding/Decoding', in S. Hall, D. Hobson, A. Lowe and P. Willis (eds) *Culture, Media, Language*. London: Hutchinson.

Hall, S. (1992) 'Cultural Studies and its Theoretical Legacies', in L. Grossberg, C. Nelson and P.A. Treichler (eds) *Cultural Studies*. New York: Routledge.

Hansen, M. (1987) 'Benjamin, Cinema and Experience: "The Blue Flower in the Land of Technology"', in *New German Critique* 40: 179–224.

Hansen, M. (1991) *Babel and Babylon: Spectatorship in American Silent Film*. Cambridge, MA: Harvard University Press.

Harraway, D. (1991) *Simians, Cyborgs, and Women: The Reinvention of Nature*. New York: Routledge.

Harvey, D. (1989) *The Condition of Postmodernity: An Enquiry into the Origins of Cultural Change*. Oxford: Basil Blackwell.

Hebdige, D. (1988) *Hiding in the Light: On Images and Things*, London: Routledge.

Hebdige, D. (1993) 'A Report on the Western Front: Postmodernism and the "Politics' of Style"', in C. Jenks (ed.) *Cultural Reproduction*. London: Routledge.

Heidegger, M. (1977) 'The Age of the World Picture' in *The Question Concerning Technology and Other Essays*, tr. W. Lovitt. New York: Harper and Row.

Hendrick, S. and Hendrick, C. (1992) *Romantic Love*. London: Sage.

Herbert, J. (1995) 'Masterdisciplinarity and the 'Pictorial Turn', *Art Bulletin* LXXVII(4).

Herman, E. and McChesney, R. (1997) *The Global Media: The New Missionaries of Corporate Capitalism*. London: Cassell.

Heron, M. (1996) *How to Shoot Stock Photos That Sell*. New York: Allworth.

Hesmondhalgh, D. (2002) *The Cultural Industries*. London: Sage.

Hiley, M. (1983) *Seeing Through Photographs*. London: Gordon Fraser.

Hirota, J. (1995) 'Making Products Heroes: Work in Advertising Agencies', in R. Jackall (ed.) *Propaganda*. New York: New York University Press.

Hirsch, P. (1972) 'Processing Fads and Fashions: An Organization-Set Analysis of Cultural Industry Systems', *American Journal of Sociology* 77: 639–59.

Huizinga, J. (1970) *Homo Ludens*. London: Maurice Temple Smith.

Illouz, E. (1991) 'Reason Within Passion: Love in Women's Magazines', *Critical Studies in Mass Communication* 8(3): 231–48.

Illouz, E. (1997) *Consuming the Romantic Utopia: Love and the Cultural Contradictions of Capitalism*. Berkeley: University of California Press.

Jacobs, D.L. (1986) 'Domestic Snapshots: Toward a Grammar of Motives', in Gary Gumpert and Robert Cathcart (eds) *Intermedia: Interpersonal Communications in a Media World*, Oxford: Oxford University Press.

Jakobson, R. (1988) 'Linguistics and Poetics', in David Lodge (ed.) *Modern Criticism and Theory: A Reader*. London: Longman.

Jameson, F. (1984) 'Postmodernism, or The Cultural Logic of Late Capitalism', *New Left Review* 146: 53–92.

Jameson, F. (1990) 'Reification And Utopia in Mass Culture', in *Signatures of the Visible*. London: Routledge.

Jay, M. (1988) 'Scopic Regimes of Modernity', in H. Foster (ed.) *Vision and Visuality*. Seattle: Bay Press.

Jay, M. (1995) 'Photo-unrealism: The Contribution of the Camera to the Crisis of Ocularcentrism', in S. Melville and B. Readings (eds) *Vision and Textuality*. London: Macmillan.

Jensen, J. (1984) 'An Interpretive Approach to Culture Production', in W. Rowland and B. Watkins (eds) *Interpreting Television: Current Research Perspectives*. London: Sage.

Jensen, K. (1991) 'When Is Meaning? Communication Theory, Pragmatism and Mass Media Reception', *Communication Yearbook* 14: 3–32.

Jones, P. (1999) "The Problem is Always One of Method . . .": Cultural Materialism, Political Economy and Cultural Studies', *Keywords* 2: 28–46.

Kaes, A. (1990) 'History and Film: Public Memory in the Age of Electronic Dissemination', *History and Memory* 2(1).

Kaplan, H. (1987) 'The Psychopathology of Nostalgia', *Psychoanalytic Review* 74(4).

Keenan, C. (1998) 'On the Relationship between Personal Photographs and Individual Memory', *History of Photography* 22(1): 60–4.

Kelly, A. (1979) 'Feminism and Photography', in P. Hill, A. Kelly and J. Tagg *Three Perspectives on Photography*. London: Arts Council of Great Britain.

Kember, S. (1995) 'Medicine's New Vision', in M. Lister (ed.) *The Photographic Image in Digital Culture*. London: Routledge.

Kember, S. (1996) '"The Shadow of the Object": Photography and Realism', *Textual Practice* 10(1): 145–63.

Kenyon, D. (1992) *Inside Amateur Photography*. London: Batsford.

Kopytoff, I. (1986) 'The Cultural Biography of Things: Commoditization as Process', in A. Appadurai (ed.) *The Social Life of Things: Commodities in Cultural Perspective*. Cambridge: Cambridge University Press.

Kozol, W. (1994) *Life's America: Family and Nation in Postwar Photojournalism*. Philadephia: Temple University Press.

Krauss, R. (1982) 'Photography's Discursive Spaces: Landscape/View', *Art Journal* 42(4): 311–19.

Krauss, R. (1984) 'A Note on Photography and the Simulacral', *October* 31: 49–68.

Kreiling, A. (1978) 'Toward a Cultural Studies Approach for the Sociology of Popular Culture', *Communication Research* 5(3): 240–63.

Krieger, M. (1992) *Ekphrasis: The Illusion of the Natural Sign*. Baltimore: Johns Hopkins University Press.

Kuhn, A. (1995) *Family Secrets: Acts of Memory and Imagination*. London: Verso.

Lanham, R. (1993) *The Electronic Word: Democracy, Technology and the Arts*. Chicago: The University of Chicago Press.

Lash, S. (1988) 'Discourse or Figure? Postmodernism as a "Regime of Signification"', *Theory, Culture & Society* 5: 311–36.

Lash, S. (1990) *The Sociology of Postmodernism*. London: Routledge.

Latour, B. (1987) *Science in Action*. Milton Keynes: Open University Press.

Lee, J.A. (1988) 'Love Styles', in R. Sternberg and M. Barnes (eds) *The Psychology of Love*. New Haven: Yale University Press.

Lefebvre, H. (1991) *The Production of Space*, trans. by D. Nicholson-Smith. Oxford: Blackwell.

Leiss, W., Kline, S. and Jhally, S. (1997) *Social Communication in Advertising: Persons, Products and Images of Well-Being*. London: Routledge.

Lippman, W. (1956) *Public Opinion*. New York: Macmillan.

Lister, M. (ed.) (1995) *The Photographic Image in Digital Culture*, London: Routledge.

Lister, M. (1997) 'Photography in the Age of Electronic Imaging', in Liz Wells (ed.) *Photography: A Critical Introduction*. London: Routledge.

Lloyd, G. (1993) *Being In Time: Selves and Narrators in Philosophy and Literature*. London: Routledge.

Luhmann, N. (1986) *Love as Passion: The Codification of Intimacy*. Cambridge, MA: Harvard University Press.

Luhmann, N. (1990) *Essays on Self-Reference*. New York: Columbia University Press.

Luhmann, N. (2000) *The Reality of the Mass Media*. Cambridge: Polity.

Lury, C. (1998) *Prosthetic Culture: Photography, Memory and Identity*. London: Routledge.

Lury, C. and Warde, A. (1997) 'Investments in the Imaginary Consumer: Conjectures Regarding Power, Knowledge and Advertising', in M. Nava, A. Blake, I. MacRury and B. Richards (eds) *Buy this Book: Studies in Advertising and Consumption*. London: Routledge.

Lutz, C. and Collins, J. (1993) *Reading National Geographic*. Chicago: University of Chicago Press.

Lyotard, J. (1983) 'Answering the Question: What is Postmodernism?', in I. Hassan and S. Hassan (eds) *Innovation/Renovation*. Madison: University of Wisconsin Press.

Lystra, K. (1989) *Searching the Heart: Women, Men and Romantic Love in Nineteenth Century America*. New York: Oxford University Press.

Marchand, R. (1985) *Advertising the American Dream*. Berkeley: University of California Press.

McDonough, T.F. (1994) 'Situationist Space', *October* 67.

McLuhan, M. (1994 [1964]) *Understanding Media: The Extensions of Man*. Cambridge, MA: MIT Press.

McQuire, S. (1998) *Visions of Modernity*. London: Sage.

Messaris, P. (1997) *Visual Persuasion: The Role of Images in Advertising*. London: Sage.

Metz, C. (1982) *The Imaginary Signifier: Psychoanalysis and Cinema*. Bloomington: Indiana University Press.

Metz, C. (1985) 'Photography and Fetish', *October* 34: 81–90.

Meyrovitz, J. (1985) *No Sense of Place: The Impact of Electronic Media on Social Behaviour*. Oxford: Oxford University Press.

Miller, J. Abbott (1999 [1994]) 'Pictures for Rent: From Stereoscope to Stereotype', in E. Lupton and J. Miller *Design Writing Research: Writing on Graphic Design*. London: Phaidon.

Mitchell, A. (1983) *The Nine American Lifestyles*. New York: Macmillan.

Mitchell, W. (1992) *The Reconfigured Eye: Visual Truth in the Post-Photographic Era*. Cambridge, MA: MIT Press.

Mitchell, W.J.T. (1986) *Iconology: Image, Text, Ideology*, Chicago: University of Chicago Press.

Mitchell, W.J.T. (1992) 'The Pictorial Turn', *Artforum* XXX: 89–94.

Mitchell, W.J.T. (1994) *Picture Theory.* Chicago: University of Chicago Press.

Mitchell, W.J.T. (2002) 'Showing Seeing: a Critique of Visual Culture', *Journal of Visual Culture* 1(2), 165–81.

Morley, D. and Robins, K. (1995) *Spaces of Identity: Global Media, Electronic Landscapes and Cultural Boundaries.* London: Routledge.

Morris, M. (1992) 'Banality in Cultural Studies', in P. Mellencamp (ed.) *Logics of Television: Essays in Cultural Criticism.* Bloomington/London: Indiana University Press and BFI Publishing.

Morse, M. (1992) 'An Ontology of Everyday Distraction: The Freeway, the Mall and Television', in P. Mellencamp (ed.) *Logics of Television: Essays in Cultural Criticism.* Bloomington/London: Indiana University Press and BFI Publishing.

Mort, F. (1996) *Cultures of Consumption: Masculinities and Social Space in Late Twentieth-Century Britain.* London: Routledge.

Mulvey, L. (1975) 'Visual Pleasure and Narrative Cinema', *Screen* 16(3): 6–18.

Nava, M. (1997) 'Framing Advertising: Cultural Analysis and the Incrimination of Visual Texts', in M. Nava, A. Blake, I. MacRury and B. Richards (eds) *Buy this Book: Studies in Advertising and Consumption.* London: Routledge.

Neale, S. (1990) 'Questions of Genre', *Screen* 31(1): 45–66.

Negus, K. (1997) 'The Production of Culture', in P. Du Gay (ed.) *Production of Culture/ Cultures of Production.* Milton Keynes/London: Open University/Sage.

Negus, K. (1998) 'Cultural Production and the Corporation: Musical Genres and the Strategic Management of Creativity in the US Recording Industry', *Media, Culture & Society* 20(3): 359–79.

Negus, K. (2002) 'The Work of Cultural Intermediaries and the Enduring Distance Between Production and Consumption', *Cultural Studies* 16(4): 501–15.

Nichols, B. (1981) *Ideology and the Image: Social Representation in the Cinema and Other Media.* Bloomington: Indiana University Press.

Nixon, S. (1997) 'Circulting Culture' in P. Du Gay (ed.) *Production of Culture/Cultures of Production.* Milton Keynes/London: Open University/Sage.

Nixon, S. and Du Gay, P. (2002) 'Who Needs Cultural Intermediaries?', *Cultural Studies* 16(4): 495-500.

Nunberg, G. (1996) 'Farewell to the Information Age', in G. Nunberg (ed.) *The Future of the Book.* Berkeley: University of California Press.

Panofsky, E. (1955) *Meaning in the Visual Arts.* Garden City, New York: Doubleday.

Peirce, C.S. (1931–58) 'The Icon, Index and Symbol', in *Collected Works*, ed. C. Hartshorne and P. Weiss, Vol. 2. of 8. Cambridge, MA: Harvard University Press.

Peterson, R. (1976) 'The Production of Culture: A Prolegomenon', in R. Peterson (ed.) *The Production of Culture.* London: Sage.

Phillips, D. (1993) 'Modern Vision', *Oxford Art Journal* 16(1).

Pinney, C. (1992) 'The Parallel Histories of Anthropology and Photography', in E. Edwards (ed.) *Anthropology and Photography 1860–1920.* New Haven: Yale University Press.

Poppi, C. (1997) 'Wider Horizons with Larger Details: Subjectivity, Ethnicity and Globalization', in Alan Scott (ed.) *The Limits of Globalization: Cases and Arguments*. London: Routledge.

Postman, N. (1985). *Amusing Ourselves to Death: Public Discourse in the Age of Show Business*. New York: Elisabeth Sifton/Viking.

Pultz, J. (1995) *Photography and the Body*. London: Weidenfeld and Nicolson.

Ramamurthy, A. (1997) 'Constructions of Illusion: Photography and Commodity Culture', in Liz Wells (ed.) *Photography: A Critical Introduction*. London: Routledge.

Ricoeur, P. (1981) *Hermeneutics and the Human Sciences*, ed. and tr. J. Thompson. Cambridge: Cambridge University Press.

Ritchin, F. (1990) *In Our Own Image: The Coming Revolution in Photography*. New York: Aperture.

Robins, K. (1996) *Into the Image: Culture and Politics in the Field of Vision*. London: Routledge.

Robins, K. and Webster, F. (1999) *Times of the Technoculture: From the Information Society to the Virtual Life*. London: Routledge.

Rodowick, D.N. (1990) 'Reading the Figural', *Camera Obscura* 24: 10–45.

Rogoff, I. (1998) 'Studying Visual Culture', in N. Mirzoeff (ed.) *The Visual Culture Reader*. London: Routledge.

Rosenblum, B. (1978a) *Photographers At Work: A Sociology of Photographic Styles*. New York: Holmes and Meier.

Rosenblum, B. (1997b) 'Style as Social Process', *American Sociological Review*, 43.

Rosenblum, N. (1997) *A World History of Photography*. New York: Abbeville Press.

Rossler, M. (1991) 'Image Simulations, Computer Manipulations: Some Consideration', *Ten 8*, 2(2).

Ryan, B. (1992) *Making Capital from Culture: The Corporate Form of Capitalist Cultural Production*. New York: Walter de Gruyter.

Salaman, G. (1997) 'Culturing Production', in P. Du Gay (ed.) *Production of Culture/ Cultures of Production*. Milton Keynes/London: Open University/Sage.

Samuel, R. (1994) *Theatres of Memory Vol. 1: Past and Present in Contemporary Culture*. London: Verso.

Scannell, P. (1996) *Radio, Television and Modern Life: A Phenomenological Approach*. Oxford: Blackwell.

Schiller, D. (1994) 'From Culture to Information and Back Again: Commoditization as a Route to Knowledge', *Critical Studies in Mass Communication* 11(1): 93–115.

Schiller, H. (1991) *Mass Communications and American Empire*. Oxford: Oxford University Press.

Schudson, M. (1986) *Advertising: The Uneasy Persuasion*. New York: Basic.

Sekula, A. (1981) 'The Traffic in Photographs', *Art Journal* 41(1): 15–25.

Sekula, A. (1982) 'On the Invention of Photographic Meaning', in V. Burgin (ed.) *Thinking Photography*. London: Macmillan.

Sekula, A. (1989) 'The Body and the Archive', in R. Bolton (ed.) *The Contest of Meaning: Critical Histories of Photography*. Cambridge, MA: MIT Press.

Sekula, A. (1999) 'Reading an Archive: Photography Between Labour and Capital', in J. Evans and S. Hall (eds) *Visual Culture: The Reader*. London: Sage.

Silverstone, R. (1993) 'Television, Ontological Security, and the Transitional Object', *Media, Culture and Society* 15(4): 573–98.

Silverstone, R. (1999) *Why Study the Media?* London: Sage.

Simmel, G. (1997 [1910]) *Simmel on Culture: Selected Writings*, eds D. Frisby and M. Featherstone. London: Sage.

Sinclair, J. (1987) *Images Incorporated: Advertising as Industry and Ideology*. London: Routledge.

Singer, I. (1984) *The Nature of Love*. Vols 1 and 2. Chicago: Chicago University Press.

Slater, D. (1983) 'Marketing Mass Photography', in H. Davis and P. Walton (eds) *Language, Image, Media*, Oxford: Blackwell.

Slater, D. (1995a) 'Domestic Photography and Digital Culture', in M. Lister (ed.) *The Photographic Image in Digital Culture*. London: Routledge.

Slater, D. (1995b) 'Photography and Modern Vision: The Spectacle of "Natural Magic"', in C. Jenks (ed.) *Visual Culture*. London: Routledge.

Smith, L. (1992) 'The Politics of Focus: Feminism and Photography Theory', in Isobel Armstrong (ed.) *New Feminist Discourses: Critical Essays on Theories and Texts*. London: Routledge.

Snyder, J. (1980) 'Picturing Vision', *Critical Inquiry* 6(3): 499–526.

Soar, M. (2000) 'Encoding Advertisements: Ideology and Meaning in Advertising Production', *Mass Communication and Society* 3(4): 415–37.

Solomon, R.C. (1981) *Love: Emotion, Myth and Metaphor*. New York: Anchor.

Sontag, S. (1977) *On Photography*. New York: Doubleday.

Spence, J. (1986) *Putting Myself in the Picture*. London: Camden.

Spence, J. and Holland, P. (eds) (1991) *Family Snaps: The Meanings of Domestic Photography*. London: Virago.

Steichen, E. (1986 [1955]) *The Family of Man*. New York: Museum of Fine Art.

Stein, S. (1992) 'The Graphic Ordering of Desire: Modernisation of a Middle-Class Women's Magazine 1919–1939', in R. Bolton (ed) *The Contest of Meaning: Critical Histories of Photography*. Cambridge, MA and London: MIT Press.

Tagg, J. (1988) *The Burden of Representation: Essays on Photographies and Histories*. London: Macmillan.

Thompson, J.B. (1990) *Ideology and Modern Culture: Critical Social Theory in the Era of Mass Communication*. Stanford: Stanford University Press.

Tolson, A. (1996) *Mediations: Text and Discourse in Media Studies*. London: Arnold.

Tomas, D. (1996) 'From the Photograph to Postphotographic Practices: Toward a Postoptical Ecology of the Eye', in T. Druckery (ed.) *Electronic Culture: Technology and Visual Representation*. New York: Aperture.

Tomlinson, J. (1999) *Globalization and Culture*. Chicago: University of Chicago Press.

Trachtenberg, A. (ed.) (1980) *Classic Essays on Photography*. New Haven: Leete's Island Books.

Tucker, A. (1973) *The Woman's Eye*. New York: Knopf.

Turow, J. (1997) *Breaking Up America: Advertisers and the New Media World*. Chicago: University of Chicago Press.

Vidler, A. (1993) 'Bodies in Space/Subjects in the City: Psychopathologies of Modern Urbanism', *Differences* 5(3).

Watney, S. (1999) 'On the Institutions of Photography', in J. Evans and S. Hall (eds) *Visual Culture: The Reader*. London: Sage.

Wernick, A. (1991) *Promotional Culture: Advertising, Ideology and Symbolic Expression*. London: Sage.

Wilkinson, H. (1997) '"The New Heraldry": Stock Photography, Visual Literacy, and Advertising in 1930s Britain', *Journal of Design History* 10(1): 23–38.

Williams, V. (1986) *Women Photographers: The Other Observers, 1900 to the Present*. London: Virago.

Williamson, J. (1978) *Decoding Advertisements: Ideology and Meaning in Advertising*. London: Marion Boyars.

Index